TOP SECRET/ MAJIC

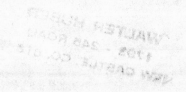

TOP SECRET/ MAJIC

Stanton T. Friedman

MARLOWE & COMPANY

First Marlowe & Company edition, 1996

Published by
Marlowe & Company
632 Broadway, Seventh Floor
New York, NY 10012

Manufactured in the United States of America

Library of Congress Cataloging-in-Publication Data

Friedman, Stanton T.

    Top secret MAJIC / Stanton T. Friedman.
       p.   c.m.
    Includes index.
    ISBN 1-56924-830-3
    ISBN 1-56924-741-2 (paper)
    1. Unidentified flying objects—Sightings and encounters—New Mexico—Roswell.
2. Unidentified flying objects—Government policy—United States. 3. Conspiracies—United States.
4. Security classification (Government policy—United States. I. Title.
TL789.F68   1996
001.9'42'09789—dc20   96-47711
                                                                       CIP

To Jesse Marcel, Sr., without whose testimony
this quest would never have begun.

CONTENTS

ACKNOWLEDGMENTS

Many, many people have been helpful and encouraging in my 12 years of research on the Majestic-12 documents. Particular thanks must be given to the Fund for UFO Research and the archivists at the many archives I have visited; with special gratitude to Dennis Bilger at the Harry S. Truman Library, Herb Pankratz at the Dwight D. Eisenhower Library, Larry Bland at the George C. Marshall Archives, Ed Reese at the National Archives, and the staff at the Library of Congress Manuscript Division, the Harvard University Archives, and many others. Discussions with George Elsey, Forrest Pogue, Mrs. C. H. Humelsine, Tim Good, Nick Redfern, Tim Cooper, Robert Swiatek, John Schuessler, William L. Moore, and Jaime Shandera are much appreciated.

I am grateful to the Mutual UFO Network for publishing a number of my papers in its annual symposium proceedings, and the *International UFO Reporter* for publishing several MJ-12-related articles. Special gratitude must be expressed to my literary agent, John White, and my editor, Robert Weisser—I am sure I have stretched their patience. Of most importance have been the patience and understanding of my wife Marilyn and daughter Melissa, who have put up with my all-too-frequent trips and my obsession with Majestic-12 and crashed saucers.

You may be one of the thousands of people around the world who have first- or secondhand information about flying saucers. You may have had a sighting yourself, or know someone who has. You may have a friend or relative who was involved in one of the government agencies named in this book. You may have thought your story was not important, or you may have convinced yourself that it was all your imagination.

What you know *can* make a difference. Hundreds of people like you have been inspired after reading books or seeing TV documentaries to tell what they know. Quite often, these leads reveal new paths in the search for the truth about flying saucers, allowing researchers to corroborate older information or to uncover new witnesses and documents.

If this book inspires you to come forth with your own knowledge, don't hesitate to contact me. My telephone number is 506-457-0232; my fax number is 506-450-3832. From the United States, you can write to me at PO Box 958, Houlton, ME 04730-0958. From Canada or other parts of the world, send mail to 79 Pembroke Crescent, Fredericton, New Brunswick E3B 2V1 Canada. On the Internet, you can reach me at fsphys@brunswickmicro.nb.ca. Witnesses' names will not be used without permission. I'm willing to listen.

Stanton Friedman
Fredericton, New Brunswick

FOREWORD

In this book, Stanton Friedman does something that nobody else has ever done before: he provides virtual proof that there is a UFO coverup, and that it is regarded as a matter of the very highest importance by U.S. government agencies.

Friedman has been involved in UFO research for more than a quarter century. During that time, he has struggled tirelessly against a vast amount of resistance on almost every level. He has uncovered hoaxes, discovered hidden truths, and has fought arrogant bureaucrats and fallacy-happy UFO debunkers, not to mention other researchers eager to discredit him for their own ends. He is one of the few truly professional UFO researchers.

In these pages, he develops a detailed chronicle of a seemingly incredible reality: there is a great secret at the center of the U.S. government, and the government is guarding that secret with a zeal so fanatical that its actions appear to have crossed the border into paranoia.

To pursue his case, Friedman has spent a substantial part of his adult life struggling to extract secrets from a bureaucracy that has reduced things like the Freedom of Information Act to a grotesque,

Kafkaesque joke. Abuse of FOIA is routine in the federal system. Responses to requests that the act mandates should take only short periods are dealt with at a pace so slow that it amounts to contempt for the law. Certain requests that Friedman initiated in 1988 have yet to be acted upon.

The remarkable thing is that Friedman has kept at this for so long. Being a professional UFO researcher doesn't return much money. The public recognition is at best a very mixed bag. But Friedman is among a small group of brave and determined people who have persisted for years.

He offers a remarkably cogent case for the authenticity of a number of documents relating to the coverup. Notable among these are the Cutler-Twining memo of 1954 that refers to MJ-12, the group of high-level scientists and military personnel who oversaw the recovery and analysis of UFOs in the 1940s and 1950s, and which may still exist today. Another astonishing document that has stood up under his close scrutiny is the Eisenhower briefing of 1952, which offers a short background regarding the status of the recovery of debris and extraterrestrial biological remains.

Both of these documents have been extensively debunked in the UFO press, but Friedman's very close and painstaking analysis leads one to doubt not their authenticity, but the veracity and motives of some of the people who have taken such pains to deny their validity. Some of these individuals are shown to have ignored and even doctored evidence in their zeal to prove the documents false. It would now seem essential for them to prove that they are not working in furtherance of a conspiracy of silence before they can be trusted further.

More important even than these documents, though, is an event that took place in the late 1970s, which Friedman precipitated along with the Citizens Against UFO Secrecy (CAUS), and which proves, beyond any doubt, that there is a coverup.

Under FOIA, CAUS asked to obtain UFO information from the CIA. The CIA claimed that it had none. After the demand was made through federal judge Gerhard Gesell, the CIA produced documents, some of which suggested that other agencies, including the National Security Agency, also had files. A request to the NSA for its documents was turned down. Further court action elicited none of the 156 documents which were withheld.

CAUS then asked Gesell to request to see the documents that he might rule on the legality of the NSA's actions. Incredibly, the NSA refused even to do this. Instead, it produced an affidavit saying why they should be kept secret.

To read this affidavit, Gesell had to be security cleared Above Top Secret. When he had read the affidavit, the judge agreed that nobody should be allowed to read the documents—not even himself! When the issue was brought before the Court of Appeals, that tribunal concurred with Gesell and the NSA that they didn't need to know. The appeals court, which normally takes months and even years to decide issues, handed down its opinion in a matter of days. Whatever was in that affidavit was so convincing that they agreed *without question* to continue the coverup.

This certainly reveals one thing: those documents contain information that is spectacularly and incredibly secret. What sort of information might produce a need for this unprecedented level of concealment is unknown. The secret must be different from the other secrets held by the federal government. It is hard to conceive of anything so dangerous that it could not be revealed even to a security-cleared federal judge in the privacy of his chambers. It is almost as if the judge himself would have been placed in some sort of jeopardy if he knew the secret. Arguably, Friedman and CAUS were dealing with the most jealously kept secret in American history.

What the secret might be is another question. There has been a lot of speculation, of course. For example, it has been suggested that, since the aliens are so secretive themselves, they are forcing our government to maintain its part of the coverup.

However, the real reasons for it may be much more down to earth. It is more likely that the coverup of this most important of all information has been going on so long that it has become self-perpetuating—revealing it now would cause the public to realize that it had been lied to for years in ways so fundamentally irresponsible as to make the government unworthy of the public trust.

Friedman provides his own fascinating insights into why this material was held to such extremely rigorous standards of secrecy, and details some remarkable stories about this secrecy, including an extraordinary close encounter that had tragic results for some of the military personnel involved.

His argument concerning the existence of a coverup is devastatingly powerful, even terrifying, and the complicity of the powerful national press seems inescapable and tragic. Friedman documents the *Washington Post* responding to him in a completely inappropriate manner when he questioned some facts it had reported in relation to Congressman Steven Schiff's request for the General Accounting Office to investigate the 1947 Roswell incident.

This terribly provocative book is not only the history of an appalling secret that is probably the central reality of our times, but also of the life of a man who has been fighting to reveal that secret for most of his adult life. The vilification and scorn that has been heaped upon Stanton Friedman is amazing, and it can be safely assumed that this book will receive the same sort of treatment from the press.

That this will not stop him is fortunate. Friedman is the sort of man who, after being thrown down a cliff, simply gathers himself up and starts climbing again.

A shadow hangs over our world, and it is the shadow of this secret. We have reached a terrible place indeed in the history of our republic when the servants of the people would keep the most vital information they possess—indeed, the most vital information any human institution has ever possessed—from the people.

It is to be hoped that Friedman and his successors will one day write the complete history of this dreadful secret, so our nation will be cleansed at last of its corrosive and debilitating effects.

Whitley Strieber
May 1996

INTRODUCTION

WHAT'S A NICE NUCLEAR PHYSICIST DOING IN A PLACE LIKE THIS?

For almost 40 years, I have been researching UFOs. I have written two books and dozens of articles, have spoken before hundreds of live audiences, and have appeared on many more call-in shows on television as well as radio. I am what you might call a "personality," judging from the number of strangers who stop me on the street when I am away from home on speaking tours.

I am positively convinced that alien UFOs exist, that they are visiting earth, and that our government knows this. I do not base this on wishful thinking, nor am I some apocalyptic philosopher concerned about the coming of the millenia. My conviction comes from a scientific analysis of facts that I and other researchers have gathered over the years. This growing body (I might say mountain) of data overwhelmingly supports the idea that other civilizations, probably from nearby in our own galaxy, are checking us out from close range.

While growing up in Linden, New Jersey in the late 1940s, my best friend was Roger, who lived about a block away. Roger's brother was four years older than us, and he had a great collection of pulp magazines that he let us read. Although I went more for the adventure stories that I got out of the library, I enjoyed the sci-fi magazines, too. I was certainly excited about space travel in the late 1940s, as many of us post–World War II kids were, but in high school I was too busy with sports, the debate team, and work to follow it. After high school, my busy schedule continued as I worked my way through two years at Rutgers as a busboy in the Catskills and down on the Jersey shore. I continued my studies—and my restaurant ex-perience—at the University of Chicago.

After the University of Chicago awarded me a masters degree in physics in 1956, I got a job at the General Electric Aircraft Nuclear Propulsion (ANP) Department in Evendale, just north of Cincinnati, Ohio. As the name of the department indicates, we were working on nuclear-powered high-performance jet aircraft, and so our research was classified Secret Restricted Data. The program was jointly sponsored by the Atomic Energy Commission and the Air Force. We were at the leading edge of technology, and our program had money for exotic materials, expensive tests, and extensive cal-culations.

The department was growing rapidly. In 1958 we had perhaps 3,500 employees, of whom about 1,100 were engineers and scientists. The government provided facilities, fissionable materials, and a bud-get of more than $100 million a year. My associates—many of whom had been in the service and so were several years older—were very sharp people from whom I learned a lot. But I was anxious to assert my knowledge as well, since there was really nobody around with a long history in the field.

The emphasis of our work was developing shielding for the nu-clear reactor that was to power the aircraft. The reactor heated air to above 1,700°F for the turbines—a much higher temperature than conventional water-cooled reactors. Thus, our two primary concerns were temperature and weight, since the nuclear-powered engine re-quired a new kind of shielding that was the biggest portion of the weight of the engine. Thus I had a real opportunity to make a sig-nificant contribution through high-temperature experiments with various exotic combinations of materials. We made great strides toward our goal, and as early as 1957 we successfully operated jet engines on nuclear power.

Some time in 1958, I was ordering a batch of books from a mail order company. I needed one more choice so we wouldn't have to pay shipping charges, and so I was idly leafing through the catalog. My eye fell on a blurb about *The Report on Unidentified Flying Objects* by Air Force Captain Edward J. Ruppelt, who had headed the Air Force Project Blue Book in the 1950s at Wright-Patterson Air Force Base in Dayton, just up the road.

The Air Force was very exciting to me. The experiments I was involved in were conducted at a nuclear testing facility operated by Convair at the end of a runway at Carswell Air Force Base in Fort Worth, Texas, and when I was there I used to enjoy watching the many different planes taking off and landing. The huge, lumbering B-36 was built at Convair in Fort Worth, as was the sleek, high-performance B-58 bomber. The Air Force's flagship B-52 bombers were there as well.

While I neither knew nor cared much about flying saucers, I figured that Captain Ruppelt probably knew what he was talking about. What if there really were alien spacecraft, perhaps using nuclear power for high-speed travel in the atmosphere or between the stars? Our program could certainly benefit from the knowledge. Or the book might be good for a laugh.

When the books came, I read Ruppelt's first. It didn't convince me on the spot that flying saucers existed, but the captain had included a lot of hard-to-refute data. I loaned the book to my neighbor, Charlie, also an engineer and about ten years my senior. I respected Charlie, and he was more convinced than I was that there really was something to this UFO stuff. His opinion that Ruppelt's data was sensible heightened my interest in the subject. (More than a decade later, when I spoke to a chapter of the Institute of Electrical and Electronic Engineers in Connecticut, Charlie's first words when he came up to me with his wife were, "We knew you when you didn't believe in flying saucers.")

* * * *

A couple of years later, I was working at Aerojet General Nucleonics near San Francisco. I had become disenchanted with the ANP program, as it had gone through several budgetary ups and downs and it lacked the kind of leadership it needed to compete for research and development funding. Aerojet General was much smaller than GE-ANP, and I was now considered an expert in the field. Due in part to my expertise, Aerojet General won a contract to develop very-high-performance, extremely compact nuclear reactors to provide electric power for space vehicles.

Unfortunately, not too long afterward, the ANP program was canceled and Pratt & Whitney, GE's major competitor, was given the compact reactor contract. It had expensive facilities that Aerojet General could not match, and their design used liquid metals such as sodium, potassium, or lithium to cool the reactors. Since I liked California, I managed to get work on other proposals for Aerojet General, including the development of a nuclear rocket. We won that contract, too, but the work was mostly done elsewhere.

I wound up consulting with other parts of the company on a compact, transportable reactor that could be set up quickly to produce power at remote installations. Since this was at the height of the cold war and Americans were worried about the Russians raining missiles down on us, I was also involved in a proposal to review Soviet scientific literature to determine their capabilities in regard to nuclear power in space—whether it be to power radar, weapons, or other systems.

We won that competition, and I spent well over a year as project engineer for the "Analysis and Evaluation of Fast and Intermediate Reactors for Space Vehicle Applications." Although the program's title was impressive, it was really just a one-person operation. The contract was administered out of the Air Force's Foreign Technology Division at Wright-Patterson back in Ohio—coincidentally the same division that administered Project Blue Book, the most extensive and more or less unclassified study of UFO sightings done by the U.S. government.

Over the next year and a half, I made a number of trips back to Dayton to meet with my project monitor and to review huge collections of abstracts of Soviet technical literature at the Battelle Memorial Institute in Columbus. I also met with the new Project Blue Book head, Major Friend, on several occasions. Although I had security clearance to work on the program, the Foreign Technology office was in a vault inside a vault, and I was admitted only with an escort.

During this time, I had happened upon a privately published version of U.S. Air Force Project Blue Book Special Report 14 at the nearby University of California, Berkeley, library. I had already read more than a dozen UFO books thanks to a very helpful local librarian, but none had mentioned Special Report 14 by name. By nature, I'm a facts and figures man, and now I was in data heaven. The Special Report had more than 240 charts, tables, graphs, and maps. It covered over 3,000 sightings of which more than 600 could not be identified by the professional investigators.

The organization that actually did the work of collecting, reviewing, and evaluating the sightings was none other than Battelle Memorial Institute. They found that the better the quality of a sighting, the more likely it would remain unidentified after investigation by the scientists involved.

Whoever compiled the report did quality evaluations of each reported sighting. They characterized the sightings into "knowns" (aircraft, astronomical, etc.), "unknowns," and "insufficient information," and also cross-compared the "unknowns" with the "knowns" using six characteristics—including apparent size, shape, speed, and color. The researchers found that the probability of "unknowns" simply being missed "knowns" was less than one percent!

As I sorted through this mountain of data, I became more and more certain that the government's own information strongly indicated that a significant number of UFO sightings were probably of alien vehicles. I also recognized that the Air Force, in its October 1955 press release about the study, flat-out lied.

The report was never publicly distributed by the Air Force, although they gave very wide distribution to the press release, a comic-book style drawing of a "flying saucer," and what the Air Force said was a summary of the Blue Book report—which did not include any of the fascinating data in all those tables. Naturally, they didn't say who did the work or where it was done or even give the title of the program. Undoubtedly, if "Project Blue Book Special Report 14" had been mentioned in the press release, some intrepid reporter would have asked, "What about Reports 1-13?"

For my Foreign Technology project, I wrote two final reports. The first, for general consumption, was basically an unclassified bibliography listing Soviet publications on every aspect of technology related to building nuclear reactors for space applications. The second was highly classified, had a very limited distribution, and included my evaluation of Soviet capabilities vis-a-vis U.S. technology and my prediction that the USSR would very soon be building nuclear reactors for space applications. (When the Soviet Cosmos 954 satellite, with its nuclear reactor, reentered the atmosphere and crashed in the Canadian wilderness, I was probably one of very few Americans who were delighted to hear the news. My report had been right on! Cosmos 954 was about the thirteenth such satellite the Soviets had orbited, and the total eventually reached more than thirty. Even now, the United States has launched only one nuclear reactor into space. There was a great fuss in the press about possible radiation damage to caribou and lichens, but I never saw one report that mentioned the real significance of the satellite—that the Soviets were well ahead of us in providing power for military applications in space.)

Because of my own experience with the Foreign Technology Division and Battelle, I was absolutely convinced that a highly classified report, most likely Special Report 13, had been written with the good stuff in it. But the Air Force got away with their totally misleading press release. At the time, no one asked about it.

While at Aerojet General, I joined the Washington-based National Investigations Committee on Aerial Phenomena (NICAP) and the

Tucson-based Aerial Phenomena Research Organization (APRO). Both are gone now, but they did lead me to other interested professional people. Many of us at Aerojet General ate our lunches at our desks, and we often discussed outer space, flying saucers, and security. I wrote to Aime Michel, a French researcher who had written two excellent books on UFOs, for ideas on how to get more involved in the field. His advice was, "Don't bother. It's much too frustrating."

This advice was not a deterrent to me, for I had other influences. While working on Aerojet General's design of a nuclear fusion rocket for deep space travel using newly discovered superconducting materials, I came in contact with John Luce, probably the best scientist I have ever known. Luce, who had been head of the Oak Ridge National Laboratory's nuclear fusion department, joined Aerojet General as director of research. John was a true leader of men although he never went to college. Apparently, this was no drawback, for he received an honorary Ph.D. and more than 40 patents for high-tech devices. He was a world-renowned leader in fusion and plasma physics devices, and was always doing things that other experts said couldn't be done.

His work demonstrated to me a very important maxim: technological progress comes from doing things differently in an unpredictable way. Thus, the future is not an extrapolation of the past. For example, rockets propelled by nuclear fusion, the process that produces the sun's energy, are as much of an advance over our present chemical-fuel rockets as microintegrated circuitry is over the vacuum tubes that powered our first computers. Using the right materials in a properly designed nuclear fusion rocket, one can eject particles having *ten million times* as much energy per particle as in the chemical rockets we use now. Yet most academic reports about interstellar travel assume the use of primitive chemical rockets in calculating how long it would take us to reach other stars. If we extrapolate from the past, interstellar travel is impossible. If we do things differently than in the past, interstellar travel becomes feasible.

* * * *

In early 1963, I moved to General Motors' Allison Division in Indianapolis, where I oversaw the shielding work on the military compact reactor program. Much of my time was spent looking over the shoulder of our nuclear subcontractor in White Plains, New York.

My son has hemophilia, and so I had become active in the local chapter of the National Hemophilia Foundation. Needing a fascinating speaker for a fundraising dinner, I contacted Frank Edwards, a well-known reporter who was on the board of NICAP and was quite outspoken about his conviction that some UFOs were extraterrestrial and that the government knew about it. The speech went over very well.

My next stop as an itinerant nuclear physicist was Westinghouse Astronuclear Laboratory near Pittsburgh, where I was involved in research on shielding for a nuclear rocket engine. Once again, I found many of my colleagues very interested in UFOs. Frank Edwards sent me a copy of his new book, *Flying Saucers—Serious Business,* and after I read it, I called Frank to see how I might help spread the word. Having traveled extensively and met media people everywhere, he gave me some leads, including the producer of a talk show on KDKA, the biggest radio station in Pittsburgh. I called and offered to appear to talk about UFOs. The producer was relatively cold to the idea, and said he would get back to me. It seemed like a brush-off, but not too long thereafter, they called me at 6:30 P.M. for a 7:00 show. Their other guest had canceled—could I make it?

Luckily, I lived close to the station and got there on time. Unluckily, it was baptism by fire. The host knew little about the topic and made ridiculous charges about UFOs and those who were interested in them. I didn't know how to handle the situation, and did the best I could. I apparently did well enough, for a woman who was a technician at Westinghouse heard it and asked me to talk to her book review club, which was reading Edwards's book. And so it was in her living room that I gave my first UFO lecture, for free. I did a number of such presentations on what I came to call the chicken-and-peas circuit.

*   *   *   *

As I gave more lectures, I found that I enjoyed speaking and that people believed me no matter what I said. After all, I was a nuclear physicist for Westinghouse, which in Pittsburgh, with its numerous nuclear divisions and research facilities, were gold-plated credentials. The blind acceptance frightened me—now I knew how the demagogues of the twentieth century had had such success. I wanted people to think, to explore, to look at the data and make up their own minds. I decided that I would try to reach more technical groups, who presumably wouldn't accept everything I said as gospel.

I didn't want to jeopardize my job, so I asked my boss if management had any restrictions on employee speaking engagements. The response was that I could speak where I wanted and say what I wanted on my time, so long as I made clear that the opinions expressed were mine and not those of my employer. I could even identify myself as a Westinghouse nuclear physicist. They could not have been fairer. (Even in recent months I have found that many scientists in Europe are afraid to speak out about UFOs for fear of retribution by management.)

I convinced a Westinghouse colleague to have me as a speaker for a joint meeting of the local sections of the Institute of Electrical and Electronic Engineers (IEEE) and the American Institute of Aeronautics and Astronautics (AIAA), to be held at the Mellon Institute. He was program chairman. I told him a lot of people would come, and all I wanted in return was the cost of a babysitter and dinner for my wife and me.

When we went to the the preprogram dinner at a hotel across the street from the institute, I thought I would be eating my words instead. Only about two dozen people showed up at dinner. However, when we walked into the auditorium, my faith in my colleagues was borne out. The hall was packed, and people were still sifting in. By the time I started speaking, more than 400 people were in attendance.

My lecture—"Flying Saucers *Are* Real!"—was designed to raise the objections of the skeptics and then demolish them with facts. I leaned heavily on Special Report 14 for my data, and I could tell that the audience was interested. This was just the sort of presentation they could relate to. I recognized a number of high-level people from Westinghouse and other area corporations, and the question-and-answer session went on until the janitor chased us out. There were no hostile questions. People came at me not only with questions, but with money. I sold eight copies of Special Report 14 and took orders for ten more. Even more gratifying, as after my radio stints, a number of listeners asked how they could dig deeper into the subject, and I was able to refer them to our very active UFO group in Pittsburgh, the UFO Research Institute.

UFORI had begun as a subcommittee of NICAP, and it expanded rapidly. It funded meetings, published a newsletter, investigated UFO cases, had a 24-hour answering service, and distributed scientific materials. I was elected president in 1968. Our goals were to get instrument data during a sighting and to educate the public via the media to the existence of alien spacecraft. I also contributed a paper to Congressional hearings on UFOs held on July 29, 1968.

Some time after the IEEE-AIAA session, I was driving to work with a woman named Jo Ann, who was a supervisor at Westinghouse. She had received her Ph.D. from Carnegie-Mellon University, and in casual conversation, I told her I would like to speak at CMU. She said, "Talk to the dean." Unthinkingly, I replied that I had spoken with a professor there who expressed no interest. She looked at me. "Talk to the dean, Stan. He's my husband!"

I called her husband, and it turned out he had heard some of my appearances on KDKA. He said he would be delighted to have me speak at the university. After we settled on a date and time, he asked me how much money I wanted. Thinking quickly—I would have to take a half-day off from work—I said $100, hoping for $50. "Sold!" he said. Then, because Jo Ann knew me, he let me in on what the other speakers in the series were getting paid: $1,200-$1,500! He also was kind enough to give me the name of the agency through which he had booked the other speakers. After my Carnegie-Mellon lecture, which went extremely well, I called the agency and they booked me to speak to the Engineering Society of Detroit for the astronomical sum of $300 plus travel expenses. That lecture was truly a turning point. It sold out three weeks in advance for 1,000 people. I was now a professional speaker.

In the coming months, I spoke at a number of gatherings of the IEEE, AIAA, and other technical societies. I also received a request from a colleague at Los Alamos National Laboratory to speak to the local section of the American Nuclear Society. My host and I were both delighted when a crowd of 500 showed up for the lecture and stayed for an enthusiastic question-and-answer session. But I wasn't surprised, for the man responsible for obtaining the copy of Special Report 14 that I had found in the Berkeley library had been a scientist there. Their library had lots of UFO books. Ironically, at the time, I knew nothing about UFO crashes in New Mexico, specifically the Roswell incident, with which I was to become so closely linked. But twenty-five years later when I spoke at Los Alamos, my lecture title was "Crashed Saucers in New Mexico." I was certain that pieces of the wrecked saucers went to Los Alamos for testing, since that installation had very high security and some of the finest scientists and equipment in the world. I suspect that some of those very scientists were part of the overflow audience at my presentation.

In the meantime, my work on the nuclear rocket program at Westinghouse was rewarding. I was planning and evaluating radiation shielding measurements made during full-power tests at the nuclear test site in Nevada and low-power tests at our local facility. I developed a new technique for evaluating nuclear heating rates in our control devices and even wrote an unclassified paper about it. As arcane as this sounds, one of the highlights was listening over the public address system in Pittsburgh to a full-power test of our NRX-A6 system in Nevada. The reactor was only five feet by six feet in size, but it produced 1,100 megawatts, or about half the capacity of the mammoth Grand Coulee Dam.

Running at temperatures close to 4,000° F, cooled by hydrogen gas, the reactor roared away while we listened for signs that it was breaking up. Estimates for how long it could run ranged from five to forty minutes, but the reactor lasted for the entire hour-long run. It was shut down only because the hydrogen used to cool the core was exhausted. The test was tangible proof of the success of our work.

Less than a year later, Los Alamos operated their slightly larger Phoebus 2B nuclear rocket reactor propulsion system at a power level of 4,400 megawatts, the highest-powered reactor ever operated in the free world at that time. Unfortunately, by then the nuclear rocket program was dying. There were substantial cutbacks in spending, and neither politicians nor bureaucrats had courage enough to back the program, even though the rockets showed real promise for getting astronauts to Mars or to help establish a base on the moon or provide transfer capabilities from earth orbit to lunar orbit. I got caught in a major layoff, and went full-time on the speaking circuit.

Lecturing full-time put a lot of stress on my family. My younger son's hemophilia caused him to have unpredictable and very painful bleeds. My daughter is deaf, and needed special schooling. My wife had had a serious bout of mental illness and was hospitalized for months. I had my hands full dropping off my two-year-old daughter at one babysitter and my four-year-old at another before heading to work. Finally, I hired a housekeeper who could look after the family so I could keep my sanity. During this time, my wife and I separated. The break-up was rough on all of us, and especially my 14-year-old son.

I was traveling a lot, and was feeling terrible about my inability to help out at home. Then what I thought was a great opportunity opened up for me. I was hired to work for McDonnell Douglas in Santa Monica, California, under Dr. Robert Wood, a scientist who had a long-time interest in UFOs. One of his people had heard a talk I gave at the Westinghouse Research Laboratory, and recommended me to work on trying to back-engineer flying saucers using some Blue Sky (far-out thinking) funds available through the Manned Orbiting Laboratory program at McDonnell. I packed up a bunch of furniture, clothes, and household goods and headed across country.

But during the trip, I heard a radio report that the program had been canceled. What could I do? I reported to the personnel department, which was already in shock. "We are laying off 5,000 people," they told me, "and you want to begin work?"

Even so, they honored my contract and let me stay for three months. I researched magnetoaerodynamic propulsion systems (similar in principle to an electromagnetic submarine developed by a Westinghouse scientist) that might explain the hypermaneuverability of flying saucers and their ability to overcome the obvious problems of heating, drag, sonic boom production, and reduced radar cross sections. I found references to hundreds of papers in the mostly nonacademic literature. The great majority were classified, indicating the government was certainly interested in such technology.

My three-month stay at McDonnell Douglas was followed by six months at TRW Systems, where I worked on the Pioneer spacecraft that have now left the solar system. When that contract ended, I was back full-time on the lecture circuit. Except for consulting work, I was finished with industry for good, and became the only space scientist known to be devoting full time to ufology.

Much of what I learned in industry has come in handy during my ufological research. Every report or paper I wrote and every claim I made at group meetings had to be justified by logic and evidence to colleagues and supervisors. I couldn't get by on research by proclamation, and often I had to say that there wasn't enough evidence to justify any conclusion. I learned early on that absence of evidence is not the same as evidence for absence. And through my own classified research, I learned that secrets can certainly be kept; that an enormous amount of extraordinary scientific work is done in classified programs that the public never hears about.

Thus, the data presented in this book is the result of long, painstaking research, and the logical connections that I make are based on my almost 40 years' acquaintance with high-tech matters and high-security procedures. Far from being a story that only techno-nerds would relish, the chase for details about extraterrestrial visitors and our government's interest in them (and denial of their existence) makes one of the fascinating adventure stories of our time.

The objective of this book is to review a very substantial amount of research that has been done since receipt of the first Operation Majestic-12 documents in late 1984. In addition, more recently received MJ-12 documents will be presented here for the first time ever in a public report. In many ways the chase has been fascinating and very frustrating as well. It is complicated by the simple fact that, if the documents are genuine, they deal with a very highly classified matter. I worked as a nuclear physicist with a Q clearance (required for work on highly classified nuclear projects) under security from 1956 until 1970 and have over the years visited a total of 15 document archives and have a very healthy respect for national security. There is no question that the U.S. government is able to keep secrets, including those about UFOs.

Over the years, I have become accustomed to dealing with opposing viewpoints. But the attacks on the documents presented herein have been intensive indeed. The arguments have been raging for many years. With this book, the data is on the table. Make up your own mind.

THE ROSWELL CRASH
AND MAJESTIC-12

For a period of about five years after I moved to southern California in 1969, I had worked on a number of magazine articles about UFOs with the late Bobbi Ann Slate Gironda. It was a good relationship. I knew my way around the scientific research and security matters, and knew how to verify the authenticity of material. Bobbi had the rare ability to make this information accessible to nontechnical readers.

In 1973, Bobbi had interviewed a forest ranger about his UFO sighting. During their conversation, the ranger had said that if she wanted an even better story, she ought to talk to his mother, Lydia Sleppy. When we called her shortly thereafter, she first related a sighting of her own, which had occurred while she was living in New Mexico. But then she told us of something far more important.

Back in 1947, when she was working at a radio station in Albuquerque, New Mexico, she had taken a call from their affiliate in Roswell, nearly 200 miles southeast. The caller described how a saucer had crashed outside of town, had been recovered by the Army Air Force group stationed at the Roswell base, and was being taken to Wright Field (now Wright-Patterson Air Force Base) in Ohio.

Newspapers all over the country had been carrying front-page

stories about "flying saucers" for many days after private pilot Kenneth Arnold's famous June 24, 1947 sighting of nine disc-like objects
moving "as a saucer would if it was skipped across the water." Arnold
timed the objects' flight between two mountain peaks and figured
out that they were traveling at a velocity of over 1,500 miles per hour!
(At that time, the aircraft speed record was only 625 miles per hour.)
By early July 1947, there had been more than 1,500 sightings reported across the United States, in Canada, and in other countries.

As Sleppy's informant dictated his story to her, she typed it out
over the newswire. Suddenly, her transmission was interrupted, and a
message came back to her—"STOP. DO NOT CONTINUE THIS
TRANSMISSION." Although from our vantage point it is not surprising that the station's teletype was being monitored, what with so
much classified government and military activity in New Mexico, it
certainly was a shock to Lydia. Later, when she talked to the person
who had called her, he wouldn't talk about it.

A crashed saucer and a 26-year government coverup. Bobbi and
I set out to verify Lydia's story. We actually located some people who
had worked with Lydia at that time. However, they either did not
know about the event or had selective amnesia, and the trail turned
cold. I tucked the story away as one of those fascinating leads that
one hears but about which little can be done. More than 15 years
passed before I spoke to Lydia again.

On January 11, 1977, I was in Minnesota to give a lecture at the state
university campus in Morris, 26 miles from the Dakota border. The
temperature that evening was 41° below zero, but even so, I spoke
to a full house. After the lecture, I went out for a pizza with an old
acquaintance, Bill Moore, who had attended the program. Bill and
I had met in Pittsburgh a decade earlier when I was very active in
UFORI while working at Westinghouse. He was interested in
UFOs, but had been only peripherally involved in UFORI, most of
whose board members were scientists.

We talked at some length. He was teaching high school in
Herman, about 10 miles away, but was interested in a wide variety

of topics. We had other conversations over the next year about UFO research that later developed into actual projects.

On February 20, 1978, I was in Baton Rouge to lecture at Louisiana State University and was doing three separate interviews at a local television station. Over coffee, the station manager, who was a little embarrassed that the third interviewer was late, told me, "The person you really ought to talk to is Jesse Marcel. He handled pieces of one of those flying saucers when he was in the service, a long time ago." The man was absolutely offhand about this remark, but I sat right up and pumped him for more information. Finally, he said, "Well, Jesse and I are old ham radio buddies. He lives over in Houma. He's very straightforward and trustworthy."

I had a very busy day and a great crowd at LSU. The next day while I was waiting to catch a plane to my next stop, I got Marcel's telephone number from information and called him. He told a fascinating story of having been the base intelligence officer at Roswell Army Air Field in the late 1940s. He was eating lunch at the officer's club when he took a call from the local sheriff who mentioned that some sheep rancher had come in with pieces of strange wreckage. By prearrangement, the sheriff was supposed to notify the base of anything that might be related to the base's people or equipment.

Marcel went down to the sheriff's office to check out the debris, and knew immediately that it was nothing that he had ever seen in his extensive Army Air Force experience. He talked to the base commander, Colonel William Blanchard, who told him to get out to the ranch for a firsthand look. So, with a Counter-Intelligence Corps agent named Cavitt, Marcel followed the rancher out to his place in a remote area that wasn't really on any road. Since it was dark, they camped out overnight. The next day, the rancher showed them the wreckage strewn over an area about three-quarters-of-a-mile long and hundreds of feet wide. Marcel and Cavitt brought back an Army carry-all and a Buick full of fragments—a mere fraction of the wreckage on the ranch.

There were several kinds of very strong, lightweight materials which Jesse could not identify. There were I-beams with unusual symbols along the inside that were as light as balsa wood but which could not be cut, broken, or burnt. There was a foil-like material that when crumpled would go back to its original shape uncreased. And he remembered some thin material that couldn't be broken through with a sledgehammer.

After stopping at home late that night and showing some of the wreckage to his wife and son, Jesse brought the debris back to the base. On July 8, 1947, Colonel Blanchard ordered the base public information officer, Walter Haut, to issue a press release announcing the recovery of a crashed saucer, and instructed Jesse to put the wreckage on a B-29 and fly with it to Wright Field in Ohio, the normal destination for captured enemy equipment. They were to make a stop in Forth Worth, Texas, at the headquarters of the 8th Air Force, of which his group, the 509th Composite Bomb Wing, was a part. (At that time the 509th was the only atomic bombing group in the world.) When they arrived in Fort Worth, General Roger Ramey, head of the 8th Air Force and Blanchard's immediate superior, instructed Marcel to say nothing and told the press the material was just the wreckage of a weather balloon radar reflector. Jesse went on back to Roswell, but his picture was in newspapers across the country over the next few days as part of the Army's campaign to scotch the flying saucer stories.

This conversation was the beginning of a long, intensive effort on my part to dig out the truth about what happened at Roswell. Marcel's story and others related to the crash and recovery of an alien craft near Roswell and another one elsewhere in New Mexico have been told and retold in various articles, books, and movies (see Sources), so there is no need to recapitulate them. But as a result of publicity and hard research efforts, I and other investigators have continued to turn up new witnesses and leads that have brought the truth closer to the light of day.

Another very important event took place on October 24, 1978. That was the day I met Vern and Jean Maltais after my lecture at Bemidji State University in Bemidji, Minnesota. They quietly told me of an old friend of theirs, a civil engineer named Barney Barnett who lived for a while in Socorro, New Mexico. He had told Vern and Jean that he had come across an almost-intact saucer stuck in the ground with four strange bodies around it. The military had come along, and told him and a nearby archaeological expedition to leave the area immediately and never say anything about the event, ever. The Maltaises had no date for the Barnett story. The very next day, I met with Bill Moore at colleges in Thief River Falls and Crookston, Minnesota, where I was lecturing, and passed on the Barnett story for follow-up.

In January 1979, Bill came across the story of Hughie Green, an English actor, who described how, while driving across the United States in the late 1940s, he had heard an incredible story about the recovery of a crashed flying saucer in New Mexico on several radio stations. But when he got to the East Coast, there was nothing more. Bill contacted Green, got a date for the event (early July 1947) that led him to check out newspaper stories at the University of Minnesota Periodicals Library. He found articles dated July 8, 1947 about what had happened to Jesse Marcel! Thus, we were able to verify the accuracy of Marcel's memory. Now we had a solid date for which to look at other newspapers. These additional reports gave the names of a number of people we could contact—if we could find them. Our research effort intensified.

Three months later I was in Houma, making one of a number of stops with a crew filming what eventually became the 93-minute documentary *UFOs Are Real*. Brandon Chase was the producer, and I was technical advisor and one of the scriptwriters, as well as an on-screen commentator. (According to a recent ad in *Omni*, more than 100,000 copies of the video have been sold.) We interviewed Jesse Marcel at length. As of 1980, when the book *The Roswell Incident* (by Moore and Charles Berlitz) came out, Bill and I had talked to about 60 people in conjunction with the event.

Bill and I continued our research and publicity efforts. When Bill was promoting *The Roswell Incident* in 1980, he was approached by Richard Doty—an "insider"—who arranged to meet with him. At the meeting, Doty showed credentials indicating that he worked for

the Air Force's Office of Special Investigations (OSI). Bill established a good relationship with Doty, who said he wanted to get the
UFO information out and would try to help quietly in any way he
could. We would have to be cautious about anything that was given.
It was a fascinating contact with the "underworld" of Air Force intelligence that continued for several years.

In August 1980, I moved from Hayward, California 3,500 miles
east to Fredericton, New Brunswick, Canada, my second wife's home
province. Proposition 13 had passed in California, slashing education
budgets and thus my income from lecturing at California community
colleges. Before we left, I had been contacted by a company that
wanted to produce a fictional movie about UFOs. Jaime Shandera
was to be the director, and they wanted me as a consultant. Since
they also needed somebody to help out with the script, I recommended Bill Moore, who had written and directed plays. Although
we had several meetings and shot some scenes, the project fell apart
for lack of funding. But the end result was that Bill, who had by that
time moved to Arizona, hit it off with Jaime. With me back in the
East, Bill (who was now in southern California, too) and Jaime
began to work together on UFO contacts while staying in touch with
me by telephone and at various conferences and meetings that we
all attended.

Then, in December 1984, the Majestic-12 documents showed up
on Jaime Shandera's doorstep.

To be more exact, a roll of undeveloped black-and-white 35mm
film came in the mail to Shandera's home in Burbank in a double-
wrapped plain brown envelope with no return address and an
Albuquerque, New Mexico postmark. Why was it sent to Jaime?
One possibility is that it was well-known that Shandera had been
working closely with Bill Moore and myself on the Roswell crash
story, and that together with Bill, had had many contacts with insiders, some of whom were connected with OSI in Albuquerque.

Bill and Jaime's meetings with Agent Doty and others had left
them with the impression that these insiders were interested in hav-

ing the facts about flying saucers released to the public, in a manner that would protect their identity and their status. But we may never know.

After Bill and Jaime developed the film, they called me. What they found on the film were duplicate sets of eight pages of documents that were classified TOP SECRET/MAJIC, with a title page declaring "Briefing Document: Operation Majestic 12 Prepared for President-Elect Dwight D. Eisenhower: (Eyes Only) 18 November, 1952." The second page of the set listed the members of the Majestic-12 group, all of whom were dead. Then they read to me the third page: "On 24 June, 1947, a civilian pilot flying over the Cascade Mountains in the State of Washington observed nine flying disc-shaped aircraft traveling in formation at a high rate of speed. . . . In spite of these efforts, little of substance was learned about the objects until a local rancher reported that one had crashed in a remote region of New Mexico. . . . On 07 July, 1947, a secret operation was begun to assure recovery of the wreckage of this object. . . ."

Incredible as it sounded, the documents on this film dealt with the New Mexico crashes as well as with the government's efforts to keep them secret. According to the briefing, the wreckage of a crashed flying saucer was recovered by the U.S. government 75 miles northwest of Roswell in early July 1947. Four small alien bodies, apparently ejected from the vehicle, were found two miles east of the main wreckage site. The government took into its possession the wreckage and the bodies for careful study and evaluation, and in September 1947, officially established Operation Majestic-12 as "a top secret Research and Development/Intelligence operation responsible directly and only to the President of the United States."

This "preliminary" briefing for Eisenhower notes that the characteristics of the humanlike bodies were different from those of *homo sapiens*, that there were strange symbols on the wreckage which had not yet been interpreted, that there had been an increase in UFO activity in 1952, that there had been another crashed saucer recovered in December 1950, and that it was strongly recommended that Operation Majestic-12 be kept accountable only to the President.

A contingency plan for release of information had been prepared. The security markings indicate that the original is copy one of one. Apparently no other copies were made at that time. (See Appendix A for a full transcript of the documents on the film.)

The last page of the documents on the film was marked "Attachment A." This was a brief memo from President Truman to Secretary of Defense James Forrestal, dated September 24, 1947, authorizing Forrestal to proceed with Operation Majestic-12 with advice from noted science and technology administrator Dr. Vannevar Bush and the Director of Central Intelligence, who at that time was Admiral Roscoe H. Hillenkoetter (listed as the briefing officer on page 2 of the document).

I was very excited about this discovery, but I also knew that we had to be very, very cautious with it. There was no question that if the TOP SECRET/MAJIC Eyes Only briefing document for president-elect Eisenhower was genuine, it was one of the most important classified government documents ever leaked to the public. Of course, the first question was whether these eight pages were legitimate.

There were three possible answers to this question. First, the entire roll of film could be disinformation or a hoax. Despite the supposed power of the media, it is relatively easy for the government and powerful people to disseminate misleading but believable information to the public. One need only think of the dirty tricks campaigns of the Watergate era to understand how this works, or the carefully staged press conferences during the Gulf War in 1991.

In addition, there have been a wide variety of private frauds associated with UFOs over the years. People created fake photographs. Individuals claimed credentials they didn't have, experiences they didn't have. Some created false physical traces where a UFO supposedly had been seen on the ground. Some sought fame and fortune for their UFO-related experiences.

For example, in the 1960s an evangelist named Frank Stranges exhibited a dried devilfish in a velvet-lined casket and charged admission to view the "alien" body. Frank had served time for trying to smuggle a load of marijuana into the country, according to his parole officer. He is still on the convention and conference circuit authoritatively making wild claims.

Not only are there plenty of pro-UFO conmen, but there are also a number of unscrupulous UFO debunkers who make up phony experiences, documents, and photos to try to show that UFO investigators are all gullible fools. Bill Moore and I had tangled more than once with such people, many of whom were connected with the Committee for the Scientific Investigation of Claims of the Paranormal (CSICOP). Were these mysterious documents intended to fool us into going public so that these debunkers could say "Gotcha!" and discredit not only us but the entire Roswell story as well?

Second, the documents could contain some truth mixed with some phony material, sending researchers off on a wild-goose chase and keeping the secrets for that much longer. Perhaps there was a Majestic-12 group, but it dealt with something entirely different. Third, they could be plain straight legitimate. We had to establish which answer was correct.

There are many complications involved in assessing the validity of these documents, and their evaluation is much more complex, in a sense, than the original crash-retrieval story. Based on my decades of research into the Roswell incident and subsequent coverup, I am certain that alien bodies and wreckage were retrieved. Based on my detailed study and investigation of the overall UFO phenomenon beginning in 1958, I am equally certain that (1) some UFOs are intelligently controlled extraterrestrial spacecraft; (2) the subject of flying saucers represents a kind of cosmic Watergate, wherein a relatively small group of people in government have known about the visitors for many years; (3) none of the anti-UFO arguments made by a small but vocal group of debunkers stand up under careful scrutiny; and (4) visits by extraterrestrial space vehicles and the successful 50-year government coverup of the best evidence (alien bodies and wreckage) is the biggest story of the millennium.

Certainly it seemed very reasonable that after recovering a

crashed flying saucer and alien bodies, some sort of high-security organization would have been established to deal with the implications. The very-high-security Manhattan Project during World War II would have provided an excellent model, especially since many of the activities controlled by that project took place in New Mexico.

This does not mean that I or other legitimate UFO researchers believe every UFO story that comes down the pike. I have what I call a "gray basket" for all those stories which have not yet been validated and may or may not be true. Neither myself nor Bill nor Jaime were ready to accept the briefing as genuine without validation.

As Bill read me the list of Majestic-12 members, it was immediately obvious that the group was an all-star cast made up of top-level personnel in the armed forces, the intelligence community, and the scientific community. All of the members (with one exception) certainly had the highest security clearances, meaning they would have had access to documents that touched on the most sensitive national security matters. This would have been extremely important, as we knew that, despite denials, the U.S. government considered the subject of UFOs to be classified above Top Secret. In 1979 I had obtained a copy of the so-called "Smith Memo" of November 1950, a formerly Top Secret Canadian government memo which included this paragraph:

> I made discreet inquiries of the Canadian Embassy in Washington and obtained the following information about flying saucers: (1) the subject is the most classified in the United States, even more so than the H bomb; (2) flying saucers exist; (3) their modus operandi is as yet unknown, but there's a small group working under Doctor Vannevar Bush; and (4) the entire subject is considered of enormous significance by the United States authorities.

The most bothersome thing about the list—the one major item that made me think the documents were frauds—was the presence of Harvard astronomer Donald Menzel. His was the only name that had not surfaced in our continuing research on the Roswell incident. By the time Jaime received the film, we had contacted 92 people concerned with the incident. We had been checking at various archives on who was doing what in the government in July 1947. We had looked at White House logs of Truman's visitors, newspaper articles around that time which mentioned government officials and their whereabouts and activities, and cross-contacts between people who would have some reason to be involved with UFOs. We had reconsidered a September 23, 1947 letter from General Nathan Twining describing a number of government organizations that were to be notified of news on the UFO scene. (See Appendix B.)

All of the other men on the Majestic-12 list made sense as part of a group dealing with UFOs. But not Donald Menzel. People don't require high-level security clearances to be Harvard astronomers. And for years, Dr. Menzel had been the primary debunker of UFOs in the United States, if not the world.

THE DOUBLE LIFE OF DR. MENZEL

When Bill Moore told me that Donald Menzel's name was on the list of Majestic-12 members, my first reaction was that the document must be a hoax.

Donald Howard Menzel was known in ufological circles since the early 1950s as a total skeptic. He authored or co-authored three debunking books and made frequent public statements that all UFO sightings could be explained as common natural or manmade phenomena. How could such a skeptic have possibly been a member of a group dealing with the crash and recovery of flying saucers and alien bodies?

I didn't like Menzel. We had never met, although we spoke once on the phone. I had read his three anti-UFO books and many of his articles, and I felt that Max Planck was thinking of people like him when he said, "New ideas come to be accepted, not because their opponents come to believe in them, but because their opponents die and a new generation grows up that is accustomed to them." In my opinion, Menzel took an *a priori* approach to explaining UFO sightings—he started with the presumption that the sighting was caused by some common phenomenon, and then made the facts fit the presumption.

Menzel and I had only one close encounter. I was scheduled to speak to the Harvard Engineering Alumni Association, and I called him earlier that day. When I introduced myself, he said icily, "Yes, I know all about you."

"Oh. You read my congressional testimony?" I replied in a civil tone.

"No, but I have seen memos and letters about you. You can't be a scientist and believe in UFOs!"

I had to laugh, although I did the best I could to cover it. This was a Harvard scientist and professor, supposedly trained to reserve judgment until all the facts are known. I commented that surely he wasn't serious, and he started to rant at me about science and UFOs. I broke in and said, "Dr. Menzel, I didn't call to argue with you. I called to give you my personal invitation to my lecture tonight at the Harvard Engineering Alumni Association meeting."

Menzel's reply was terse. "I won't be there."

So for me, Menzel always stood for all those rigid UFO debunkers whose approach seems to be "Don't bother me with the facts, my mind is made up."

Although I didn't like the man personally, I actually found his role in the UFO controversy puzzling rather than maddening. Here was a famous astronomer whose reasoning about UFO sightings could be picked to pieces by a first-year physics student. Over and over again, he adjusted the facts to match his explanation.

Menzel testified in congressional hearings on UFOs on July 29, 1968, and in a meeting session on UFOs sponsored by the American Association for the Advancement of Science in Boston in December 1969. One observer at the Boston meeting indicated that Menzel almost had a heart attack and appeared much more upset than the situation warranted, especially during the testimony of Dr. James E. McDonald, professor of physics at the University of Arizona. McDonald had interviewed over 500 UFO witnesses, and provided tremendous evidence that destroyed the theories of Menzel and another debunker, Philip Klass.

I was also mystified by the fact that I found proof in the Air

Force files that Menzel had a copy of Project Blue Book Special Report 14, but he never mentioned it in any of his three books or numerous papers! This official database is unique, and one would expect it to be acknowledged by any scientist with a serious interest in flying saucers.

And why would a Harvard professor of astronomy, hardly a high-security-level position, be working with the other people on the Majestic-12 list? These included the first four directors of the CIA (or its forerunner), the first Secretary of Defense, and Vannevar Bush, who headed the wartime Office of Scientific Research and Development and was in charge of the Manhattan Project and other high-security military research projects.

I sat down in my office and thought this over. Could I have been wrong about Menzel's intentions? I started rereading my files on the other people listed in the document, all of whom had popped out in one way or another in our attempts to fathom the government's early UFO operations. In my papers on Vannevar Bush, I found a pertinent letter I had copied at the Library of Congress. The January 14, 1951 letter was to Bush from Robert Proctor, a member of the very old Boston law firm of Choate, Hall, and Stewart:

> I am happy to inform you that the Air Force central loyalty security board has under date of January 11, 1951, advised Dr. Donald H. Menzel and myself of Dr. Menzel's complete clearance with respect to loyalty and security charges brought against him by the U.S. Air Force. The letter of the executive secretary of the board advising of this determination contains the following paragraph:
> "I am pleased to inform you that the board determined that on all the evidence reasonable grounds do not exist for the belief that you are disloyal to the Government of the United States and that reasonable grounds do not exist for the belief that your immediate removal would be warranted by the demands of national security. This decision has been approved by the Assistant Secretary of the Air Force (Management)."

I know that you will be hearing directly from Donald Menzel, but I am, in accordance with my commitment to you, advising you immediately of this result because of your great interest in the matter. In doing so, I want to express personally my very sincere appreciation of the all out help which you provided in presentation of his case.

Now I looked at this letter in a new light. Why had Menzel been in danger of losing an Air Force security clearance? Why did he have such clearance in the first place? I knew he had been in the Navy during World War II. What connection was there between Bush and Menzel? Why did Bush give his "all out help" at the hearing?

There was no mention of Menzel's loyalty hearings in the *New York Times* (they were commonly reported in that communists-under-every-bed era). Freedom of Information requests to various government agencies and the National Archives brought no information. I contacted Choate, Hall, and Stewart and learned that there had been more than a week of hearings in May 1950 that produced over 1,300 pages of testimony, and that one of Menzel's staunchest defenders had been Vannevar Bush!

I then determined that, in addition to the huge correspondence about UFOs by Menzel at the American Philosophical Society Library in Philadelphia, there were also substantial holdings at the University of Denver, where he had been an undergraduate, and at Harvard.

Gaining access to the Harvard papers took some doing. I had to get written permission from the chairman of the astronomy department and the director of the Smithsonian Observatory. I also needed to obtain Mrs. Menzel's permission to read his unpublished autobiography. I was finally granted permission by the Harvard folks, and visited Cambridge in April 1986. (The Fund for UFO Research paid my travel expenses.) The evening of my first day at Harvard, I and several people from the astronomy department visited Mrs. Menzel. She was most charming and cooperative, and I got her permission as well.

Most of my questions to her focused on the loyalty hearings, not on flying saucers. I did ask her casually about her husband's classified work; she indicated she knew nothing about that. From my own extensive work on classified nuclear programs, I knew this was the truth: you simply don't tell your family the details of what you are doing on highly classified programs.

Thanks to Joan Thompson, who worked in the astronomy department at Harvard and has a longstanding interest in UFOs, I was able to ask a number of other people in the department about Menzel, too.

Once inside the Harvard archives, things were not so hospitable. The Finders Guide, a sort of index to the Menzel papers, gave no indication of any documents on UFOs. There was no copier in the facility for researchers to use. As at all archives, I had to list the boxes I wanted to search, wait for an attendant to bring them from the vaults, go through them folder by folder, return them to the attendant, and write another request. I had only three days at Harvard, as I was scheduled to go to Princeton to search Forrestal's papers.

Faced with all these innocuous file folder titles and being under time pressure, I decided to make a stab in the dark and start with Menzel's correspondence with President Kennedy. Frankly, I was curious as to why there even was such a file. (It turns out that Kennedy was on the Board of Overseers at Harvard, had chosen astronomy as his special interest area, and was well-acquainted with Menzel.) To my surprise, the correspondence showed that Menzel led two separate lives.

Publicly, Menzel was a famous astronomy professor serving on international committees, leading solar eclipse expeditions, establishing solar observatories, supervising graduate students, and debunking UFOs.

Privately, he did highly classified consulting work for federal intelligence agencies, primarily with the huge National Security Agency (NSA), and for more than thirty corporations on such matters as radio wave propagation, cryptography, and apparently, alien interstellar spacecraft.

(None of the several biographies of Menzel deal at all with his close connection with intelligence agencies. The articles in *Current Biography*, the McGraw-Hill *Modern Scientists and Engineers, Who's Who*, and the eight-page appreciation by his former student and long-time colleague Leo Goldberg in the April 1977 *Sky and Telescope*, mention his UFO debunking, but do not even hint at his connections with the NSA, the CIA, the military, or Vannevar Bush. Discretion and patriotism were two prominent features of his fascinating career.)

Two quotes from letters to Kennedy (there are many others) show Menzel's intelligence involvement and his discretion. Speaking of the NSA and its predecessor U.S. Navy agency in an August 13, 1960 letter, he said, "I have been associated with this activity for almost 30 years and probably have the longest continuous record of association of any person in the country. I still keep my close association with them. Properly cleared to one another, I should be able to help in this sensitive area." (The NSA has a strong UFO connection. It has refused to release 156 UFO documents or even an unexpurgated version of a 21-page Top Secret affidavit to federal judge Gerhard Gesell justifying the withholding of the documents. About 75 percent of the version of the affidavit eventually released under FOIA is blacked out.)

On November 3, 1960, again about the NSA: "I have been a consultant to that activity with Top Secret clearance and have also had some association with the CIA. Obviously in an unclassified letter, I cannot go further into detail."

So Menzel did belong with the other high-security-level members of Majestic-12! Among other fascinating facts, my three days at Harvard revealed the following:

- Menzel stated to Kennedy that he had had a Navy Top Secret Ultra Security Clearance, even at the time that the Air Force was trying to withdraw his much lower-level Secret clearance.
- Menzel's association with Vannevar Bush dated back to at least 1934, according to both Bush and Menzel. Bush at that time was

a dean at MIT and was working on development of one of the first analog computers. Menzel was interested in this system for astronomical calculations. It is clear from Bush's loyalty hearing testimony that he had contact with Menzel during World War II when he was serving in Washington on various projects and that that association continued after the war. (Bush never discussed classified details at the hearings, since his testimony was unclassified.)

• Menzel was known for his outstanding discretion about classified material. Many of those who testified on his behalf at the loyalty hearings, including Bush, stressed his total trustworthiness with regard to security. I have talked to numerous others who knew Menzel, including two people who worked for him during the war on classified projects. There was also testimony at the loyalty hearings from his Ph.D. advisor at Princeton. They unanimously agreed that he was extraordinarily discreet.

• Menzel would have been well aware of the uses of disinformation by governments. For example, he knew what was done to keep the Germans and Japanese from suspecting that the Allies had broken their secret codes.

• Menzel had learned Japanese during his work in cryptography. (He was involved in this field before, during, and after the war.) He was an ideal person to analyze the symbols on the Roswell crash debris, since he had the high-level security clearance to go with his cryptographic skills and understanding of an entirely different—"alien"— symbolic language.

• According to the notebook he kept listing travel expenditures, he made frequent trips to Washington, D.C. and New Mexico from 1947 to 1949 on government business. The trips to New Mexico were ostensibly for the establishment of the Air Force-sponsored Sacramento Peak Observatory, which is not far from Roswell.

• He was well acquainted with Detlev Bronk and Lloyd Berkner, other members of MJ-12, as well as most of the other top scientists of the 1950s.

• In his autobiography, Menzel wrote that he had written articles for newspapers as well as science fiction. He also mentioned that he had done work for the CIA and had written a Top Secret document about the NSA which had reached Ike and hopefully done some good. (The Eisenhower Library was unable to locate a copy of the NSA memo, illustrating the researcher's nightmare—even decades-old classified material is still not accessible at archives.)

Now my confusion about Menzel was giving way to the certainty that he was the best suited of all the members of Majestic-12 to provide disinformation to the general public. He had written science fiction and popular newspaper articles about science. That his UFO efforts were disinformation is fairly clear if one carefully reviews criticisms of his UFO investigations by myself; Brad Sparks, a West Coast researcher who did a devastating critique; the late Dr. James McDonald in his congressional testimony and elsewhere; and optical physicist Dr. Bruce Maccabee, former Chairman of the Fund for UFO Research. For instance, Menzel often claimed sightings were mirages, or sun dogs. McDonald, whose specialty was atmospheric physics, clearly demonstrated that such explanations didn't stand up to quantitative analysis of those well-known phenomena. In some cases, Menzel invented fictional concepts such as "reflections from clouds" to explain sightings. When you carefully examine the data used by Menzel to justify certain conclusions about specific UFO cases, you find that it doesn't stand up. And Menzel was too smart not to know he was putting out nonsense.

A very important aspect of Menzel's professional persona was that, unlike the great majority of astronomers, he incorporated practical engineering considerations into his work rather than being strictly a theorist. During World War II, for example, he used what he knew about blocking out the main body of the sun when viewing solar prominences to help pilots deal with Japanese fighters diving at them out of the sun. After the war, Menzel had a running battle with Dr. Harlow Shapley, technically his boss at Harvard, about the need for more precise engineering work when designing an observatory in South Africa. Shapley did what Menzel considered a slapdash job, and that telescope was never as useful as it might have been if the proper engineering had been done. And Menzel consulted with corporations such as Lockheed and McDonnell Douglas on numerous high-tech, high-security projects that required him to apply theory to practical matters.

So he was a man who was ready, willing, and able to get his hands dirty with equipment. It is interesting that, according to the MJ-12 briefing document, Menzel pushed for an origin of the wreckage as outside our solar system. This opinion is consistent for a mind that understands technical applications.

By contrast, Dr. J. Allen Hynek, also an astronomer and the Project Blue Book scientific consultant for 20 years, throughout his career refused to do any kind of research on the engineering aspects of interstellar flight. He often said that if the thickness of one playing card were the distance from the earth to the moon, the distance to the nearest star would be 19 miles of playing cards. He was implying that the ratio of the distances gives the ratio of the travel times. This was proof enough for Hynek that interstellar travel was impossible.

What Hynek failed to consider, and what Menzel would have known, was that the playing-card analogy was false. If you double the velocity of a moon rocket after it leaves the earth's gravitational field and begins coasting toward the moon, it will arrive 20 times faster, not twice as fast!

Despite these qualifications, many people have objected to the notion that Menzel could publicly attack ufologists and explain away all UFO sightings while in private being on the inside. They find it impossible that someone could keep the two lives so discrete. How could he not tell someone—his close friends, his family—about his secret work?

As someone who has worked on classified projects for many years, my answer is straightforward: It was easy. There are many popular examples of people who have led double lives. Take Burgess, MacLean, and Philby, the three Soviet spies who were very high up in British Intelligence. They fooled their associates, family, and friends, for more than 15 years in a high-stakes endeavor in which discovery meant imprisonment or banishment. Dr. Klaus Fuchs was a scientist who, while working at Los Alamos, turned over considerable top-secret information about the U.S. atomic bomb to the Soviets. His traitorous activity came as a complete shock to his associates, and he didn't even do it for the money. Aldrich Ames sold secrets to the Soviets for many years while seeming to be a dedicated CIA agent. And these spy cases are just the ones we know about!

Perhaps a better example of this discretion is given in *The General and the Bomb,* William Lawren's biography of General Leslie Groves, who directed the day-to-day operations of the Manhattan Project. On the morning of August 6, 1945, Groves's wife received a phone call from an officer in her husband's office at the Pentagon suggesting that she listen to the radio for an important news announcement at noon. The announcement, of course, was about the atomic bombing of Hiroshima. As she listened to the announcement, she realized that this event probably meant that her son would not be sailing off to the war in the Pacific, and thought how considerate it was for the officer to notify her. The last sentence of the bulletin noted that the bomb had been developed under the direction of her husband. That was the first she knew about what he had been doing for the previous three years!

The strongest proponents of the idea that secrets can't be kept are those people who haven't kept secrets. I have talked to dozens of World War II generals, officers, and intelligence agents in my attempts to learn more about classified government programs. Universally, they have agreed that secrets can be kept; that people with high-level clearances simply do not tell their families or friends anything about their classified knowledge and work. There are two obvious reasons for this. First, to tell others is to put them at risk of kidnap and torture by enemies or terrorists. Second, those with high security clearances have in general accepted the validity of the notion that highly classified information should not be distributed to people who don't have a need to know it.

Besides their agreement on how individuals keep secrets, every one of the oldtimers I spoke with also agreed that there are "black budget" programs which the public will probably never hear about. *New York Times* correspondent Tim Weiner has won two Pulitzer Prizes for investigative journalism. In his solidly documented book *Blank Check: The Pentagon's Black Budget* (Warner Books, 1990), he makes a strong case for an annual black budget beyond direct congressional control of $34 billion!

Menzel and all others who had high-level clearances during World War II learned to be discreet. Vannevar Bush himself was famous for his insistence on compartmentalization of classified information, in which not even people cleared at the highest levels know everything about a project. (Bush gave glowing testimony about Menzel's discretion at the loyalty hearings.) Even J. Allen Hynek admitted that he knew of Bush's penchant for compartmentalization from his work under Bush at the Applied Physics Laboratory at Johns Hopkins University. Bush's strong views about security were well known down the line.

To establish Menzel's own ability to segregate his activities, one has merely to consider that he could have saved himself a great deal of grief at the Air Force loyalty hearings by stating that he had an active Navy Top Secret Ultra clearance. Yet he didn't do so, even though he later described the extended period surrounding the hearings as the worst time of his life. The hearings were held in May 1950, but it wasn't until January 1951 that the Air Force cleared his record. During that whole period, Menzel was living with uncertainty.

Amongst the charges against him for disloyalty were that he had led an eclipse expedition to the Soviet Union in 1936. Also, that he had said nice things about the Soviet war contribution at a government dinner honoring Soviet-American wartime friendship; and that his wife had given a pair of stockings to a Soviet astronomer to take home to his wife! He was also charged with guilt by association—Shapley, Menzel's Harvard boss, had a reputation as a communist sympathizer. The people who made the charges against Menzel didn't even show up at the loyalty hearings. The hearings were a travesty, but Menzel didn't go public with his great distress—

not even to a number of his World War II colleagues, with whom I spoke, who never even learned of the hearings.

Some people, such as Menzel's friend Dr. Ernest Taves, who coauthored his last UFO book, maintain that while Menzel was indeed the perfect person to be called in on such an event as the crash of a flying saucer, there would have been no need for secrecy past the first few months. However, little reflection is needed to recognize the national security aspect of crashed saucers at a time when the cold war was heating up: military exploitation of the technology of the saucers and the need to classify the information Above Top Secret to prevent enemies from learning about the work. Menzel's many decades of highly classified research and his responses at the loyalty hearings clearly indicate his unwillingness to reveal classified information to anyone without a need to know (including President Kennedy).

It is questionable that our top scientists would be able to divine the technological secrets of flying saucers in a matter of decades, let alone a few months. It would be like giving Christopher Columbus a nuclear submarine in 1492 and asking him to build one for his transoceanic voyage.

Since it was clear from his comments to Kennedy that Menzel had the facilities for storing, preparing, shipping, and receiving highly classified documents, I made a serious effort to find out who did his postwar classified work for him. After considerable sleuthing, starting with older secretaries at Harvard, I eventually found a woman who had been a student in one of Menzel's prewar cryptography courses, was his assistant in Washington during the war, went back to Harvard with him after the war, and wound up marrying one of his graduate students. He was so much like a father to her that her wedding took place in his house.

In late 1986, I tracked her down in retirement. Yes, she had a very good recollection of her association with Menzel; however, she was very concerned about revealing classified data. I assured her of my own discretion, and we made an appointment for me to visit her.

However, she soon called back to cancel, with a very lame excuse. She had clearly talked to some people, and she was spooked. From my contacts at Harvard, I learned that she had talked to Menzel's daughters and wife, and she was very worried. I have had subsequent phone conversations with her and she always steers as far from MJ-12 as possible. I had the impression that she knew what I was talking about, but felt that she couldn't say anything because of security.

While pursuing this source, I located a man who had worked at Engineering Research Associates (ERA) in Minnesota after World War II. This company had been started by some of Menzel's wartime code-breaking associates at the suggestion of James Forrestal, who was then Secretary of the Navy. The company became the forerunner of a host of major computer corporations.

A Minnesota member of the Mutual UFO Network, a major UFO organization, had told me about this scientist, who remembered working with Menzel many years earlier. I checked and found that Menzel had actually been offered full-time employment at ERA, but declined the opportunity. The scientist told me that one summer, Menzel suddenly had to drop his consulting work and leave in a hurry for some very highly classified project. As casually as I could, I asked, "What year was that?" and I shut up. A heartbeat passed. "Oh," he said, just as casually, "it must have been 1947."

As I followed the Menzel trail, I occasionally revealed my preliminary findings to others. One of these people was a professor at Harvard who had known Menzel very well for a couple of decades. This man had taught a course on the making of the atomic bomb, and so knew far more than most academics about how classified the project was and how closely the scientists involved in the project were spied upon and followed. However, he was not aware of Menzel's cryptographic skills, his CIA and NSA activities, or his knowledge of Japanese. I finally asked him the question that was really bothering me because I didn't know Menzel personally: "You knew him very well. How do you feel about the notion that he could have known all about crashed saucers and alien bodies and still have issued loads of disinformation?"

His answer shocked and amused me. "He would have loved it. He would have been in on the biggest story of the century and he could show how smart he was by pulling the wool over everybody's eyes!"

My research so far has not revealed a "smoking gun" pointing to Menzel's involvement in Operation Majestic-12. This is not surprising, in light of the Above-Top-Secret nature of the project. (Recall the Smith memo of November 21, 1950.) What I have been able to do is to demonstrate that Menzel could very well have been part of such a high-level group despite his public persona, and that his inclusion on the Majestic-12 briefing document is thus no deterrent to that document's validity. Menzel had the right kinds of specialized theoretical and technical knowledge; he had written fiction and nonfiction for popular consumption; he had the right security clearances; he maintained a long and patriotic involvement with highly classified work; he had a close association with the other top-level people listed as being involved in Majestic-12. Being on the inside of one of the most important projects ever conceived postwar probably appealed to his ego and would very likely have soothed any concerns he had about misleading the public and other members of the scientific community. In addition, he would have recognized the need for protecting the technology associated with saucers, and of the need to prepare the public for the shattering notion that the planet was being visited.

Menzel's scientific contacts and influence were worldwide, and so his word would have the effect of keeping other professional astronomers and scientists away from the UFO question. This would have been desirable for any Top Secret organization, since even innocent prying might have revealed the existence of the crashed-saucer project and other intelligence activities concerning UFOs.

Delving into the Menzel connection has also made certain bits of trivia seem more significant. Menzel developed the habit of doodling little drawings of "Martians" that were even collected and published. His wife even gave me one of his drawings. After reading an article I published about Menzel, a scientist who was aware of these pictures wrote me that he now understood why the doodling. Menzel really knew what the aliens looked like!

And in his 1968 congressional testimony, Menzel had commented that, if aliens had been visiting earth they would have certainly wished to talk to the National Academy of Sciences, of which he was a member. His whole tone implied that, since they haven't asked for an appointment, they must not be coming here. It would certainly appear that he may have been the one Academy member who actually did talk to an alien!

As for me, the most important result of my findings about Dr. Menzel was that they encouraged me to plunge deeper into an investigation of the Operation Majestic-12 documents. If they were real, they indicated a massive, decades-long coverup of alien visits to our planet. If they were fraudulent or intentionally misleading, they were put together by somebody on the inside who knew that Menzel would pass muster. None on the outside knew that.

OTHER MAJESTIC-12 MEMBERS

During my two decades of research related to UFOs and six years of intensive work on the Roswell crash before Jaime Shandera received the Majestic-12 documents, I had discovered possible connections between crashed saucers and all of the people listed as being part of the Majestic-12 group, except for Menzel. Now that the probability of Menzel being an insider as far as UFOs were concerned was established, the credibility of the list of members of the group was complete.

(Later, I interviewed General Arthur E. Exon, commander of Wright-Patterson Air Force Base in the mid-1960s. He had heard a lot of scuttlebutt about crashed saucers and aliens while stationed at Wright Field in 1947, as commander of the base in 1964 and 1965, and later while on assignment at the Pentagon. I met with him and we had several telephone conversations. He could find no reason to quarrel with the three primary MJ-12 documents or the list of original members.)

The original twelve-man group included six civilians and six military personnel. Of the military people, there were two each from the Air Force, the Navy, and the Army. There were outstanding research and development organizers and very strong intelligence community leaders, trained and tested in the crucible of war.

General Nathan Twining was certainly no surprise as a member of MJ-12. Twining was one of the four people on the list who were still alive when I started my Roswell quest, but according to his wife, one of his sons, and his former pilot, he was suffering with Alzheimer's disease. His papers had been donated to the Library of Congress, and I managed to get approval from his son to view them. Unfortunately, the great bulk of the papers were still classified. I put in requests for classification review of a number of boxes, and eventually made a couple of important discoveries in a folder labeled TOP SECRET EYES ONLY: two memos from Robert Cutler relating to Operation Solarium.

In Twining's correspondence files, I also found materials of interest. Twining had planned to fly to Seattle on July 16, 1947 to review the new B-50 bomber being built by Boeing and to do some fishing with old friends.

The West Coast trip had clearly been planned for a long time (with confirmed arrangements by June 2), but it was suddenly canceled. Earl Schaefer, vice president of Boeing-Wichita (Kansas) had written on July 10 asking Twining to stop by to see the prototype XL-15 liaison plane on his way to Seattle. In his July 17 response to Schaefer, Twining said "with deepest regrets we had to cancel our trip to the Boeing factory due to a very important and sudden matter that developed here. . . . I have been away quite a bit the last couple of weeks. . . ." Newspaper articles quoting Twining about flying saucers clearly established that he was in New Mexico around July 9. This strongly suggested that the very important and sudden matter was connected with New Mexico around the time of the Roswell crash.

Several years later, one of Twining's children gave me the name of the general's pilot, whom I managed to locate and eventually meet in person. He allowed me to copy many pages of his flight log:

- On Monday, July 7, 1947, they flew from Wright Field in Ohio (Twining's base) to Alamogordo Army Air Field in New Mexico.

The trip took six and a half hours.

- On Friday, July 11, they flew back to Wright Field, making stops at White Sands Missile Range and Albuquerque (Sandia and Kirtland Army Air Field). The return flight took eight hours and forty minutes.

This was Twining's only trip to New Mexico during the summer of 1947.

On July 8, Colonel Blanchard at Roswell Army Air Field ordered Lieutenant Walter Haut to put out his press release about the strange wreckage that Mac Brazel found on the Foster ranch. So why did Twining fly to Alamogordo rather than Roswell the day before this announcement? A growing body of evidence indicates that there was actually a crash west of Socorro, New Mexico in the Plains of San Agustin on about July 2, which got no press coverage and which may well have been tracked by radar at the White Sands Missile Range. That installation was preparing for a rocket launch on July 3, and standard procedure was to track weather balloons with radar to determine high-level winds starting 72 hours prior to launch, with other readings 48, 24, and 4 hours prelaunch. (These radar sets all used vacuum tubes, and were normally left on around the clock when they were needed.) Newspaper articles say the launch was postponed because there had been an accident in which several people were injured with a toxic substance.

If the radar had tracked the UFO down, that would explain the prompt appearance of the military at the crash site and their quick expulsion of Barney Barnett and the archaeology group from the area. Surely if something had been tracked down, there would have been subsequent aerial reconnaissance from Alamogordo, which was much closer than Roswell.

Alamogordo was the home to a contingent of Twining's Air Materiel Command scientists and of numerous rocket scientists, including the German contingent under Werner von Braun. Probably the recovery near Horse Springs, New Mexico, at the western edge of the Plains of San Agustin would have stimulated careful monitoring of all press wire service transmissions to assure that no story went out. Radio station personnel from Roswell have said they were called from Washington and told to discontinue coverage of the Corona crashed disc story or lose their licenses. It is very likely not a coincidence that President Truman met with New Mexico Senator Chavez on July 9 with no reason being given.

It is important to remember that Roswell was basically a Strategic Air Command base whose primary purpose was not research and development, but rather the training of a powerful force of heavy bombers in the new tactics of atom bombing. It had very high security, but with an entirely different mission from nearby White Sands, Alamogordo (now Holloman), and Kirtland.

Thus, General Twining would be an obvious choice for a control group concerning the recovery and study of crashed flying saucers. He was young and vigorous and had numerous engineers reporting to him in both Ohio and New Mexico at the time of the early UFO crashes. Even the media recognized him as an appropriate source. Many July 8, 1947 newspapers that had the article about the Roswell recovery also used a wire story from the *Oregonian* in Portland, Oregon. (The *Oregonian* was one of the first papers to report Kenneth Arnold's sighting of nine flying discs flying at high speed over the Cascades on June 24, 1947.)

> The *Oregonian* said today that Major General Nathan F. Twining, Chief of the Materiel Command, told it flatly that the "flying saucers are not the result of experiments of the armed services."

> "Neither the AAF nor any other component of the armed forces had any plane, guided missile or other aerial device under development which could possibly be mistaken for a saucer or formation of flying discs. . . . Some of these witnesses evidently saw something, but we don't know what we are investigating."

The July 14 *Alamogordo Daily News* noted that Twining had been at the base on July 11 for a "routine" inspection. No pictures were taken, and the inspection was carried out with a very high-powered team, indicating that it was hardly routine. Clearly Twining had already been tasked to look into the possibility of secret government projects related to high-performance aircraft.

Another piece of correspondence from Twining led me down a different path. The 1969 Condon Report—a 965-page volume whose official name was *Scientific Study of Unidentified Flying Objects* and which was the final report of an Air Force-sponsored study at the University of Colorado under the direction of Dr. Edward Condon—included a letter from Twining to Brigadier General Schulgen at Air Force Headquarters (Appendix B). The letter was featured in the 1979 documentary *UFOs Are Real,* and its major implication was the reality of intelligently controlled flying discs. But there were other important aspects of the letter. At one point, the letter mentions "The lack of physical evidence in the shape of crash recovered exhibits which would undeniably prove the existence of these objects." Since the letter—dated September 23, 1947, the day before the Truman-Forrestal memo in the Majestic-12 documents—was classified Secret, it could not reference information that was above Top Secret, which the recovered wreckage would have been.

Later in the letter, Twining recommends that complete sets of all UFO data should be sent to the following: "the Army, Navy, Atomic Energy Commission (AEC), JRDB, the Air Force Scientific Advisory Group (AFSAG), NACA, and the RAND and NEPA projects." It was only well after I started investigating the Roswell crash in 1979 that I finally appreciated the importance of this listing. The last six groups were all concerned with sophisticated technology, not ongoing defense work. The common link between them was Vannevar Bush.

Back in 1982 I had noted that Bush was the prewar chairman of the National Advisory Committee on Aeronautics (NACA). During the war, he had headed the Office of Scientific Research and Development (OSRD)—the predecessor of the Joint Research and Development Board (JRDB), of which he was the first chairman, and the group out of which the AEC was formed. The JRDB had also had a hand in establishing the Nuclear Energy for Propulsion Applications (NEPA) program.

When reviewing a number of NACA documents at the Truman and other libraries, I had also noted that Twining had served on NACA and that in 1948 Detlev Bronk and General James Doolittle became members. Doolittle was one of the world's great aviators, and was one of the first recipients of a Ph.D. in aeronautics (from MIT when Bush was dean). Doolittle became chairman of NACA in 1953, was chairman of AFSAG, and was involved in a host of very highly classified intelligence-related activities throughout the postwar era, including chairing a committee to evaluate the CIA for President Eisenhower and organizing super-secret Operation Solarium in 1953.

The MJ-12 member listing suggested other links. Jerome Hunsaker of MIT had succeeded Bush as NACA chairman. Vandenberg had served on NACA. Bronk became vice chairman of NACA and had headed an OSRD Biology Committee under Bush. In one way or another, the careers of all of the men on the list were intertwined.

The first thing that strikes one about the list of Majestic-12 members is that these were all very important people. None were elected officials, but they all had very high status in the postwar period. Three of the original members were the first three directors of Central Intelligence. The Central Intelligence Group was the postwar successor to the Office of Strategic Services and the forerunner of the Central Intelligence Agency. These three and two others were high-ranking military commanders. One member was the first Secretary of Defense; another held many high-security positions under Truman. Five others were top scientists in aviation, research and development, and astronomy, and had high security clearances.

Dr. Vannevar Bush was a world-renowned research scientist who was professor and later dean of MIT between the World Wars. In the 1930s, he was one of the original developers of the analog computer—the ancestor of today's personal computers. His military-related research began during World War I, when he worked on submarine detection, but his executive ability flowered during World War II. As head of the OSRD, he led the development of the atomic bomb, the proximity fuse, radar, and at least 90 other high-tech systems with military applications. One of his most important attributes was a strong desire to make scientific developments in the art of warfare understandable to field personnel, not just Ph.Ds.

Besides his scientific work, he was a member of the War Council, served on all kinds of committees, was close to President Roosevelt, and was the world's outstanding technology administrator and developer. After the war, he stayed active in national matters, devoting himself to the unification of the armed services, civilian control of atomic energy, and establishing the National Science Foundation. He served on the board of trustees at MIT as well as numerous other organizations, and was the recipient of countless awards, including having a building named for him at MIT.

When he agreed to serve as chairman of the new JRDB in 1947, Bush wrote in his acceptance letter of "my wish ultimately to be free of governmental duties in order to return more completely to scientific matters." Considering that this chairmanship was primarily an intensive administrative job of getting together a huge number of committees spanning a broad range of technological and scientific specialties, it is not surprising that Bush wanted to drop administrative matters. Bush resigned from this position on October 1, 1948. However, it is perfectly clear that he was still heavily involved in official Washington activities. He was a member of the 1953 Rockefeller Commission, and he had ongoing correspondence with the president and many other members of MJ-12.

Bush was well known for compartmentalization of classified work. Contrary to the normally wide-ranging access permitted in most research settings, Bush insisted that working scientists be permitted access only to the classified information they needed to do their well-defined jobs. Scientific curiosity was not sufficient reason for access to classified data beyond one's own field. This was very important in the war mentality of the time, for the standards Bush set limited the damage that could be done by spies. Since no one person working on a project had complete information about it, anyone who was captured by the enemy would be able to dispense information about only that part of a technology in which he or she was personally involved.

A very large, well-organized file of unclassified Bush correspondence is at the Library of Congress in Washington. Numerous other Bush papers and a long oral history are at the MIT archives.

Dr. Detlev Bronk headed a biology-related research committee under Bush at the OSRD and went on to become the head of the National Research Council and, in addition, President of the National Academy of Sciences. He served on innumerable other scientific committees, and was an advisor to Truman, Eisenhower, and Kennedy. He was president of Johns Hopkins University, and then president of Rockefeller University in New York City. Everywhere one looked around the Washington scientific scene in the 1950s and 1960s, there was Detlev Bronk. He was named to NACA in 1948. His primary field was aviation physiology. There were at that time numerous aviation biology problems since humans were beginning to fly higher, faster, and in more maneuverable aircraft than ever before. There was nobody better equipped at that time to deal with the question of what was special about alien bodies.

Dr. Lloyd Berkner had an outstanding background as a pilot, as a scientist involved in polar expeditions, and in solving radio communications problems. He had a very strong interest in space, was head of the International Geophysical Year Program for the United States in 1958, and was the individual who announced to America that the Soviets had launched the first satellite in October 1957. Berkner became head of Associated Universities at Brookhaven, New York, and served on many national committees, including the Robertson Panel, established by then-CIA director Walter Bedell Smith in early 1953 to evaluate UFOs. (Perhaps he was there to make sure that no one without a need to know was informed about crashed saucers and Majestic-12.) Berkner was also the first executive secretary of the JRDB under Bush, and in 1960 gave great encouragement to Dr. Frank Drake's Project Ozma, the first radio-telescopic search for extraterrestrial intelligence.

Dr. Jerome Hunsaker, the first-born and last to die of the Majestic-12 group, had an illustrious career. From 1915 to 1930, he was instrumental in developing a wide variety of systems in aerodynamics, including the first airplanes to cross the Atlantic, the first wind tunnels, and various lighter-than-air vehicles. He performed all kinds of work for the Navy and later for the Army Air Force, was head of aerodynamics at MIT for decades, and succeeded Bush as head of NACA. He was at the very apex of the field of high-performance aircraft design, and trained many of the top names in that area. Many of his papers are at the MIT archives. (Interestingly, Jaime Shandera received the film of the Majestic-12 documents only three months after Hunsaker's death!)

General Robert Montague, probably the least known of all the Majestic-12 group, was a West Point classmate of General Twining's. As commander of Fort Bliss, near El Paso, Texas, he was responsible for the White Sands Proving Ground in New Mexico, not too far from the Roswell crash site. He was a well-known expert in mathematics, was on the ground in a sensitive part of the country, and had command of a lot of soldiers. According to the old generals whom I interviewed, Montague had a solid technology background and a reputation as somebody whose judgment and discretion could be trusted completely.

Montague was chosen to head the very highly classified Armed Forces Special Weapons Center at Sandia Base, now Sandia National Laboratory, adjacent to Kirtland Air Force Base in Albuquerque in early July 1947. Sandia's primary mission was to convert nuclear weapons designed at Los Alamos into easy-to-use, safe weapons systems able to withstand the harsh conditions of aircraft takeoff and landings, rocket launches, and even aircraft crashes without premature detonation.

Montague was introduced to high officials in Washington in early July 1947 by General Leslie Groves, who, because of his Manhattan Project activities, clearly had a need to know for anything that might threaten the security of New Mexico's nuclear weapons installations. Surely one of the government's fears would have been that unknown intruders were checking on highly classified facilities. Were they spies from the Soviet Union in a new high-performance vehicle, perhaps developed by German scientists?

Gordon Gray, a rich North Carolina newspaper publisher, was active in intelligence work during World War II. He later was chairman of the 5412 Committee, which was in charge of covert operations for the National Security Council (NSC) and CIA and handled matters considered too classified for the full NSC to hear. He was a protege of General George Marshall, and President Truman appointed him as Undersecretary and later Secretary of the Army. He also was the head of the CIA's Psychological Strategy Board during the Truman administration. (Most of the records of this board even from that era are still classified.) Gray later served as Special Assistant to the President for National Security Affairs, in effect the liaison between the president and the NSC. He also was a member of the President's Foreign Intelligence Advisory Board. His record over many years in Washington was distinguished, and he served several administrations in a nonpartisan fashion. He was considered one of the more brilliant men in Washington.

Perhaps more importantly, he was Eisenhower's Director of the Office of Defense Mobilization and then chairman of the 5412 Committee, whose only other members were the Secretaries of Defense and State and the Director of Central Intelligence. Stephen Ambrose, in his book *Ike's Spies*, called 5412 "the most secret committee of the U.S. government. No covert action could be taken without the prior approval of the committee." Ambrose went on to say that Dr. Richard Bissell, longtime CIA official, said that operations once approved by 5412 would not even go before the full NSC because they were much too sensitive!

Gray also served on the committee that deprived Dr. Robert Oppenheimer, who oversaw the creation of the Los Alamos laboratory and of the atomic bomb, of his security clearance, much to the dismay of many in the scientific world. Bush had defended Oppenheimer. However, there is correspondence on file for both Gray and Bush indicating that even after the Oppenheimer decision, they maintained a healthy respect for each other.

In 1988, four years after we received the Majestic-12 documents, I crossed paths with one of Gray's sons, C. Boyden Gray. I had located him in Washington, D.C., and when I called his home, I was given his office number. When I called there, the receptionist answered with "Office of the Vice President." I wondered what company he was vice president of. I spoke to Boyden for some time about his father, the respect with which he was held in Washington, and how much highly classified work he had done. I agreed to send Boyden copies of the Majestic-12 documents, about which he knew nothing. Only when I obtained his mailing address did I realize that Gray was in the office of the *Vice President of the United States,* George Bush, who was former head of the CIA. A few months later, Bush became President, and Gray served as his White House counsel. I have often wondered what kind of reaction the receipt of a Top Secret/MAJIC Eyes Only document by regular mail elicited at the top levels of government.

In 1916, James V. Forrestal began a Wall Street career as a bond salesman, but soon enlisted in the Navy to fight in World War I. After the war, he returned to Wall Street, rising to become president of Dillon, Read in 1937. In August 1940, President Roosevelt appointed him Undersecretary of the Navy, and he was instrumental in modernizing and enlarging that arm of the service. In 1944, he was appointed Secretary of the Navy. Truman named him the first Secretary of Defense after the unification of the command structure of the Army, Navy, and newly formed Air Force in September 1947. In this position, Forrestal was certainly somebody who would have been involved in an operation with the national security implications of Operation Majestic-12.

Admiral Sidney Souers was very active in Naval intelligence during World War II. A fellow Missourian, Souers was named by President Truman as the first head of the Central Intelligence Group in 1946. The next year, Truman asked him to become the first head of the NSC. His deputy at the NSC was James Lay, whom Souers groomed to take over as executive secretary. In 1950, he retired from government and went back to being a businessman in Missouri. (There is a Souers file at the Truman Library, and it is clear that Truman and Souers continued their long relationship well after Truman returned to Missouri.) However, because of his background and knowledge, he maintained an office at the White House as an advisor through 1953. Souers also served as a member of the first President's Board of Consultants on Foreign Intelligence Activities appointed by Eisenhower in January 1956. Thus, he maintained his high-level security clearance, involvement in intelligence matters, and the respect of such outstanding Eisenhower associates as Generals Omar Bradley and James Doolittle, who were also on the board. Souers had a low public profile, but judging by his correspondence, he had the full confidence of Harry Truman, J. Edgar Hoover, Vannevar Bush, and other top officials inside the U.S. government.

General Hoyt S. Vandenberg, a West Point graduate, was also very active in intelligence during World War II, was a member of the War Council, and accompanied President Roosevelt to the Yalta and Montreal conferences. He succeeded Souers as Director of Central Intelligence in 1946, but was reluctantly released to Europe at the specific request of General Eisenhower. He was named the first vice chief of staff of the Air Force under General Carl Spaatz, and succeeded Spaatz in 1948 as chief of staff. He was a close relative of powerful U.S. Senator Arthur Vandenberg.

Admiral Roscoe H. Hillenkoetter, an Annapolis graduate, was active in naval intelligence during World War II, was military attache in Europe right after the war, and was named first director of the Central Intelligence Agency (the successor to the Central Intelligence Group) in 1947. He was replaced as director by General Walter Bedell Smith in 1950, and went off for a year of sea duty in Korea, coming back to head the Brooklyn Navy Yard in 1951. In 1952 he was named head of the 3rd Naval District, headquartered in New York. There is some correspondence between him and Menzel, and he was an Annapolis classmate of Donald Keyhoe, who was head of the National Investigations Committee for Aerial Phenomena (NICAP) and an agitator against government coverup of UFO information from the 1950s through the 1970s. Hillenkoetter even served on NICAP's board of directors, though it essentially never met.

General Walter Bedell Smith, who according to the briefing documents was named a permanent replacement on Majestic-12 for James Forrestal in 1950, had an unusual career. He was the only one of the people on the list not having a college degree. He worked his way up in the military, becoming Eisenhower's chief of staff during World War II. After the war he had the sensitive, difficult role as Ambassador to the Soviet Union. He succeeded Hillenkoetter as CIA director in late 1950, and then became Assistant Secretary of State in 1953. Historians consider him the outstanding early director of the CIA.

The career paths of the thirteen men listed as members of Majestic-12 crossed again and again. Bush and Forrestal were close in Washington for many years. Not only did they meet often, according to the records in the Forrestal files at Princeton University, they even played tennis together. It is clear from the notes and correspondence between them that they liked and appreciated each other. Besides being men of vision, they were men of accomplishment, backing up their words with action.

Vandenberg and Twining were both flyers and were old friends, having had more or less parallel careers in the military beginning at West Point. In the early 1950s, Twining served under Vandenberg as vice chief of staff of the Air Force, and became chief of staff after Vandenberg died.

Souers was not only the first head of the Central Intelligence Group (followed by Vandenberg), but also became the first Executive Secretary of the National Security Council. There is correspondence between him and Bush and most of the other MJ-12 members. Hillenkoetter attended all the meetings of the NSC during his tenure as CIA director, so Hillenkoetter knew Souers well, as did Vandenberg, who succeeded Souers at Central Intelligence.

Bronk and Bush's relationship goes back to pre-World War II days, and they served together on numerous postwar committees. Not only were Bush, Bronk, and Twining all on NACA immediately after the war, but judging by the correspondence, Bronk and Bush were close. Bush even commented in one letter about his concern over Bronk's health and eyesight because of some incident.

Menzel and Bush, of course, went back to 1934 according to Bush's testimony at Menzel's loyalty hearings in 1950, and Menzel's letters to President Kennedy clearly indicate that he knew Bronk well. Menzel's papers indicate that he and Berkner knew each other's work well, and they served on the same international radio propagation committee of one of the astronomical organizations.

Bush and Vandenberg were on the War Council together. Hunsaker and Bush were together doing engineering work at MIT in the early 1930s, and it is clear from their correspondence that they knew each other extremely well. Hunsaker succeeded Bush as head of NACA when Bush was busy with OSRD.

There were close links within this group of very important people. Considering what was happening in America and around the world post–World War II, they were a natural group to be on a committee such as Majestic-12. Either by aptitude, position, or geographic location, their inclusion would be fairly obvious.

OPERATION MAJESTIC-12 MEMBERS

Name	Date of Birth	Date of Death	Age in July 1947	Field
Lloyd V. Berkner	2/1/05	6/4/67	42	Scientist, explorer; executive secretary of JRDB; leader of space program; on CIA Robertson Panel
Detlev Bronk	8/13/97	11/17/75	49	Aviation physiologist; chair, National Academy of Sciences; National Research Council; pres. Johns Hopkins, Rockefeller University
Vannevar Bush	3/11/90	6/28/74	57	Head of NACA, OSRD, JRDB; other high-security R&D positions; MIT; Carnegie Institute
James V. Forrestal	2/15/92	5/22/49	55	Secretary of the Navy; 1st Secretary of Defense
Gordon Gray	5/30/09	11/25/82	38	5412 Committee; National Security advisor; other intelligence posts; Secretary of the Army
Roscoe H. Hillenkoetter	5/8/97	6/18/82	50	Admiral; Navy Intelligence; 1st director CIA; 3rd DCI
Jerome Hunsaker	8/26/86	9/10/84	60	Aeronautical engineer at MIT; head of NACA
Donald H. Menzel	4/11/01	12/14/76	46	Astronomer at Harvard; high-security consultant to NSA, CIA
Robert M. Montague	8/7/99	2/20/58	47	General, Army; commander of Ft. Bliss; Head Armed Forces Special Weapons Center, Sandia Base
Walter B. Smith	10/5/95	8/9/61	51	General, Army; ambassador to USSR; 2nd director CIA; 4th DCI
Sidney W. Souers	3/30/92	1/14/73	55	Admiral; intelligence consultant; 1st director Central Intelligence Group; 1st DCI; 1st executive secretary, NSC
Nathan F. Twining	10/11/97	3/29/82	49	General, Air Force; Head, AMC; Air Force Chief of Staff; Head, Joint Chiefs of Staff
Hoyt S. Vandenberg	1/24/99	4/2/54	48	General, Air Force; 2nd director Central Intelligence Group; 2nd DCI; Air Force Chief of Staff

AUTHENTICATING THE MAJESTIC-12 BRIEFING DOCUMENTS

There's been a great deal of confusion within the small but vocal ufological community with regard to the Operation Majestic-12 documents. A major reason for this has been the confused, unconventional, and often incomplete way in which information has been released. Moore, Shandera, and I could not immediately release the documents because we couldn't be sure they were legitimate. That search for confirmation has taken years.

However, the first article about the Majestic-12 documents appeared in the December 1985 issue of *Just Cause*, a limited-distribution newsletter of Citizens Against UFO Secrecy (CAUS). This group was established in the late 1970s to try to pry open the government's files on UFOs using FOIA requests against the CIA, NSA, and other agencies. The editor of the newsletter is Barry Greenwood, who works for the U.S. Postal Service, and the publisher is Lawrence Fawcett, now a retired police officer. Greenwood and Fawcett had previously published the book *Clear Intent*, which focused on various government documents obtained under FOIA. What was missing from *Clear Intent* was a sense of the role of national security in the UFO question, which would explain much about why the government has gone to such great lengths to cover up its findings. At times they have taken the approach that the public has the right to know everything about everything.

The unsigned article in *Just Cause*, entitled "MJ12: Myth or Reality?" and apparently by Greenwood, included some information on the MJ-12 members, but no copies of the briefing document. *Just Cause* had been in touch with another researcher on the West Coast, Lee Graham, who has written many FOIA requests. Graham works for an aerospace firm, and claimed that he had given *Just Cause* the MJ-12 list, which he had been shown by a source in the military. He had not been allowed to copy the list, but he had taken notes. (As far as I know, the source was actually Bill Moore, who was not in the military and does not work for the government but has a fondness for playing games. As a joke, Bill once pulled out a MUFON identification card, flashed it at Lee, and indicated that he was working for the government. Lee bought it.)

The article had the right people on the list, although the information about each person was quite incomplete. Unfortunately, the information about the document itself wasn't accurate. According to the article, the document was classified "Top Secret Eyes Only" (the compartment *MAJIC* was left out). It reported that the document was nine back-to-back pages dated September 18, 1947 and signed by President Truman. (Of course, the document is eight one-sided pages. The briefing is dated November 18, 1952; the one-page Truman-Forrestal memo is dated September 24, 1947; the memo was signed by Truman, but the briefing was not signed.) The article explained the significance of the September 18, 1947 date as "the birthdate of the CIA! Is it a coincidence or a telltale clue to the document being phony? Or could this report have been one of the first orders of business for the fledgling CIA?" They were off on the wrong foot.

In the spring of 1987, Bill and Jaime were warned that very soon the briefing document would be coming out in Europe. Their informants were some insiders. Moore has since admitted that one of his major inside contacts is Richard Doty, who used to work for the Air Force Office of Special Investigations in Albuquerque. His name ap-

pears on a document out of Kirtland Air Force Base involving mul-
tiple-witness simultaneous observations of a UFO landing and taking off from the nearby Manzano Nuclear Weapons Storage area in
New Mexico.

Some have assumed that Doty provided the briefing document
in the first place. Moore and Shandera have claimed that nobody has
admitted sending the document, although the postmark on the
brown envelope was Albuquerque. It is clear from their conversations
with Doty that he knows about the document, but so far as I know,
he has never admitted sending it. I doubt that he did.

Within about a week, the London *Observer* ran a page 1 article
on the documents. The May 31, 1987 article by Martin Bailey was
headlined "Close Encounters of an Alien Kind—And Now if You've
Read Enough About the Election, Here's News from Another
World," and showed a tiny portion of the Majestic-12 document.

The article was picked up by Reuters and appeared in numerous
North American papers in the following days. When I heard about
it, I called Jaime who went out and got copies of the papers. The
Reuters account was somewhat less full than the *Observer* one. Bill
and Jaime had already been talking to their people about releasing information and immediately swung into high gear. They published a
version of the document in the Fair Witness Project publication
Focus, which Bill edits and publishes.

The timing was interesting. I was going to be in southern
California to help Bill with a national UFO conference in Burbank.
Bill was doing the local sponsorship; besides being a speaker, I was
also helping with public relations. A few days after Bill sent me a
copy of the documents as they appeared in *Focus,* I was in California
responding to reporters' questions about them. Now that I finally had
access to a full copy of the report, I was calling various archives, including the Truman and Eisenhower libraries, trying to pin down
dates and activities in particular and trying to counteract some of
the false information that was being put out by the noisy negativists.

The version Bill had published in *Focus* had heavy black censor
lines through portions of the document, especially the security mark-

ings, without any explanation of why they were there or who put them there. Nor did Bill publish an explanation about the receipt of the document. Bill later explained to me that he had put the black markings on the documents, and that what he included in the article and the markings on the documents were based on instructions from his insider contacts in New Mexico.

The fact of the matter is that the eight pages of the briefing document on the film that Jaime received were clean. There were no heavy markings. Bill had taken one set of 8 1/2" x 11" prints and run the censor lines through the security markings because getting caught with a copy of a Top Secret document didn't seem like such a good idea. That was one of the reasons he hadn't sent me a copy earlier, because taking it or sending it across national boundaries could be dangerous. From my viewpoint, I would be happy to have the U.S. government arrest me for carrying that particular TOP SECRET/MAJIC document, for that would tend to verify that the document is legitimate. If the government prosecutes, they are admitting that the briefing document is the real thing—if it were fake, they would have no case.

Bill did include another very interesting item in his article—although without providing background on it: a copy of a telex from OSI headquarters at Bolling Air Force Base to their more than 120 units around the world:

1. We have reason to believe that in the near future some or all of our field units may receive a request for information regarding UFO sightings or similar subjects. The request may originate with Stanton T. Friedman.

If such a request is received, do not repeat do not, refer the request to this HQS as required by AFR [Air Force Regulation] 12-30 AFOSI Sup 1. Respond directly to the requestor as follows: Quote. Requests for information from AFOSI files must be processed by our headquarters. Please resubmitt [sic] your request to HQS AFOSI, Information Release Division, Bolling AFB, DC 20332. Unquote.

2. Requests of this type from persons other than Friedman should also be processed the same way.

3. The original letter of request and a copy of your response should be forwarded to this HQS {XPU}, via Form 158.

4. FOIA/PA requests regarding other matters should be processed following normal procedure.

5. This special procedure is in effect until further notice.

The regulation mentioned in the telex requires that an OSI office pull the appropriate file, send it on to headquarters for review, and notify the requestor that they had done so. This would reveal that there is material responsive to the request. By ordering local offices to instruct the requestors to go through headquarters, the OSI could avoid indicating that they had any pertinent material and gives headquarters a chance to cover up. (Researchers including myself have found many documents showing that OSI is still heavily involved in UFO investigations, especially those involving military personnel.) Surely there must be something to hide if OSI personnel are told to violate their own regulations.

Articles mentioning the briefing document then appeared in the *New York Times* of June 16 and the *Washington Post* of June 28, 1987. From Bill's place, I heard all kinds of rumors. One of them came from the *Times*, whose science reporter told me that UFO debunker Philip Klass had said the briefing document couldn't be legitimate because Hillenkoetter had been sent to Korea in 1950 and didn't return until 1953. I told the science reporter that I knew that was not true, and promised to check and get right back to him. I remembered seeing information long before that Hillenkoetter did not remain in Korea long. Indeed, soon thereafter I was able to call the reporter back with the correct information which clearly established that Hillenkoetter was gone for less than a year before being stationed in New York in November 1951.

After this whirlwind of West Coast activity, I went back to quiet Fredericton with my copy of the briefing document finally in hand. It was time to do a lot of the research that needed to be done.

* * * *

In order to authenticate a questioned document, a researcher first takes it to a professional examiner. The examiner matches the paper to the time period, tests the ink, compares the signature to other signatures by the same person, and compares the typeface of the printed words to those from typewriters known to have been used in that person's office. In most cases, the expert then has enough information to decide whether the document is likely to be authentic. However, even the best expert cannot guarantee absolutely that any document is genuine, for a clever forger or disinformation specialist—especially one within the intelligence community—would have access to all the appropriate ink, paper, typewriters, signature samples, and memo formats.

In an area as controversial as ufology, the possibility of fraud or disinformation is everpresent. Thus, everything about each new find must be scrutinized in the minutest detail. The MJ-12 briefing document is no exception; in fact, because it arrived on film and we couldn't do the normal physical checks, even more attention had to be paid to its content and format.

Years ago, a woman named Pat Conklin told me a great story about her uncle, Charles Cooke, an Air Force colonel-physician who had at one time been stationed in England. While Pat and her sister were visiting him there in the 1950s, there had supposedly been a red alert at the base. He was at the base for three days and when he came home he supposedly had pictures of dead alien bodies from a crashed flying saucer. He was very sad that they had been unable to save any of the aliens. Pat claimed that her uncle was still living and practicing medicine in Tucson. She would get me his address from her mother. I casually asked for her sister's married name and where she was living.

At that time, Bill Moore was living in Prescott, Arizona, so I could have asked him to charge on down the interstate to get a look at the pictures and hear the details of the story. However, after years of chasing down leads that went nowhere, this story had a familiar ring to it. I checked the Tucson phone book at a local library and found no listing for her uncle the doctor. Doctors should have listings.

So I called Pat's sister. Yes, she said, they had an uncle named Charles Cooke who had been an Air Force colonel and had been stationed in England. However, she had never been to England and, to the best of her knowledge, Pat had never been there either. In addition, the uncle had lived near Phoenix, not Tucson, but had died seven years before!

I called information and got a listing for a Colonel Charles Cooke in the Phoenix area. When I called, I asked the woman who answered if her husband had been an Air Force colonel, a physician, and stationed in England. I was close. As her niece had said, her husband had been an Air Force colonel and had been stationed in England, but he was not a physician and he had died seven years earlier.

I relayed the story to Bill Moore, who called Pat and asked her when she had last seen her uncle. She said she had last seen him at the family reunion the year before at her Aunt Bertha's home in San Francisco. Since at the time I was living only 30 miles from San Francisco, I called Aunt Bertha and confirmed my suspicions about Pat's story—Aunt Bertha repeated the same facts that Pat's sister and the colonel's wife had told me.

Out of this frustration came two very important lessons:

- Not everything in the story was a lie. The important claims were lies, but Pat did have an uncle who was an Air Force colonel, had been stationed in England, and had lived in Arizona.
- As far as I could tell, Pat had no obvious motivation to tell me lies. Perhaps she really believed what she was saying. I do not know, and it really doesn't matter. What matters is whether she was telling the truth. Figuring out motivations I leave to the psychiatrists.

This is what we had to do with the MJ-12 briefing documents. The validity of the briefing documents would stand or fall on our ability to ferret out any false details in the documents themselves.

Obviously, it would have been wonderful to have related documents that would verify the information in the briefing. For example, it would be very useful to have attachments B through H of the briefing document, which from the contents page received would include details of the alien bodies, the materials and structures, names of investigators, and so on. Since MJ-12 appears to have been an ongoing project, documents from before and after the briefing would be important, too.

The 1952 briefing implies that the organization had been operating for at least five years, and the items noted as attachments were all done well before 1952. Using this data, I could check the dates, the events, and the people, cross-referencing them to other known sources of information.

The first and most obvious question to answer was, of course, whether a crashed flying saucer with alien bodies actually was recovered outside Roswell, New Mexico, in July 1947. After years of research by myself and others, I knew without doubt that the answer was an emphatic *yes*.

While debunkers have been attacking the Roswell story ever since *The Roswell Incident* came out in 1980, none of their arguments have stood up to careful investigation. The Center for UFO Studies (CUFOS), for example, was originally skeptical about Roswell. Don Schmitt, then the group's director of investigations, selected Kevin Randle, a prolific writer who had a long-term interest in UFOs, to help him dig deeper. Kevin, a former Air Force Reserve captain and intelligence officer, was an associate of Philip Klass and entirely skeptical about the incident. However, after making several trips to New Mexico, talking to many of the oldtimers and then locating other witnesses, both Don and Kevin became convinced that there was indeed the recovery of a crashed flying saucer and an almost immediate coverup by the government. (The pair have written articles in the *International UFO Reporter* and have coauthored two books supporting this view.)

Continued investigation of what happened in New Mexico in

early July 1947 has revealed a much more complete picture of the events. Several more crews who flew wreckage out were turned up by the late Leonard Stringfield, who collected crashed saucer stories, and by Randle and Schmitt. Other more recent research has been done, including tracking down a number of leads resulting from the *Unsolved Mysteries* broadcasts of September 20, 1989 and January 24, 1990. It is also true that, because of the publicity generated by these and later broadcasts, a number of phony witnesses have come out of the woodwork. However, I and other researchers have interviewed dozens of firsthand witnesses, seven of whom independently described the strange symbols on the wreckage and the strange characteristics of the materials.

This is all well and good, but why should you believe something that the government says did not happen? Simply because all of their explanations of the events do not add up.

For example, what about the government's insistence that what was recovered outside of Roswell was something other than a flying saucer—say, a prototype of a very advanced aircraft?

This is a very tortured explanation. Consider the claim that what was recovered was the wreckage of an Army Air Force device based on the Horton brothers' flying wing technology developed in Germany during World War II. First, I have talked with John Northrop, the inventor of the flying wing and the founder of Northrop Aircraft, whose YB-49 flying wing was flown in the late 1940s. John himself believed that some UFOs were alien spacecraft, and he even arranged for me to speak about UFOs to a group in Santa Barbara. He also related a UFO sighting by one of his pilots who was testing the flying wing at the time. The craft was clearly not a flying wing or anything like it. Second, one of the Horton brothers' flying wings is at the Air and Space Museum in Washington, D.C. The construction is two layers of plywood with sawdust and carbon in between, which hardly matches the Roswell wreckage. And appropriate personnel would have been seeking any "lost" advanced vehicle by radar, on the ground, and by plane. This clearly was not the case at Roswell.

What about a weather balloon and radar reflector, as the Army claimed, or a Japanese FUGO balloon bomb made of rice paper, as New York writer John Keel has maintained? These are out of the question for a number of reasons, of which three should suffice here. First, the amount of wreckage reported by witnesses is far more than would be produced by either a weather balloon or a FUGO. These objects are not very big. Second, when such objects come to earth, they do not scatter debris over acres of land, as witnesses have reported. They tend to land relatively softly. Third, these balloons were not made of the types of materials that eyewitnesses have reported: material that looked like the foil in a cigarette pack and that could not be torn, could not be permanently creased, could not be broken through with a sledgehammer, when crumpled returned to its original shape, and weighed next to nothing; I-beam-shaped pieces that were the weight of balsa wood but that could not be cut, broken, or burned.

Even if the materials were "ours" and had the characteristics ascribed to them by witnesses, where are they now? Extremely lightweight materials with very high strength would have enormous utility for aircraft, spacecraft, and other high-tech vehicles and products. Why are we not using that technology today? Because we very obviously are still unable to produce large quantities of such a material.

And if the materials were "ours," why was the command of the 509th Bomb Group, the group at the Roswell Army Air Field, allowed to put out a press release saying that they had recovered something that wasn't ours?

The 509th was the only atomic bombing group in the world. All the people in the unit had very-high-level security clearances; all of the officers were hand-picked. It is unreasonable to expect that if the crash was of a top-secret craft, this group would not be told, "It is ours. You do not have a need-to-know for the details of it. Please let it alone." The 509th would not then have had to deal with the question at all and would not have put out a press release at noon on July 8, 1947. The 8th Air Force command in Fort Worth would then not have had to issue a retraction that evening.

*   *   *   *

The next question about the briefing documents was actually stimulated by our diligent research. There is strong evidence that there
were two separate New Mexico crashes in 1947—the one near
Roswell and one in the Plains of San Agustin, west of Magdalena—
each including aliens, perhaps mutilated and perhaps with some
alive. Why, if the briefing is a genuine document, is there nothing
about the other crash, which many stories indicate involved the
Alamogordo Army Air Field, much closer to the site than Roswell?

Unlike the incident involving personnel from the Roswell base,
there was nothing in the press about the Alamogordo or Plains of
San Agustin activity, so from a security viewpoint it may well have
seemed appropriate for a preliminary briefing to discuss only the
crash that got national attention. Indeed, Eisenhower, as Army Chief
of Staff in July 1947, may have already been informed of this one,
although he had already announced he would be leaving the Army to
become president of Columbia University at the end of 1947.

And why is it called a preliminary briefing, anyway? What more
would there have been to report, given the list of seemingly detailed
attachments and the mention of increased activity in 1952? Suppose
there was a live alien with whom there had been communication.
This incredible and far-reaching interaction would have been considered extraordinarily compartmentalized, with details to follow
only when Eisenhower officially took office in January 1953.

Bill Moore and I met with an individual who helped prepare
daily briefings for Eisenhower while he was president. He noted that
there was some worry that Kay Somersby, Eisenhower's wartime
chauffeur with whom he was said to be very close, was a spy. Thus,
Eisenhower was not given access to everything until Somersby was
checked out. Furthermore, Eisenhower had no power as president-
elect. On any substantive issue, it was President Truman who would
make all decisions.

As I discussed in Chapter 1, I first spoke with Jesse Marcel in 1978,
and had been researching the Roswell story for years before the brief-

ing papers showed up. Independent witnesses turned up by a number of researchers said that alien bodies were recovered, as described in the briefing document. The briefing document also talks about the strange symbols on the wreckage, which we had heard about long before the document was received. So couldn't we have just made up the documents ourselves?

The answer to this question comes through a careful look at the documents and the realization that there are many details in the briefing that were not known to any of us on the outside at the time. (See Appendix C.)

Many of these details were turned up by my investigations after receipt of the document. The secret postwar life of Donald Menzel, for example, was not known to anybody in the UFO field. (The Englishman C. D. Allen claims Menzel's involvement with intelligence was well known. But the source that he references deals only with his work before and during the war, which of course was well known. It mentions nothing about his extensive activity after the war.)

We also checked the dates in the document. Take the date of the briefing: November 18, 1952. President-elect Eisenhower had a long and busy schedule that day. He came into Washington by plane from Georgia, landed to a tumultuous welcome, and rode in a triumphant cavalcade through the city to the White House with cheering crowds lining the way. He briefly met with Truman, the two men had their picture taken, and their representatives discussed certain matters. Then he motored over to the Pentagon for a 43-minute high-security meeting with the various members of the Joint Chiefs of Staff. This is established by a report in the *New York Times,* shows up on Twining's calendar, and is mentioned in Army Chief of Staff General Collins's calendar. There is no question that Eisenhower was briefed on that date, at the Pentagon in the vault where almost anybody with the right security clearance could have been present.

It might be objected that any researcher could have picked up the November 19, 1952 *New York Times* and found the reference to the Pentagon briefing. Perhaps. But in late 1989, during a visit to the National Archives, while reviewing the files of the Office of the

Secretary of Defense (OSD), which I had not previously reviewed, I discovered evidence that there were other briefings for the president-elect on November 18, 1952.

The OSD files are in the form of 3" x 5" cards, alphabetized in a special kind of filing index. Under "Briefings," an entry on card 5 for 1952 reads "18NOV52-Memo F [from] Thorpe OFDA T [to] MSA RE Briefing for President Elect, European Defense Production." Another entry begins "OFEDA 2 EMSA RE: Briefing for President Elect, International Export Controls." On card 5A is this entry: "18NOV52 memo from Nash to Secretary of Defense RE Briefings for the President Elect." I have obtained the first of these briefings, but the latter two are still classified, as are the cards from 1953 on.

So the Truman administration was making sure that there were all kinds of briefings for Eisenhower on November 18, 1952. According to Ed Reese at the National Archives, no one else had called his attention to these briefings listings, so other researchers hadn't discovered this. There, of course, may well have been other briefings from other departments in the OSD. I have not yet found reference to them although I have written numerous letters to the Eisenhower and Truman libraries and have obtained quite a bit of background information.

I also discovered that the date on the Special Classified Executive Order from President Truman to Secretary Forrestal (Attachment A of the briefing document)—September 24, 1947—is highly significant. After I had seen a full clean copy of the Majestic-12 briefing document and the Truman-Forrestal memo, I wrote to the Truman Library on June 17, 1987 inquiring about the date on the order. Their response, on June 23, 1987, was stunning:

> Our regulations do not permit us to pass on the authenticity of documents or handwriting. . . . President Truman's appointment records indicate that his only meeting with Dr. Vannevar Bush between May and December 31, 1947 was on September 24, 1947. Dr. Bush was accompanied at that meeting by Secretary of Defense James Forrestal.

I later discovered from both Bush's and Forrestal's files that the two had met for half an hour prior to their meeting with Truman and left the White House together. It certainly is conceivable that the two men prepared a memo for Truman's signature. Both men had unclassified notes about the meeting in their files—they were observed by reporters as they left the White House, so there had to be some kind of a cover story. One of the things that apparently took place at the meeting was Bush's appointment to be head of the newly formed JRDB. In any event, no other date for that eight-month period in 1947 would have the same significance since that was the only day when Bush met with Truman at the White House and Forrestal was there.

And it was not unusual that Forrestal and Bush were together. The two met quite often, sometimes more than once a week during 1947-1948. They even played tennis together, and judging by their correspondence, they knew each other very well and trusted each other. Although in his oral history, written many years later, Bush mentions that he felt Forrestal was perhaps the wrong man to be the first Secretary of Defense because he was not a strong believer in service unification, there's no question that the two served together and liked each other.

The next date mentioned in the briefing was May 22, 1949, a well-known date because that was when Secretary Forrestal died. Anyone could have found that date. August 1, 1950, "upon which date General Walter B. Smith was designated as permanent replacement" for Forrestal, is more obscure. As such, it is more significant in proving the validity of the briefing.

When I first considered this date, it was difficult to imagine what was special about it. But as I dug into the role of General Walter Bedell Smith, I learned something that, to the best of my knowledge, nobody else knew previously. I checked appointments for Truman for that date and then asked for all the dates on which Smith met with Truman. If the two met regularly once a week during that period, then the session on August 1 could have been about normal administrative matters, and as such would not corroborate the briefing. What I discovered was quite intriguing.

Whereas Hillenkoetter, Smith's predecessor at the CIA, did not meet very often with Truman, Smith did, once he was fully settled in as head of the CIA by the end of 1950. But August 1 was the only day prior to November 1950 when Smith met with Truman! It was a brief meeting, scheduled for less than 15 minutes at the West Door of the White House, off the record and no subject given. This is an area where they were not likely to be seen, and there was certainly no press coverage. None of the other meetings on Truman's calendar that day were identified by location. (Later that day, Truman met with another member of MJ-12, Gordon Gray. This meeting shows up only on the post-calendar for that day.)

This does raise a question, of course. How did whoever wrote the briefing document know that the meeting date would be of significance? Perhaps Truman had already decided that Smith would replace Hillenkoetter as Director of Central Intelligence. He certainly had full trust in Smith, who had been his ambassador to the Soviet Union from 1946 though 1949. Smith had also been Eisenhower's chief of staff during World War II. Once Truman had decided that Smith would be the next Director of Central Intelligence, he probably also decided that Smith should become a permanent member of MJ-12. The first three directors of Central Intelligence are all listed on the MJ-12 roster. It certainly seems appropriate for the fourth to be, as well.

Therefore, although there is no record of what transpired between Truman and Smith on August 1, 1950, we know that they met then and that it was their only meeting for a 10-month period. The Truman Library archivist told me that nobody else had ever asked him about the dates of meetings between Smith and Truman. It would be an incredible coincidence for a forger to pull such a date out of the air, unless he were an insider.

Continuing, the briefing mentions June 24, 1947—the date of the famous Kenneth Arnold flying saucer sighting. Nothing special there, except that the date is correct. (If this date was incorrect, the document would obviously be bogus.) The next date is July 7, 1947, when "a secret operation was begun" to recover the Roswell wreckage. Any researcher would recognize that as the date when Major Jesse Marcel and Counter-Intelligence Corps officer Sheridan Cavitt were out at the Foster ranch near Corona bringing back the first load of wreckage from the crash site. Probably much more important, as I found much later, it was also the date when General Twining flew to New Mexico from Wright Field. It has become clear that Twining, who was head of the Air Materiel Command, had been tasked to delve into the saucer situation.

On September 19, 1947, according to the briefing, a preliminary consensus was released on the covert analytical effort organized by Twining and Bush. A detailed copy of the consensus was Attachment D, which we do not have. What we do have is the flight logs of both General Twining and his pilot, who flew from Wright Field to Bolling Air Force Base (near Washington) on September 18 and returned on September 19, 1947. Twining and Bush could easily have met in Washington on that date. Twining's pilot, who became his aide and served him until 1957, said he often saw Bush and Twining together. Once again, the information in the briefing was corroborated by another source.

Interestingly, General Twining's letter to General Schulgen (Appendix B)—in which he states that the phenomenon of flying discs is real—is dated September 23, 1947. This letter was classified Secret, not Top Secret, and therefore could not have mentioned the recovery of alien wreckage. However, it certainly indicates that there was a consensus reached about the legitimacy of flying saucers and the need to get more information.

The next date in the briefing, November 30, 1947, is the date of a report on the four dead occupants of the Roswell craft supposedly given by Dr. Bronk. Although I have spent considerable time going through some Bronk papers at the Rockefeller Archives in New York (Bronk was for a time president of Rockefeller University), I haven't found anything that establishes that this is or is not a meaningful date. The briefing also mentions December 1947 as the beginning of Air Force Project Sign; this is verified.

December 6, 1950 is supposedly when a second object impacted

near the Texas-Mexico border. There is considerable indication that
something UFO-related happened on that day. There is mention in
several books of great concern at the White House when radar supposedly picked up strange vehicles, and some newspaper articles
mention it. The FBI even went on red alert over them, but the "attack force" was ultimately reported as a flock of geese, or other supposedly okay phenomena and the alert was canceled.

The other dates given in the briefing are the dates the attachments were created. We have no way of corroborating these. Thus, all
the dates in the briefing documents (except the Bronk report) are accounted for.

But why were we going through such contortions? Couldn't we just
go to the appropriate archives, ask for the relevant papers, make some
FOIA requests, and have our answers immediately?

First of all, in the case of Top Secret documents, whom do you
ask? The Eisenhower briefing is an "Eyes Only, Copy One of One"
document. It would appear that there was only one copy of the document ever made, and it was probably kept in a vault at the White
House. (An assistant to both Roosevelt and Truman told me that
highly classified Manhattan Project materials were actually stored
in the White House map room.) After requests to the Truman and
Eisenhower libraries, they both did checks of their indexes and found
no listing for MJ-12.

When you go to the Eisenhower or Truman Library, you are
told, "Here is a list of our Finders Guides. You may go through these
and select boxes you would like to see. We will bring them to you
for review." The listings in the guides (file folder titles) are sketchy
at best, and so you go through the guides and guess at which boxes
might hold pertinent information. At the Eisenhower Library alone,
there are eleven different Finders Guides for different portions of the
NSC files.

Many people who are unfamiliar with the Freedom of Information Act and how the various archives work are shocked that we
have not simply requested all the government's MJ-12 documents

and not been able to obtain other documents. Contrary to what many people assume, FOIA is not a key that opens all doors. The intent of the act was not for the government to be a search team for anyone who is curious about various and sundry topics. It is quite the reverse. The purpose is to provide public access to certain classes of documents if they can be well defined and easily sought. There are numerous exclusions, the greatest of which include matters that affect national security and intelligence activities. (See Appendix D for a list of exclusions.)

Another common misconception is that the government has to declassify everything after 20 or 30 or 40 years. While it is true that in England the Official Secrets Act does have such provisions, the United States does not. Certain documents are put under security with the proviso that they shall be periodically downgraded, but many do not have any such limitation. There is no automatic provision that any classified document will be declassified after a specified period.

It would seem logical that even if there isn't automatic downgrading of classified material, material from the 1940s and 1950s should all be declassified by now, or should at least be declassified upon request. After all, it's been 50 years. The world has changed. We won the cold war. Why keep these outdated secrets?

Unfortunately, this logic does not hold. One of the fascinating revelations I had at the Eisenhower Library was going through the voluminous NSC materials and finding file folder after file folder containing only withdrawal sheets, which indicate that Top Secret material has been removed from the file. At the Eisenhower, these are pink sheets, some noting 10 to 12 different items with cryptic entries: "Memo, TS [Top Secret], James Lay to Robert Cutler, July 16, 1954, 1 page."

There is a procedure for requesting mandatory classification review of still-classified documents. You fill out a form giving whatever information is available—the number of pages in the document, the date, the security level, and title information, if any. This is submitted to the archive, which passes the request on to the originating office,

say the National Security Council. The NSC will respond—
eventually.

The average response time to such requests for the NSC is currently more than two years. Some responses have taken as long as
six years. Part of the problem is that while the NSC may have no
objection to the release, it may insist that some other agency (or
agencies) review it as well; the CIA, for example, or the Department
of State or Department of Defense. Then the request has to be submitted in sequence to all of these.

In February 1988, I requested classification review of a number
of NSC documents. By March 1, 1990, none of my requests had
been acted upon. And of course I have been turned down on a number of requests. The materials were still classified. I went after the
Operation Solarium reports after discovering that they were listed
in the NSC files at the Eisenhower Library. I was turned down on
their release, appealed, and was turned down on the appeal. (A couple of years later, they were reviewed again and were released with
some censoring.)

In April 1990, at the National Archives, I tangled with Record
Group 341, the important Air Force Headquarters intelligence
records. (More about these records in Chapter 5.) The listing for the
group is titled "Preliminary Inventory of the Records of
Headquarters United States Air Force," compiled in 1963. The listing is 56 pages long and includes 512 entries. The total volume of the
records is 9,787 cubic feet covering the period 1939-1955—the
equivalent of 1,000 four-drawer filing cabinets. The size of the individual entries ranges from 1 inch to 1,743 feet! Entry 63 has 19 feet
of "Orders and Memoranda, with Background Correspondence
Relating to Personnel Actions 1948-54." Unfortunately, there are no
Finders Guides for any of the entries and most have not been classification-reviewed. Entry 23, for example, includes 51 feet of Top
Secret incoming and outgoing messages.

I asked about the availability of 24 entries. There is no listing of
availability, so Ed Reese had to check each entry for its location in
the vault and then check to see if there were labels on that entry's

boxes indicating the box had been reviewed and could be served to researchers. Fifteen of the 24 entries had no boxes available and three had only one box available. Of a total of about 721 boxes in the 24 entries, only 75 could be brought to me! In several of the folders, a majority of the items had been withheld even for 1947 and 1948! Clearly, there had been a great deal of Top Secret material, and much of it is still classifed after more than 40 years.

The Freedom of Information Act, even in those situations in which it does apply, requires that you identify the record you are seeking, for the government cannot do a blind search. Since there are no Finders Guides for any of these entries, you can only request classification review of these items based on the cryptic notes on the withdrawal sheets. This cannot be done by mail or phone, but requires sheet-by-sheet review.

Similarly, at the National Archives Civilian Reference Branch, which houses the official NSC files, I was told that at most 15 percent of these files for the Eisenhower years are available. Of 85 "P" documents (1947-1959), only 27 had been declassified and listed. Of 229 "Mill" documents for 1948-1960, only 22 are available. As another example, there were 20 pages of General Twining's 187-page mail log for 1954 withheld as of 1989 for security reasons and listed only by page number!

Thus, from a practical viewpoint it is impossible to gain access. Individuals, even those who are supported by grants (as my early MJ-12 research was supported by the Fund for UFO Research), do not have the time, the money, or because of security, the opportunity to follow the maze through to the end.

There is an additional hurdle to getting official confirmation on the reality of Majestic-12. If it was a highly classified program, as seems to be the case from the TOP SECRET/MAJIC markings, the *MAJIC* would be a need-to-know compartmentalized limitation, and with "Eyes Only" and "One of One," there would be very few people in government who would know about the program. Most people in government, if asked "Do you have any information on Majestic-12?" would say quite honestly that they had never heard of it. And suppose a request was made of somebody who *did* know of the organization. What could that person say? If the very existence of the organization was classified, then even a knowledgeable person would be bound to deny its existence.

This would not mean that information did not exist. Over the years, I have spent many weeks at 15 different archives. Although some of those archives certainly have compartmentalized Top Secret documents, I have never yet been able to see any. The Eisenhower Library admitted having a drawer full, but could not even search it for material with the terms *Majestic, MAJIC,* or *MJ-12.* Indeed, even at the highest levels of government there is compartmentalization of data. If an official does not need to know of the existence of a report or the information in a report, he does not get to see it. Period.

One illustration of this is a many-page formerly Top Secret listing of pre-1960 NSC documents that I saw. One of the entries said "Title classified for security reasons." The very title of the report was still classified above Top Secret!

Another difficulty in gaining access to highly classified material is the profusion of so-called "black budget" programs. These programs are not accountable to Congress, and their budgets come out of other programs where there is very little oversight. In a March 18, 1990 article, the *Washington Post* estimated that such programs run by the National Security Agency alone cost $10-$15 billion a year and employ 160,000 people. Most people have never even heard of the NSA.

We know that the NSA was involved in UFO activities from a long legal battle between CAUS and the NSA. In the late 1970s, CAUS had asked the CIA to do a search for their UFO material. The search turned up almost 900 pages of UFO material and a listing by date of 57 documents originating with other agencies. Eighteen of those documents were from the NSA. When an FOIA suit was filed against the NSA, they did a court-ordered search and found 239 UFO documents, of which "only" 160 originated with the NSA. However, after eliminating four of these, the NSA absolutely refused to release any of the remaining 156 documents, even refusing to show them to federal judge Gerhard Gesell, who was presiding over the case. Even the agency's 21-page Above Top Secret justification to Judge Gesell for not releasing any of the documents, when finally obtained under FOIA, was 75 percent expurgated!

What about the other 79 UFO documents found by the NSA that originated with other agencies? Twenty-three of these were supposedly from the CIA, and I requested those under FOIA in late 1984. Thirty-five months later, the CIA released nine documents, all of which were press abstracts of Eastern European newspaper articles about UFOs. The Soviets had these the day they were published. The other 14 were withheld on grounds of national security. I appealed the withholding of the remaining 14 documents, and two years later, at the end of 1989, the CIA responded. Eleven of the documents were withheld in their entirety because of national security. Very small portions of the other three—such as eight meaningless words on a page (document reference, information location, etc.)—were released.

Back to the information in the briefing. Since Roscoe Hillenkoetter is listed as the briefing officer, we had to ask if there were any indications that Hillenkoetter could not have been the briefing officer on November 18, 1952. Also, were there any indications that the language of the briefing document was not the sort that he would use? As noted above, one early objection was that Hillenkoetter was sent to Korea in late 1950 after he finished his job as head of the CIA. According to one skeptic he didn't return until 1956. More careful investigation revealed that while he did go to Korea, he served there for only 11 months, came back to the United States in 1951 to serve as head of the Brooklyn Navy Yard, and then in late 1952 was made head of the 3rd Naval District headquartered in New York, serving in that position until 1953. So he was not in Korea or any other distant location on November 18, 1952. He was stationed in New York City and certainly would have made trips to Washington without any trouble.

With regard to the language of the briefing, at the suggestion of Connecticut lawyer Robert Bletchman, I obtained copies of more than twenty different notes, memos, and other writings by Hillenkoetter during one of my visits to the Truman Library. Bletchman gave these and the briefing to Dr. Roger W. Wescott, a world-class linguistics expert. Wescott holds a Ph.D. in linguistics from Princeton, has written more than 40 books on linguistics and anthropology, and has lectured at Princeton, Harvard, Oxford, and other top schools around the world. At the time, he was professor of anthropology and linguistics at Drew University in New Jersey, although he has since retired. Here are his comments on the Hillenkoetter material:

> In my opinion, there is no compelling reason to regard any of these communications as fraudulent or to believe that any of them were written by anyone other than Hillenkoetter himself. This statement holds for the controversial presidential briefing memorandum of November 18, 1952, as well as for the letters, both official and personal.

Some people are upset that Dr. Wescott didn't make a positive statement that his work proves that Hillenkoetter wrote the briefing. Obviously, no such statement could be made. Somebody working for the CIA, for example, could have read Hillenkoetter's papers and simulated his style.

I located Mrs. Hillenkoetter in the hope of gaining access to his papers. She stressed that he intentionally did not keep his papers, precisely because he didn't want somebody going through his files! The CIA refused to provide copies of memos or briefings by Hillenkoetter. Some files from the 3rd Naval District are at the National Archives branch in Bayonne, New Jersey. Unfortunately, these papers are not well filed.

Because skeptics have been unable to come up with items of substance in their dealing with Operation Majestic-12, they have mounted a strong attack on various peculiar aspects of format and style. Klass and others have repeatedly claimed that the document is a forgery because the date format is "wrong." In the briefing document, there is a consistent pattern of day-month-comma-year for the dates, rather than month-day-comma-year. In addition, a zero is consistently used as placeholder in front of a one-digit date; for example, *01 August, 1950*. Klass and others claim that this format wasn't used until computers were in widespread use, years after the date of the briefing.

It turns out that Bill Moore, in a number of letters to Klass, used a similar date format, and Klass implies strongly that the briefing document must have been forged by Moore. Klass never mentions that he has letters from Moore that don't use this date format. He also doesn't mention that many examples of similar date formats have turned up in a variety of places in the same time period as the briefing. It was apparently standard for NATO for many years. Timothy Good's book *Above Top Secret* includes several examples, and I have picked out examples in some of the older documents I have been through. If Hillenkoetter did prepare the briefing for Eisenhower, then it was one military man briefing another military man. In addition, Hillenkoetter had served in Europe, and the French use this date format.

More importantly, if you spend sufficient time doing actual work in archives going through many papers of a particular individual, you find many different date formats, many different letter formats, and many different style formats emanating from the same office. For example, in letters from MJ-12 member General Walter Bedell Smith to General George Marshall—personal notes, birthday notes, thanks for the greetings, and so on—there are four different date formats: 29 December 1952; 26 October, 1954 [note the comma]; Oct. 7, 1954; and 12/29/54. Three of these letters were handwritten and signed by Smith himself, including the one with the day-month-comma-year format. These came from the Marshall Archives of which much more will be discussed later.

And where would Hillenkoetter have had the briefing typed? Clearly, it would have been at a very high security level. At 3rd Naval District headquarters? Who there would have had a need-to-know for Majestic-12 information, which was considered to be accountable only to the President? Since Hillenkoetter was head of the CIA from

1947 to 1950, he should have been able to have it typed by somebody with a need-to-know within the CIA.

In 1952, that somebody would have been Hillenkoetter's successor, Walter Bedell Smith, who supposedly became a member of Majestic-12 in 1950, replacing Forrestal. It shouldn't have been a problem for Hillenkoetter to go to Smith. In addition, since General Smith had worked so closely with Eisenhower in Europe during World War II and was from the same branch of the service (as opposed to being an admiral like Hillenkoetter), it would not be surprising if Hillenkoetter had asked Smith's advice about the format for the briefing and what style Eisenhower liked.

That Smith would have been consulted about any briefings for president-elect Eisenhower in November 1952 seems reasonable from a comment in Eisenhower's book *Mandate for Change.* On the same page where he mentions his meeting with Truman, Eisenhower notes that at Truman's instruction, he was briefed on national security and defense matters during the election campaign by none other than CIA Director Smith. In addition, in a letter from Smith to Truman dated January 9, 1953 that I discovered, Smith recounted how many times he had briefed Eisenhower and Adlai Stevenson about national security matters during and after the election campaign.

Smith stated that each would have been briefed four times during the campaign (June to November 1952) and that Eisenhower had been briefed by Smith himself four times after the election. The Eisenhower Library has the dates of two of the briefings (2-2:30 P.M. on November 28, 1952 and 2:30-3 P.M. on December 19, 1952) and I have tried to get copies of what transpired at these official briefings, but neither the Truman nor Eisenhower libraries has that information. I made an FOIA request to the CIA and paid search fees. More than two years later they replied they could find nothing in response to my request! I appealed, and three years passed before they once again claimed they had no responsive documents. It is highly improbable that the CIA has no record of briefings by its director to a president-elect, especially since the dates and times for two of them were provided.

It must be stressed that the MJ-12 documents were prepared by people who never expected that they would serve any other purpose than to provide information to the recipients. They were classified documents with very limited distribution, with certainly no Freedom of Information Act in existence or even contemplated in the late 1940s and early 1950s. Format was of much less concern then than we seem to think it should be today. In our computerized world, it is very easy to have the same document format for an entire office or an entire government department. But in the precomputer government, a lot of the typewriters were manuals, and the formats were often as not determined by the department head's proclivities or a secretary's experience, not some database.

There is no rule that people in government must use a particular format for internal documents, and they certainly don't stick to one. For instance, I have copies of three different brief memos from Allen Dulles, then CIA director, to Colonel A. J. Goodpaster, staff secretary to President Eisenhower. All three were typed in November 1956, and all three have different date formats. In fact, on one of them, the date is stamped in, not typed. There are other style differences between the memos, although they convey basically the same type of information. (They are cover letters for memorandums that Dulles thought would interest Goodpaster.) They were typed on different typewriters, and one of them even uses a different letterhead.

Another concern about format and style is the use of the term *Executive Order #092447* that identifies the Truman-Forrestal memo on page 6 of the briefing. Obviously, the numbers signify the date of the memo. People have checked a whole host of available unclassified executive orders, including those proclaiming various special days, and find that this number doesn't fit that numbering system at all.

However, this is not the problem it might seem to be. If the briefing is genuine and was typed for the November 18, 1952 session, then this may very well have been the first time the memo was referred to as an Executive Order. When the memo was first created in 1947, it may not have been thought of as an Executive Order in the official sense. The principals had no idea of the scope of the activ-

ity, how long it would go on, or how soon there might be a con-
frontation with aliens or with the public demanding evidence. It appears to be the kind of thing that was done to provide Forrestal with
authorization should one be necessary for use of government funds
or personnel for the effort.

And since a Democratic administration was passing the torch to
a Republican one, the Trumanites would have to call the memo something official to justify things on a rather formal basis. Eisenhower, a
former military commander, was accustomed to dealing with orders
of one kind or another, and the Truman administration might have
wanted to provide him with some kind of formal authorization.

A peculiar thing about the date on the Truman-Forrestal memo
itself is that it has two different aspects. The word *September* is po-
sitioned well below the *24, 1947*. In addition, the two parts of the
date are in different typefaces. If you compare the comma in the text
to the comma in the date, the dissimilarity is apparent. This implies
that the date might have been added later or someplace else.

We have some NSC memos from Lay where the date is done
with one size type and the text with another. This certainly implies
that the memos were put in two different typewriters. There is no
reason to doubt the legitimacy of these memos.

The someplace else is suggested by the period after the date.
While there are occasional items from Truman's office with the period after the date, the great majority do not use that style. One office that almost invariably used a period after the date was that of
Vannevar Bush. Not only did his secretaries put a period after the
date, but they also put a period after the typed-in closing name.

And why would the memo be signed? If some kind of Executive
Order was given to Forrestal, then his original would have Truman's
signature, but the White House copy would not. It might have had
a rubber stamped original "signed by Harry Truman" on it.

The memo was prepared and signed by Truman and kept by
Forrestal. Copies were perhaps made for Bush and for CIA Director
Hillenkoetter, both of whom are mentioned in the memo and were
extremely well known for their discretion. Forrestal remained in of-

fice until he resigned in March 1949, was soon hospitalized, and committed suicide in May 1949. There is a real question as to what happened to his files. Would he have had a copy of this memo in his files, and were they automatically turned over to his successor, Lewis Johnson? We simply do not know.

What we do know is that Forrestal was mentally unbalanced for months before his suicide. There was even an active FBI investigation because he requested that agency to check out people who were "spying" on him, amongst other paranoid manifestations. Because of this situation, possibly Hillenkoetter or Walter Smith decided that any authorization to Forrestal that they were going to present to Eisenhower would need to have Truman's signature on it to guarantee its authenticity. Bush was still around, and his files would have had a copy and the signed letter from Truman of October 1, 1947. Truman himself might have added the signature, or perhaps Smith had the file copy from Hillenkoetter's files and knew that Eisenhower would want to see a signed copy or original.

Ah, yes—Truman's signature. One of the most serious charges made by Philip Klass toward the end of 1989 was that the signature on the Truman-Forrestal memo is identical to that on a brief letter from Truman to Bush on October 1, 1947. Thus, he claimed, the Truman-Forrestal memo was a forgery, making the entire MJ-12 briefing a fraud. His reasoning was that supposedly no two signatures are identical. If they are, one must be a forgery.

In a Winter 1987-1988 *Skeptical Inquirer* article, Klass included pictures of the signature part of each memo and measurements of the lengths of different portions of the Truman-Forrestal signature (done by Bill Moore). He didn't include measurements for the Truman-Bush signature, nor did he show the White House letterhead. In other of his writings, he states that the signature on the Truman-Forrestal memo is actually 1.032 times longer than that on the Truman-Bush memo. He explains this difference by stating that the photocopying process normally stretches the type in a document, and that it would have taken a forger three copies to make the fake.

If he *had* included the measurements for the Truman-Bush signature and the letterheads of both memos, readers would have been able to make certain judgments for themselves:

- The signatures are clearly *not* identical. When you hold the two up to a light one behind the other, as Klass recommends, they do not match, even allowing for the supposed "stretching."
- The Truman-Forrestal *Harry* is 1.012 longer than the Truman-Bush *Harry*, the Truman-Forrestal *Truman* is 1.032-1.04 times longer than the Truman-Bush *Truman*, but the letterhead is exactly the same length for both. Clearly, to claim evidence of photocopying, the type on a sheet of paper would have to be stretched by the same ratio on all parts of the paper.
- What about comparisons between other pairs of Truman signatures? Truman signed tens of thousands of letters, memos, and other documents. In a family letter after his astonishing election victory in November 1948, Truman noted that he was signing thank-you notes at the rate of 500 per hour! If there are other signature pairs that are very similar, then the closeness of the Truman-Forrestal and Truman-Bush signatures means nothing.

Klass made various other claims. He ballyhooed a small slip of the fountain pen in the upper right part of the *H* on both signatures as proof that the two signatures were identical, and claimed that a forensics expert (a former CIA agent) assured him that the typeface of the Truman-Forrestal memo is that of a Smith-Corona typewriter not available until the mid-1960s. Both of these claims are spurious at best.

- The thickness of the ink mark by the *H* in each memo is different. In addition, I have copies of at least three legitimate Truman signatures, all of which have the same kind of mark by the *H*.
- Other examiners disagree with Klass's CIA source about the typewriter used for the text of the memo. There seems to be no doubt, however, that the typewriter used for the *24, 1947.* portion of the date does match the time period. If a forger had access

to the older typewriter, why would he use it for only one portion of the date instead of for the whole memo?

Klass also wrote of a "smoking gun" proving the fraudulence of the MJ-12 documents in the Winter 1990 *Skeptical Inquirer* article "New Evidence of MJ-12 Hoax." His major reference in that article was the book *Questioned Documents* by Albert S. Osborn, which Klass says was published in 1978. Klass quotes: "The fact that two signatures are very nearly alike is not alone necessarily an indication of forgery of one or both, but the question is whether they are *suspiciously alike*" [Klass's emphasis]."

What Klass did not reveal in the article was that Osborn's thousand-page book was actually published in 1910, with a second edition in 1929! Osborn was born in 1858 and died in 1943. The chapter from which Klass took his quote is titled "Traced Forgeries," which were a major legal problem before copy machines. Three sentences after Klass's quote, Osborn wrote, "It should be understood that *suspicious identity* [Osborn's emphasis] is that which suggests the tracing process and which is not inconsistent with the theory of tracing." Klass also ignored the footnotes to the sentence he quoted, to legal references from 1903, 1904, 1900, and 1879. The first one deals with four identical signatures on a will by a man more than 80 years old! None of this has anything to do with legitimate signatures by people who sign loads of documents every working day. And finally, even Osborn admits, on the same page as the Klass quote, "*In some cases such* [identical] *signatures can be found*" [Osborn's emphasis].

This carries the analysis of the MJ-12 documents themselves about as far as it can go. Surprisingly, nothing that we had found or that others had alleged indicated that the documents were anything other than legitimate. Barring independent confirmation of the briefing, you either believed its validity or you did not.

As mysteriously as we had received the MJ-12 documents, we found our first confirmation.

THE CUTLER-TWINING MEMO

The MJ-12 group was a collection of high-powered individuals—some of the prime movers and shakers of the postwar period. None were elected officials. However, such a group was not self-contained—it required various support and technical people to help it do its work. Given the dispersed nature of the group, these assistants would have been in many different departments in different locations. Classified laboratories all over the United States would have been involved. And as administrations changed, as key individuals retired, moved on, or died, the composition of the support staff would change as well. Few of these people would have known all of the details, but they participated in the paper trail that even such a compartmented organization as MJ-12 had to produce.

One of the highest-placed of these personnel was a man named Robert Cutler. Judging by his book *No Time for Rest,* written about his life in government, Cutler was a fascinating personality. He was a bachelor, a banker from Boston, and a man who worked hard and took his responsibilities very seriously. He was a general during World War II handling administrative work, served on the CIA's Psychology Strategy Board after the war, and was very active in

Eisenhower's 1952 presidential campaign. He was a man of many accomplishments but a relatively low profile by Washington standards.

In July 1954, Cutler was Special Assistant for National Security to Eisenhower. He had been responsible for overseeing the actions and activities of the National Security Council, sat in on all its meetings, and technically was the liaison between the NSC and the president, working very closely with James Lay, executive secretary of the NSC. The NSC during Eisenhower's administration was not a high-profile organization, as it became in Oliver North's day. However, it was still a very important group, and Ike used it far more than Truman did. There were many meetings, and much of what it did was considered privileged information to the president. That was its role: to provide guidance and advice to the president.

In this role, the NSC prepared all kinds of position papers, almost all of them classified, especially with regard to foreign affairs. These often went through numerous revisions. Copies of proposed changes would go to dozens of officials for comment and emendation. All of these changes would be synthesized by Cutler and Lay, and then sent back around for additional comments. Thus, Cutler and Lay were paper-pushers supreme, responsible for tracking a load of classified material.

July 14, 1954 was probably a day like so many others in Washington. James Lay came back to his office from a meeting with President Eisenhower at 2:30 P.M. At 4:30, he took a short call from Eisenhower. When he put down the phone, he perhaps beckoned to a secretary and started dictating some work. The secretary took down the dictation, most likely returned to her desk and typed up the material, including the following memo:

MEMORANDUM FOR GENERAL TWINING

SUBJECT: NSC/MJ-12 Special Studies Project

The President has decided that the MJ-12 SSP briefing should take place <u>during</u> the already scheduled White House meeting of July 16, rather than following it as previously intended. More precise arrangements will be explained to you upon arrival. Please alter your plans accordingly.

Your concurrence in the above change of arrangements is assumed.

ROBERT CUTLER
Special Assistant
to the President

When it was finished, the security marking TOP SECRET RE-STRICTED SECURITY INFORMATION was typed on the memo, and it was sent on its way. A perfectly normal occurrence.

More than 30 years later, in March 1985, I was visiting Washington, D.C. to present a paper at an international conference on food irradiation. I had some spare time and checked in with Ed Reese at the Modern Military Branch of the National Archives. Ed told me that the archives were classification-reviewing Air Force Headquarters intelligence files. Since UFO information was normally handled by the intelligence departments of various government agencies, it seemed logical to expect that in this material, dating back to the earliest days of the Air Force, there would be some UFO-related items.

Ed referred me to the classification division at the archives, and I eventually spoke with Jo Ann Williamson there. Jo Ann told me that the review would be finished in about a month. I went home.

A classification review doesn't mean blanket declassification. It means every document in a file is examined by people—usually military reservists—with appropriate clearance and need-to-know who follow guidelines laid down by the originating agencies to decide what can be released and what must remain classified. Sometimes, a document as a whole is declassified although it may contain small deletions (names of people or agencies, perhaps). Such a review is painstaking, especially with intelligence files since they deal with a wide variety of subjects.

Three months later, and after many phone calls, I finally determined that Entry 267 from Air Force Record Group 341 had been reviewed. I notified Moore and Shandera about this, and also that I had discovered a 1948 Top Secret UFO document that had been released. (Another Top Secret document was also released about the same time dealing with a sighting by powerful U.S. Senator Richard Russell of Georgia on a trip to Eastern Europe.)

While I was waiting for the classification review to be completed, Jaime Shandera and Bill Moore had received several peculiar postcards with provocative riddles on them. The return address on one was "Box 189, Addis Ababa, Ethiopia," and it was postmarked New Zealand. Considering that Jaime and Bill were in contact with government insiders, we knew it was easy enough for someone to put a postcard in an envelope, send it overseas, and have someone else mail the postcard back here. Moore read one of the cards to me over the phone, and we tried to puzzle it out. It mentioned Reese's Pieces and also Suitland, a repository for government files—and a sort of annex of the National Archives—that I had visited in March. We decided that it would be a good idea for somebody to go to Washington.

In early July, Bill and Jaime flew to Washington and started going through the boxes of Entry 267. During the course of several days, they had gone through 120 boxes and found about 75 pages that looked worth copying. As strange as it sounds in this era of instantaneous computerized searches, that was a good piece of work.

None of the millions of older documents in most government archives are computerized. The standard procedure at an archive is for a researcher to sit in a guarded area and request to see certain boxes. At some archives there are Finders Guides that list the titles of the file folders in each box. At others, the Guides are so general as to be next to useless, leaving the researcher to guess what boxes to request. The archivists bring the boxes to the researcher on a cart—six or eight or twelve or eighteen at a time, depending on the individual repository's rules. Each box is about twelve inches high and six inches wide with a hinged lid and a label on the end and contains file folders holding the documents. Although the folders have titles, they don't give any indication of what the individual documents are (letters, memos, etc.) within the folder, and a researcher must go through the file piece by piece looking for appropriate material. Under the watchful eye of an archivist sitting at a nearby desk, the researcher pulls one folder out of the box, goes through it, puts it back in the box, and then takes out another folder. When the researcher is done with one batch of boxes, the cart is rolled away, and after a while a new load is brought in.

Original documents cannot be removed from archives. (Thieves have on occasion "borrowed" papers with signatures of famous people, but that's an entirely different matter.) Prior to 1990, to get pages copied the researcher indicated the selections by inserting a special sheet of paper marking the place of each. The clerks in the archive would eventually make the copies and mail them to the researcher along with a bill of 35 cents a page.

Archives not only don't let you bring any original documents out, they won't allow you to bring anything into secure areas. All of your belongings—briefcases, notebooks, jackets, even scrap paper—are placed in a locker outside the secure areas. If you require notepaper while you're working, the clerks give you some—from inside.

The boxes at the National Archives are stored in locked vaults, and boxes containing any classified material at the presidential libraries are also stored in vaults. Only approved people, normally employees with security clearances, can go into the vaults. Remember the last scene of the movie *Raiders of the Lost Ark*? That's what the vaults are like—huge areas with floor-to-ceiling shelves and rows of closely packed boxes as far as the eye can see.

I had earlier had the privilege of being in a vault at the National Archives, closely escorted by Ed Reese. We were trying to determine what material was in which of the more than 300 boxes of the files of the JRDB, an organization with subcommittees on everything from biological warfare to missiles and rockets. The material had been classification-reviewed, and so there was a long list of all kinds of material available, but no correlation between the lists and the boxes. I selected a number of items on the lists, and then went down with Reese into the vault. He checked particular boxes to see whether my requests were in them. Otherwise, he would have had to bring up the box, talk to me, take the box back down, bring up another one, and so on. This way we could proceed quickly to find at least some of the materials I was looking for. I, was, of course, in his sight all the time.

Bill and Jaime found that much of the material in Entry 267 was still classified, as indicated by withdrawal sheets in place of the still-classified documents. These sheets had only cryptic summaries; for example, "Memo three pages, Top Secret, Bill Jones to Robert Smith, July 22, 1953." To get a chance of seeing this material, they would have to request a mandatory classification review—the painstaking, frustrating experience that can take years.

While putting one file folder back in a box and pulling out the next file, Jaime discovered a piece of paper between the files: the July 14, 1954 memo from Robert Cutler to General Twining. The box in which Jaime found this document? Box 189.

The memo is a carbon copy in blue ink on onionskin paper. The message is straightforward and simple—the complete text appears above. It refers to an NSC/MJ-12 Special Studies Project briefing. The paper is old, and has a watermark. There is aging around the edge of the paper. There is a slanted red pencil mark through the unusual security marking in the upper right corner. The text doesn't provide a clue as to the subject matter of the project—it is clearly a simple administrative notice that a briefing will take place during an already scheduled meeting rather than after, as originally planned. The word *during* is underlined. There is no signature on the memo, nor even an */s/* next to Cutler's name indicating that he had signed the original.

However, if this innocent little note is genuine, it means that there was an NSC/MJ-12 Special Studies Project group working on a highly classified project. And therein lies the controversy surrounding this innocent little note. Since the discovery was revealed in 1987, people have misrepresented the memo's text, tried to disprove its authenticity, and even smeared the reputations of the discoverers. Debunkers clamor that the typeface is all wrong. Cynics have claimed that Moore and Shandera planted the memo themselves and then "discovered" it—an impossibility given how archives operate.

Bill called me after he and Jaime left the archive for the evening. He read the memo to me and described how Jaime found it. The memo had no relation to anything else in Box 189, which lent greater credence to the riddle postcards.

As with any new bit of UFO documentation, we tried to make meticulous checks on the memo's authenticity before revealing its existence to the world. The process is like running down clues in an involved mystery—there is a lot of legwork that must be done, but each step takes you closer to being sure.

To begin, Bill and Jaime clearly saw the watermark with the name of the manufacturer—Fox Paper—when they held the paper up to the window of the office in the archive. (Several years later, Ed Reese allowed Bruce Maccabee and I to photograph the memo, providing a permanent record of the color of the paper and the markings as well as the watermark.) Moore contacted Fox Paper in Wisconsin, talked to their watermark expert, and determined that this paper was made only in bid lots between 1953 and the early 1970s. The government bought a great deal of the paper, and the bid lot limitation meant that it wouldn't show up in retail stores all over the country—only major customers such as the government would buy it. So we know that the paper fits the time scheme, it would have been available in a number of government offices, and it would generally not have been available to the public.

Besides the paper checking out, the language, style, format, and typeface of the memo appear to be genuine, especially when compared to other memos from Cutler that are known to be valid.

As Bill read the memo to me over the phone, I was immediately reminded of a July 13, 1953 Cutler-Twining memo we had found in late 1981 in General Twining's papers at the Library of Congress Manuscript Division. Inside a box of material that had been declassified, we found a folder labeled TOP SECRET EYES ONLY—normally the most-classified material. Two memos in the file—both from Cutler—dealt with Operation Solarium. One was dated June 25, 1953, and was routed through the Secretary of Defense and then on to General Twining, who was at that time the Air Force chief of staff. The other was dated July 13, 1953, and was sent directly to Twining. Here is the text of the latter memo, which Cutler signed:

MEMORANDUM FOR GENERAL TWINING

The President expects you to attend the Extraordinary Meeting of the National Security Council in the Broadcast Room of the White House, Thursday, July 16, at 9:00 A.M. It is advisable not to plan any other engagements before 6:00 P.M. on that day.

Due to the nature of the Meeting, it is necessary to take special security precautions and to maintain absolute secrecy regarding participation in, as well as the substance of, the Meeting. It is requested that you enter the White House grounds via the Southeast Entrance not later than 8:45 A.M. and descend from your car at the South (Diplomatic) Entrance of the Mansion. Your car should be discharged and not wait anywhere in the vicinity of the White House.

The President expects you to lunch with him at the White House at 12:30 P.M.

In order to avoid communication on this subject, it is understood that in the absence of contrary word your concurrence in the above arrangements is assumed.

ROBERT CUTLER
Special Assistant
to the President

The concluding words of the two memos are virtually the same.

Another similarity in wording is the indication that specific details will be given at the meeting only. The June 25, 1953 memo says, "The program will be explained in detail at the meeting"; the 1954 memo says, "More precise arrangements will be explained to you upon arrival."

In addition to similarities in what the memos say, there are similarities in what they don't say. Neither gives any clue as to the subject of the meetings to which they refer—another indication of authenticity.

Although it would seem that a highly classified memo would give full details because only a select few would see it, the opposite is actually the rule. I have seen many declassified Top Secret memos that give very little information, and I have determined through interviews with officials that this is standard practice. The less information in a memo between people the better, for it makes life a lot simpler from a need-to-know standpoint. As long as the ultimate recipient knows what is being discussed, then the people between the sender and recipient—secretaries, couriers, and so forth—need not be made aware of the subject, even though they might have appropriate clearance.

Verification of another peculiar aspect of the 1954 Cutler-Twining memo—the absence of a signature or /s/, since Cutler generally signed his memos—came from another source. Robert Todd, an unusual researcher on the East Coast who has written well over 1,000 FOIA requests, sought more information about Cutler's activities in July 1954. From the Eisenhower Library, he obtained information that Cutler was on an extended trip to Europe when the memo was typed! This piece of the authenticity puzzle was of major importance, for if there *had* been a signature or an /s/, the document would have to be bogus. Cutler couldn't be in Europe and in his office at the White House on the same day.

One of the most virulent attacks on the memo came as no surprise. It was from Philip Klass, who for more than two decades has been attacking anything pro-UFO. He has published four books about UFOs; has written a number of articles, especially for the *Skeptical Inquirer;* and is head of the UFO subcommittee of the self-anointed Committee for the Scientific Investigation of Claims of the Paranormal (CSICOP). He is aware of Project Blue Book Special Report 14, yet he claims there are no UFO sightings that cannot be explained and never mentions Special Report 14 in his books.

Klass has been attacking the MJ-12 items right from the start. One of his contentions was that the Cutler-Twining memo could not be authentic because the typewriters in use in the White House at that time did not have that typeface. The memo was typed in a large pica face, and Klass maintained that the White House used only the smaller elite face at that time. As he wrote to me on January 16, 1989:

> I challenge you to produce known-to-be-authentic White House business letters/memoranda written by Cutler or Lay during the 1953-1955 time period which use a typeface identical in size and style to that used in the <u>alleged</u> Cutler-Twining memo of July 14, 1954.

(Lay was a career public servant who had worked in Army Intelligence during World War II. In 1954, Lay was executive secretary of the NSC, having succeeded Sidney Souers in that position in 1950. Prior to that, he had been Souers's assistant. Lay stayed on as executive secretary right through to the end of the Eisenhower administration.)

Klass enclosed nine samples of Cutler NSC memos from that time period, all in elite type. To "provide motivation," he wrote, he offered me $100 for each such verified document I could provide him, to a maximum of $1,000.

A solid-looking argument, and he was risking money, too. Copies of this challenge were sent to many people. However, Klass ignored research done by Dr. Bruce Maccabee and Robert Swiatek of the Fund for UFO Research, who earlier spent time going through portions of the declassified NSC material from the Eisenhower era then available at the National Archives. Although there weren't that many declassified NSC documents, these researchers determined that the NSC had at least three different typewriters in use at the time: two with different pica faces as well as one with an elite face.

I knew Klass's statement that the White House didn't use pica typewriters was untrue even without Maccabee and Swiatek's work. I had in my own files numerous memos from Cutler and Lay typed in a pica typeface. I mailed him copies of twenty of these, and a month later, copies of fourteen more pica memos from Lay that I found at the Eisenhower Library. On March 3, Klass sent me a check for $1,000. It appeared that the primary debunker of UFOs was satisfied that the typeface of the Cutler-Twining memo was legitimate.

*   *   *   *

Another challenge to the document came from a less-expected quarter—the Eisenhower Library. In the May 31, 1987 London *Observer*
article that discussed the MJ-12 briefing document, writer Martin
Bailey had also mentioned the Cutler-Twining memo. While con-
tacting various archives about the memo, Bailey called Jo Ann
Williamson at the National Archives. She made a flat statement that
the Cutler-Twining memo was a very strange document. Bailey
quoted Williamson as stating, "It [the memo] was found in the files
of the US Air Force Director of Intelligence and is certainly genuine,
but we have found no minutes of the MJ-12 meeting which was
scheduled for at least two days later. It is very surprising that there are
no other papers on MJ-12 and we have no idea what it was."

Williamson was, in a sense, caught between a rock and a hard
place with the Cutler-Twining memo definitely being found in her
facility, but having no backup information. She put out a listing of
the archive's somewhat negative comments because she got so many
requests for information. She had apparently talked to the Eisenhower Library to get their views as well.

As often happens, a number of the statements in her review were
misleading because they lacked context. For example, Williamson
mentioned that there were no NSC meetings on July 16, 1954.
However, the Cutler-Twining memo does not specify that the briefing will take place during an NSC meeting, but an "already scheduled
meeting." The meeting could have been of the Joint Chiefs of Staff,
the cabinet, or any one of a number of other groups.

Similarly, the Eisenhower Library originally contributed a statement to the effect that all carbons of Cutler's memos were done on
onionskin paper with a certain watermark that was different from
that on the Cutler-Twining memo. They made it sound as if they
had done a complete search of NSC materials. What they really
meant was all of the small number of carbons they had examined.
Obviously, they did not search all of the 250,000 pages of NSC material in their archive, which include tens of thousands of pages by

Cutler, because they do not have the personnel to attempt such a study. They later changed their statement after I pointed out a number of copies done on onionskin paper with differing watermarks.

Bailey went on to quote Barry Greenwood as a UFO writer who raised an intriguing question about a very sophisticated fraud: "There are some things that look wrong with the White House memo. For example, it is unsigned. It is just possible that it was manufactured by someone waiting to prove the existence of MJ-12 and then inserted into Air Force Intelligence records which had recently been opened up to the public. The hoaxer would then have ordered a copy from the National Archives which would carry the official declassification stamp. MJ-12 may well have existed, but more research is needed to authenticate the documents."

A seemingly logical argument—if the reader is unaware of archive procedures. If one looks at the original of the Cutler-Twining memo, one is struck not only by the fact that it's in blue ink, apparently from carbon paper, but that there is a short red pencil mark drawn on a slant through the security marking. Of course, in a photocopy it's hard to tell that it is pencil, and it is certainly impossible to tell that it is red. During my own visit to the Eisenhower Library after the Cutler-Twining memo was found, I noted in a file consisting mostly of original documents a number of cases of such slant red pencil marks through the security markings.

Recalling the Cutler-Twining memo, I asked the archivist if there was any significance to the red mark. His response was affirmative. When it is decided that a document can be declassified, he told me, a slant red pencil line is run through the security markings. I did not know this previously; nor did Jaime or Bill, which points to the memo being a legitimate document. Whoever put it in Box 189 at the National Archives was apparently well aware of the red pencil convention. It would have been a perfectly natural thing for somebody accustomed to such matters to do, such as the members of the many four-man teams of classification reviewers. (The National Archives would not identify the team members to me.)

Other objections to the memo related to the security markings. The NSC claimed to the National Archives that the security designation on the memo—TOP SECRET RESTRICTED SECURITY IN-FORMATION—was not used until the Nixon administration. This objection is more transparent than it first seems. I have reviewed a number of NSC documents from 1953 that were stamped RE-STRICTED SECURITY INFORMATION. There was one that had an additional SECRET on it; another one was stamped CON-FIDENTIAL RESTRICTED SECURITY INFORMATION. Normally, when there is CONFIDENTIAL and SECRET prior to a subsequent designator such as RESTRICTED DATA (which is used for nuclear information), there will also at some point be TOP SECRET RESTRICTED SECURITY INFORMATION.

In addition, in my ongoing work in the archives, I had noted oc-casional security markings that I would see only once. TOP SE-CRET CONTROL is one example. However, just because a marking is found only once is no indication that it is fraudulent.

Another example is the marking COSMIC, which turns out to be a NATO security marking. I came across it once at the Eisenhower Library. When I asked that library for samples of doc-uments with the COSMIC marking from the Eisenhower admin-istration, they said, "Well, they're all classified, but here's some declassified material dating back to when Eisenhower was Chief of the Allied Forces in Europe." Sure enough, the marking COSMIC showed up a number of times.

Since no one searched all the NSC materials at the Eisenhower Library, the NSC's claim that the security marking TOP SECRET RESTRICTED SECURITY INFORMATION was not used sim-ply has no documentary basis.

Another objection was that the security markings are not rubber-stamped top and bottom but are merely typed in the upper righthand portion. Some people are convinced that government rules require that documents be stamped top and bottom in large letters with whatever the security indications are. The answer to this once again lay in the NSC files at the Eisenhower Library. Over and over again in those papers, variations on the normal crop up. Often the security markings are typed rather than rubber-stamped; sometimes they are a mix. Sometimes they are top and bottom, sometimes only top; sometimes in the upper and lower righthand corners, sometimes in the center. There obviously are no hard and fast rules, especially for information that was intended to be for internal use only.

The Cutler-Twining memo passed muster as to the kind of paper, the language, and the typeface. But there were still other questions about it that had to be resolved.

One of those queries was why would a memo be sent out under Cutler's name when he wasn't there? A good question, and one that has a good answer. In his FOIA searches, Robert Todd turned up another pertinent memo from Cutler, this time to James Lay and Lay's close associate, J. Patrick Coyne, who actually worked for the FBI. In this memo, dated July 3, 1954, Cutler gave Lay and Coyne specific instructions about how to handle his duties while he was away in Europe. In a separate paragraph, Cutler notes, "Keep things moving *out* of my basket."

On March 6, 1990, I received the first response to my mandatory classification review requests of February 1988, which I discussed in Chapter 4. Of the dozens of documents that I had requested, only one document had been acted upon: a message from Lay to Cutler dated July 16, 1954, just two days after the Cutler-Twining memo (which is why I requested it). It was transmitted electronically by General Paul Carroll, White House Secretary, to Cutler in Europe. It is a quick review of the activities at the July 15, 1954 NSC meeting as originally instructed by Cutler to Lay in his July 3, 1954 memo. The last two lines of this memo are: "Hope you will recuperate, rest and enjoy yourself for few days before returning. Will try to have everything tidy and not too much pressure upon you when you return." According to the Eisenhower Library, the message was a blue carbon on onionskin without a watermark and there is no heading on the stationery. Clearly, Lay was handling things for Cutler.

Lay and Cutler worked very closely together. They sat next to

each other at the weekly meetings of the NSC. They handled paperwork together, and appear to have gotten copies of each other's
memos. For example, Lay's name is on the distribution list for
Cutler's June 25, 1953 memo to the Secretary of Defense.

Since Cutler gave Lay specific instructions to keep things moving out of his basket, it is logical that Lay would have sent the memo
to Twining in Cutler's name, since Cutler was Eisenhower's man. But
logic isn't enough to make a solid case. I needed more information
before I could feel secure about this hypothesis.

I next determined from White House schedules that Lay and his
assistant S. Everett Gleason had met with Eisenhower off the record
at 2:30 P.M. on July 14, 1954, and that, according to the White House
phone logs, Eisenhower and Lay had a brief conversation at about
4:35 P.M. Eisenhower could have asked Lay to notify Twining of a
slight change in plans which would influence Twining's schedule, since
a briefing was to take place during an already scheduled meeting rather
than after it as originally planned. One can envision a phone conversation in which Eisenhower tells Lay, "With regard to the matter we
discussed earlier, there's been a slight change in plans. Please notify
Twining that the briefing will take place during the already scheduled
meeting, rather than afterward." Lay could have dictated a short
memo that didn't reveal anything classified, but told Twining everything he needed to know. The secretary would have put the memo into
the secure pouch for delivery to Twining over at the Pentagon by
courier, and Twining would make appropriate arrangements.

Certainly, most civilians wouldn't address a four-star general with
language like "your concurrence in the above arrangements is assumed," but as shown by Cutler's 1953 memo to Twining, it was
something he did. And Lay would have known this from his close association with Cutler.

Another question, also raised by Klass, was that neither
Eisenhower's nor Twining's calendar for July 16, 1954, the date on
which the briefing mentioned in the memo was to take place, says
anything about an MJ-12 briefing. Doesn't this absence establish
that there was no such meeting?

No. What it does establish is that nothing was listed on the official calendars. First, Twining's schedules were unclassified—theoretically, any private citizen could have requested them. Judging from the memo, the MJ-12 briefing was highly classified.

Second, it is common for government and military officials to be present at only parts of meetings listed on their calendars. For example, the daily log for Twining on January 25, 1960, when he was chairman of the Joint Chiefs of Staff, shows that he was at the Conference of Governors on Civil Defense from 9:15 in the morning until 10:30, when he had a meeting with President Eisenhower. After leaving the president, Twining went back to the governors' conference. (The log was in Twining's papers in the Library of Congress Manuscript Division.) President Eisenhower, as well as other presidents before and after him, very often stayed for only part of cabinet meetings, letting Vice President Nixon run parts of the meetings. And the other cabinet members would generally stay only for the portions of the meetings that directly concerned them, especially with regard to highly classified matters. The Postmaster General, for instance, might not have had a need-to-know for important defense or atomic energy information and would not be present during those segments.

Third, I found out that there may be multiple versions of important officials' calendars. For example, August 1, 1950 is listed in the Majestic-12 briefing document as the day on which General Smith was designated as a permanent replacement for Secretary Forrestal. When I wrote to the Truman Library requesting Truman's calendar for that date, I was sent a listing that was prepared ahead of time. When I visited the library, however, I discovered the list of meetings that Truman actually had that day. It includes five meetings that weren't on the preliminary sheet!

We know that Eisenhower and Twining were both in Washington on July 16, 1954. Eisenhower's docket included a meeting of his cabinet from 9:30 *a.m.* to noon. Twining had a Joint Chiefs of Staff meeting from 11 A.M. to 11:55 A.M. and continuing from 2 P.M. to 4:15 P.M. Travel time between the Pentagon and the White House is only a few minutes. Twining could have opened the meeting of the Joint Chiefs, slipped out to see Eisenhower, and then come back to the Joint Chiefs.

We cannot prove that such a meeting took place. Eisenhower was famous for committing as little information to paper as possible, for he was very concerned about security as befits the commander who oversaw the invasion of Normandy. And we have myriad examples of Eisenhower's failure to mention meetings which we know took place. Take what happened on November 18, 1952, the day of the MJ-12 briefing. Eisenhower had a 43-minute meeting at the Pentagon with the various members of the Joint Chiefs of Staff. We know that the meeting took place. The Eisenhower Library has detailed information about who was in which car, what the order of the cars was, and the detailed schedule for the day, including the briefing at the Pentagon. And yet, in his book *Mandate for Change*, Eisenhower made no mention of the Pentagon meeting. Not only that, but in five other books about the Eisenhower presidency by close associates, there is no mention of the briefing.

Thus, it appears that the Cutler-Twining memo is the real thing, indicating that there was a Top Secret MJ-12 group. Now we had to turn to other sources to find out more.

GOVERNMENT TREATMENT OF MAJESTIC-12 AND ROSWELL

The U.S. government had been relatively silent about UFOs since closing the old Air Force Project Blue Book in 1969. I made sporadic attempts using FOIA in the late 1970s to get information from the government, but learned quickly that there was very little chance of finding a smoking gun. The fact that no one sees special compart-mented Top Secret documents, along with the many restrictions on FOIA requests, makes it easy for any government agency to withhold documents.

This is not to say that useful information cannot be obtained, just that it is almost invariably meaningful only when put together with other information. For example, when CAUS went after the CIA's UFO information, they were told there was none. When the case went to court, the CIA "found" almost 900 pages about UFOs, most of it relatively dull and none of it classified above Secret. But the CIA did provide a list of 57 UFO documents originating with other agen-cies. Only the originating agencies could declassify these. Thus, al-though CAUS didn't get much new from the documents themselves, they could now prove that there were many different government agencies collecting information on UFOs: the Defense Intelligence

Agency, the Army, the Navy, the Air Force, the State Department, and the super-secret National Security Agency. Eighteen documents about UFOs in the CIA files were listed as being from the NSA.

As discussed in Chapter 4, an FOIA request was made in 1979 to the NSA for the 18 NSA UFO documents (listed by date only) found by the CIA. The NSA turned the request down cold on the grounds of national security, and an appeal was also rejected using the same excuse. Thanks to the efforts of CAUS, its attorney Peter Gersten, and a grant from the Fund for UFO Research, the case was brought to federal court in 1980, where Judge Gerhard Gesell directed the NSA to search its files for UFO materials. When the NSA came back to court, they announced they had found 239 highly classified UFO documents, 79 of which originated with other agencies, including 23 from the CIA which that agency had not found in its own search. That left 160 NSA UFO documents. Four were thrown out as being nonresponsive, and the other 156 were withheld by the NSA. Why? National security.

CAUS tried a different legal tack, requesting that Judge Gesell be shown the 156 documents, all of which were certainly pre-1980 and many of which dated back to the 1950s. CAUS wanted the judge to determine whether the NSA was properly invoking national security. (There is legal precedent for the request.) However, the NSA refused to show any of the UFO documents to Judge Gesell. Previously, the NSA had provided Gesell with an unclassified justification based on national security and "sources and methods" information that they said could not be released to the public. But this time they gave him a 21-page Above Top Secret affidavit justifying the withholding. They also had to give the judge an Above Top Secret security clearance just so he could review the affidavit in chambers. Naturally, attorney Gersten was not able to view the affidavit. The judge stated in his finding that "the in-camera affidavit presents factual considerations which aided the court in determining that the public interest in disclosure is far outweighed by the sensitive nature of the materials and the obvious effect on national security their release may well entail."

Judge Gesell agreed with the NSA; we couldn't have the 156 NSA UFO documents. We lost a chance to look at the documents, but we won something perhaps more valuable in the long run: a high-level legal opinion linking UFOs and national security. The Air Force, however, had for decades been claiming that UFOs do *not* represent a threat to national security. Surely, therefore, the UFO information should be segregatable from intelligence sources, methods, and techniques, all of which understandably could be withheld.

Based on this logic, we filed another appeal, this time with the Federal Court of Appeals in Washington, D.C. This involved both oral and written arguments. Normally the Court of Appeals takes two months to reach a decision. Only five days after the three-judge tribunal was shown the NSA's Top Secret affidavit, it agreed with the lower court. CAUS then attempted to have the case submitted to the Supreme Court, but the Supreme Court declined to review it.

We did at least receive a copy of the NSA's affidavit within a few months of an FOIA request. Seventy-five percent of the material was blacked out! Clearly the NSA was able to segregate the blacked-out Above Top Secret information from the releaseable information. But for some reason they couldn't seem to be able to do this for the 156 withheld documents.

At most of my lectures now, I recount the story of this legal battle and show the censored pages. It's a guaranteed laugh for the audience, and it proves that the NSA is withholding information about UFOs.

Unfortunately, the papers don't give us much insight into what is being withheld. You might well expect that, since the major job of the NSA is to listen in on military communications around the world with extraordinarily sophisticated listening devices and decoding systems, many of the 156 documents came from electronic intercepts about UFO encounters by foreign military personnel.

In 1977, I learned of one such encounter when I met someone who had worked for the NSA at Boca Chica Naval Air Station in Florida while he was in the military in 1967. My informant told me

this story in private after hearing my lecture. I assured him I would
not use his name, but I confirmed his version with another man who
had been stationed there at the same time.

Boca Chica is the base closest to Cuba. It's dull duty. You must
be a linguist with fluency in at least Russian and Spanish for that
base. Listening in on run-of-the-mill military communications is not
very exciting. However, in this instance, Cuban Air Defense
Command reported a UFO heading toward Cuba from the north-
east in broad daylight at an altitude of 30,000 feet and a speed approaching Mach 1—about 760 miles per hour. Two Cuban
MIG-21s were scrambled to intercept the UFO. They approached it,
radioing that it should leave Cuban airspace. They communicated
back to their base that the UFO was a bright metallic sphere, had
no appendages or markings, and was neither changing its course nor
acknowledging the warnings.

By now the UFO was over Cuba, and the base commanded the
pilots to shoot it down. The lead pilot armed his missiles and secured
a radar lock-on. Suddenly, the wingman was screaming over the radio
that the lead plane had disintegrated! The UFO took off straight up
to 100,000 feet and moved off southeast at Mach several.

The man who related this story to me noted that when they sent
a spot report of these communications to headquarters, they got an
unusual response. They were told not only to list the plane loss as
equipment malfunction, but to send the original tapes to headquarters! Normally, transcripts of the communications—time lines and
words as translated—were fine. I asked my informant whether headquarters might have wanted to try to get the exact words from the
tape. He said that was possible.

Robert Todd made several FOIA requests to get the official
records on this event. The FBI and the Air Force responded very
strongly, threatening Todd and demanding copies of the report I had
given Todd and the identity of the informant. (I had not provided the
man's identity.) I was very concerned when Todd told me of this official reaction. I was living in California at the time, my wife was
visiting family in eastern Canada, and I was at home with two handi-

capped children. I was the only one who knew the informant's name, and I wasn't about to give it up. Nevertheless, I felt somewhat intimidated and spent several sleepless nights listening for knocking at my door. I made a number of phone calls to colleagues explaining the story, so that if anyone was listening in they would know that others knew what was happening. As far as I know, no one carried through on any threats.

Sometime later, I had my own cloak-and-dagger contact with the government. When the NSA revealed they had found 23 CIA UFO documents, I naturally filed an FOIA request with the CIA. When the agency finally responded after 35 months, they sent me a letter outlining appeal procedures and noting that, if I had any questions, I should call a certain number and ask for Chris. Just Chris.

I decided to play the game. When I called Chris, he pressured me not to appeal the decision. "You don't expect to get anything, do you?" This time, I was more amused than intimidated, and I appealed anyway. As explained in Chapter 4, the CIA responded 24 months later in a totally unsatisfactory, but not unexpected, fashion.

It may appear that a few dozen documents is hardly a strong indication of great CIA interest in UFOs. However, recall that the original court case brought by CAUS had revealed almost 900 pages of material, and these pages had internal references to some 200 other documents, none of which were ever released. And I have good reasons to believe the CIA has a lot more than that.

John Marx is a lawyer who has managed to obtain a great deal of information about mind-control experiments conducted, usually illegally, in the early 1960s by the CIA and a number of subcontractors. His first FOIA release from the CIA was 400 pages of documents. He yelled and screamed. As a lawyer practicing in Washington, he could easily take the agency back to court, so he was given another box of 400 pages. More fussing; more boxes. He eventually wound up with *40,000 pages,* and he still didn't get all the material. So the minuscule amount of UFO material we have received so far is probably just the barest tip of the iceberg.

*   *   *   *

Other government agencies have their own ways of dealing with people who ask too many questions. For instance, when visiting the Project Blue Book files at the National Archives in Washington in the late 1970s, I had noted that they had added about 2,000 pages of Air Force OSI material, all declassified. Recognizing that this probably meant that there were many other documents that were not declassified, I made an effort to obtain them from the Air Force. They responded to my request with doubletalk, intentionally mis-interpreting my request. I dissected the doubletalk, sent another let-ter, and got more doubletalk. I wrote another letter and finally heard from a section chief in OSI, Noah D. Lawrence, who said they had done everything they could to assist me. (They had done nothing.) He was gracious enough to provide me, per my request, a list of the addresses of all OSI offices at Air Force bases around the world.

The next I knew about this was the copy of an order from Lawrence to all OSI offices that Bill Moore printed in *Focus*. The order, of course, instructed OSI field offices to violate their own reg-ulations when confronted by FOIA requests from UFO researchers in general and me in particular. (See Chapter 4.) So what did the OSI have to hide? It clearly wasn't going to be of much use to ask them directly.

Even members of Congress are not immune from such treat-ment. In the early 1990s, momentum was building through the ef-forts of the Fund for UFO Research, associated with Karl Pflock, to get congressional involvement, especially with regard to the Roswell event. In addition to support for research by myself and others, the Fund had sponsored a gathering of Roswell-related witnesses. The culmination of these efforts was a collection of notarized statements from these witnesses and a 105-minute *Recollections of Roswell* video-tape including the statements of 28 of the witnesses.

When *Crash at Corona* was being publicized in Washington, D.C, in the summer of 1992, Dr. Jesse Marcel—the son of the late Jesse Marcel, the Army Air Force major who first saw the Roswell wreckage in 1947—was brought in from his home in Montana. Dr.

Marcel is a medical doctor, a flight surgeon, a pilot in the reserves, and has served on a number of military aircraft accident investigation teams. As an 11-year-old, he had handled wreckage that his father brought home from the Roswell crash site. He and I and members of the Fund briefed various Congressional staff personnel about saucer crashes in New Mexico and the intimidation of various witnesses.

As a result of these briefings and the responsiveness of the staff people, Congressman Steve Schiff of New Mexico made a request of Secretary of Defense Les Aspin for a full briefing about what had happened at Roswell. (Fred Whiting, himself of the Fund, had been a Congressional aide and Karl Pflock's wife worked in the office of Congressman Schiff.) Schiff had also received a number of statements and requests from constituents and others in New Mexico indicating that there had been strong witness intimidation, and they wanted the truth about what had happened in New Mexico 45 years before.

Normally, when a congressman asks for a briefing from the DOD, he gets it. There was no response. A second request also brought no response. Finally, the request was passed to the Congressional Liaison office and Schiff got a three-sentence letter from the Air Force stating that his request had been referred to the National Archives, which had the Project Blue Book files. The National Archives responded to Schiff that they had no records on the Roswell incident, as they had been saying to others for many years!

Because of this stonewalling, at the end of 1993 Schiff turned to Congress's investigative arm, the General Accounting Office (GAO), to search for government records with regard to the Roswell incident. He wasn't looking for "everything" about flying saucers, or really anything about flying saucers. He was simply looking for records of the highly publicized Roswell event. In 1947, the commander of a major Army Air Force group had made an official statement that a flying disc had been recovered. This was followed by an official statement by the head of the 8th Air Force that what was recovered was just a weather balloon radar reflector. There had been a special flight of a B-29 from Roswell to Fort Worth, Texas. There also had, according to an FBI memo, been a special flight up to

Wright Field with the wreckage. Surely there should be records somewhere.

But before the GAO could make its report, the Air Force struck back. Not surprisingly, a former OSI disinformation specialist, Colonel Richard L. Weaver, was the point man.

I had bumped up against Weaver and his colleagues before. In late 1993, Nicholas Redfern, an English researcher, had sent me copies of two letters from Colonel Weaver, then Deputy for Security and Investigative Programs at the Pentagon. These letters were totally negative toward MJ-12. The first letter said, "this is in response to your FOIA request concerning the so-called Majestic 12 or MJ-12. We have no documents responsive to your request," and continued:

> Having said that, however, I can state that the Air Force considers the MJ-12 (both the group described and the purported documents) to be bogus. In fact, we mark the copies of the documents that come into our possession with the annotation "NOT AN OFFICIAL AIR FORCE DOCUMENT, NOT CLASSIFIED, SUSPECTED FORGERY OR BOGUS DOCUMENT." Such marking only proves to believers that we are obviously part of a gigantic ongoing coverup regarding the documents. These markings do, however, alert persons who may come into contact with them, that they are not really dealing with TOP SECRET CLASSIFIED DOCUMENTS and do not have to employ security measures to protect them (usually at great cost and inconvenience to all concerned).

Colonel Weaver even sent Redfern a copy of the Eisenhower briefing document, minus certain key identifying features but marked *BOGUS* on every page in two-inch-high letters in black ink. You might say he was emphasizing his comment.

The second letter from Weaver was in response to Redfern's request for information about potential criminal code violations that may have been violated by authors of UFO hoaxes. "As I previously stated," Weaver wrote, "no one has been interested in seriously pursuing the issue which is universally viewed in security and investigative circles as an obvious hoax."

Since Weaver had offered Redfern a seemingly official opinion, one must presume his office had done a detailed investigation of the MJ-12 documents. I sent a strong letter to Weaver on February 13, 1994, reviewing the evidence and making an FOIA request for any and all memos, letters, and documents on which Weaver based his official statement that the MJ-12 documents were a hoax. No response. I wrote again on April 3. This time Weaver wrote back: "We have no records responsive to your request." That was all. I sent a strong appeal, to which no reply had been received by April 1996. Is it stupidity that made Weaver think that UFO researchers don't talk amongst themselves? Or is it simply arrogance born of decades of unchallenged Air Force misrepresentation that allowed him to proclaim whatever he wanted?

This attitude was demonstrated by another Air Force officer, Lieutenant Colonel Thomas W. Shubert, Congressional Inquiry Division, Office of Legislative Liaison, whose job is to respond to inquiries by members of Congress on behalf of their constituents. In early 1994 Michael Atkins of the state of Washington sent me a copy of a gem from Colonel Shubert to Senator Patty Murray of Washington. It repeats totally misleading claims dating back to December 1969, when Project Blue Book was closed.

Because I always run down every lead (you never know when a break in the dam will occur), I wrote to Shubert, stressing the many problems with the Air Force's response. (See Appendix E.) After waiting months for a reply, I tried calling Shubert, and was told by a major that the office only responds to members of Congress. So I sent Shubert's letter and my critique to other elected representatives. Senator Slate Gordon of Washington tried to rattle the Air Force's cage, but unsuccessfully. In response to my FOIA requests, I received copies of dozens of similarly false and misleading letters from the Air Force to other elected representatives asking about Roswell.

Although they regularly make themselves out to be the public's watchdog, no media group has had the courage yet to blow the lid off this cosmic Watergate despite the unambiguous evidence of official lying, ignorance, or both. The *Washington Post* made numerous factual errors when it reported in January 1994 that the GAO had agreed to seek the paper trail about Roswell for Congressman Schiff. I left phone messages for reporter William Claibourne three times. No response. The *Post* Ombudsperson did respond to my calls, and asked that I send information, which I did. Then nothing.

On September 8, 1994, the Air Force executed an astonishing preemptive strike by releasing "their report" on Roswell. This was a clear violation of their agreement with the GAO. They and all other agencies approached by the GAO were to make all files available which might contain relevant information, not pick and choose on their own.

The officer listed as the author of the Air Force report was none other than Colonel Weaver, so I was not surprised that the report was loaded with false information and used the standard tactics of the propagandist: selective choice of data, name-calling, and false reasoning ad nauseum. (My 27-page detailed critique of the Air Force's report is entitled "The Roswell Incident, the USAF, and the *New York Times.*") The Air Force report concludes that what was recovered near Roswell wasn't a flying saucer with alien bodies; nor was it a weather balloon and accompanying radar reflector, as claimed by 8th Air Force Commander Roger Ramey back in 1947. Instead, according to Weaver, the wreckage probably consisted of balloons, radar reflectors, sonobuoys, and miscellaneous junk from a highly classified Project Mogul balloon assembly. Weaver's report, while only 23 pages long, made much ado about a 1,000-page collection of supporting documents at the Air Force Library at the Pentagon.

An associate was lucky enough to gain access to a set of the supporting documents. However, media personnel were denied access to the material—and for good reason. In November 1995, the attachments and the original report were published by the Government Printing Office as an impressive-looking, two-and-a-half-inch-thick, heavily illustrated report entitled *The Roswell Report: Truth*

Versus Fiction in the New Mexico Desert costing $52. In it was more information about Project Mogul than anybody would ever want.

Weaver, as it turns out, has taught courses to OSI personnel on the uses of disinformation. Project Mogul was no revelation; its existence had been known for decades. None of the technology was highly classified. The project's objective—to develop a constant-altitude balloon which could monitor sounds produced by a Soviet nuclear explosion thousands of miles away—had been highly classified. (Project Mogul began in 1946. The first Soviet nuclear explosion took place in 1949, and was detected by analyzing air samples gathered by U.S. aircraft, not by Mogul devices.)

Each Mogul ensemble consisted of 20-25 balloons tied together with twine at about 20-foot intervals and included sonobuoys, ballast containers, radio gear, and other equipment. The balloons used in June 1947 were standard neoprene weather balloons, which turned to gray ash after weeks in the sun. The radar reflectors consisted of foil over a frame of balsa wood sticks with tape holding the whole business together like a child's kite. Supposedly the tape had strange pastel flower symbols on it and the balsa wood was soaked in something to make it tougher. But no matter how tough they made the wood or the foil reflectors, this standard junk simply does not relate to the extraordinarily strong, lightweight material that Roswell witnesses have described.

Weaver had no qualms about making other misrepresentations. He attempted to tabloidize the story by claiming, "In 1978, an article appeared in a tabloid newspaper, the *National Inquirer* [sic], which reported the former intelligence officer, Marcel, claimed that he had recovered UFO debris near Roswell in 1947. Also in 1978 a UFO researcher, Stanton Friedman, met with Marcel and began investigating the claims that the material Marcel handled was from a crashed UFO." This implies that I get my leads from tabloid newspapers.

I did talk to Marcel in February 1978, but it was on the phone after I was referred to Marcel by the station manager of a Baton Rouge television station, who knew Marcel. I met with Marcel in May 1979, when making *UFOs Are Real*. More importantly, the

National Enquirer (not *Inquirer*) article Weaver references didn't appear until February 1980, and it was based on a December 1979 interview with Marcel by outstanding *Enquirer* UFO reporter Bob Pratt—who had gotten Marcel's address from me! By that time, Bill Moore and I had done almost all the research reported in *The Roswell Incident*. We spent an enormous amount of time, money, and effort locating witnesses, taking testimony, and tracking down our own leads. There was no tabloid influence.

Weaver quoted from a July 8, 1947 FBI memo referring to the wreckage recovered by the 509th, but left out an interior clause which totally changes the meaning: "Further advised that the object found resembles a high altitude weather balloon with a radar reflector *but that telephonic conversation between their office and Wright Field had not borne out this belief.*" He quotes at length from a July 9, 1947 *Roswell Daily Record* article "Harassed Rancher Who Located 'Saucer' Sorry He Told About It," but leaves out this all-important part of Brazel's quote: "I am sure what I found was not any weather observation balloon." He also doesn't mention, as is noted in several books, that Brazel was brought back into town after showing the wreckage to Marcel and Cavitt on July 7 and given a new story by the military.

Weaver talked to several persons connected with Project Mogul, and also with Sheridan Cavitt, the Counter-Intelligence Corps man who went out to the Brazel ranch with Marcel. Cavitt, who is on a military pension, is quoted as saying, "The area of this debris was very small, about 20 feet square and the material was spread on the ground, but there was no gouge or crater or other obvious sign of impact. I remember recognizing this material as being consistent with a weather balloon. We gathered up some of this material which would easily fit into one vehicle."

Simple, straightforward, and certainly false. Since 1980, when I located him, Cavitt has spoken on numerous occasions with researchers such as Bill Moore, myself, Don Schmitt, and Kevin Randle. Never did he say anything like what Weaver claims he said. Rather, he has steadfastly claimed he had nothing to do with the incident, even claiming at one point that he wasn't even in Roswell at all that week. The July 9 *Roswell Daily Record* article that Weaver quoted from also included Brazel's statement that the wreckage was "scattered over an area 200 yards in diameter." Major Marcel testified in the 1979 documentary *UFOs Are Real* that the wreckage covered an area three quarters of a mile long and hundreds of feet wide.

Even if we could believe the claim that the wreckage was from a Mogul ensemble, the Air Force report doesn't stand up. One of the report's attachments states that the reason Marcel and Blanchard didn't recognize the wreckage was that there were 23 balloons, sonobuoys, and other debris. How could an ensemble that extensive (it would have been at least 500 feet long) come down in an area "about 20 feet square"? How could it "easily fit into one vehicle"?

Weaver had already left his Pentagon assignment by the time the report was released, having been transferred back to the OSI office at Langley Field, Virginia, and was unavailable for interviews. But his disinformation continued to flourish. His original debunking was covered in gory detail in a long front-page article in the *New York Times* of Sunday, September 18, 1994. The article, by Pulitzer-winning science reporter William Broad, touted the "discovery" of the Project Mogul explanation. The article was syndicated, and appeared on the front page of many other newspapers. But it was obvious that Broad had done little independent research himself—he bought the Weaver bunk hook, line, and sinker.

For instance, although he talked to some Project Mogul specialists, Broad didn't note that C. B. Moore, the key engineer on the project, had been interviewed years ago by Bill Moore and also by Don Berliner and myself. If he had, he would have known that this explanation was not new. The language of his article was also extremely biased against ufologists. He used such terms as *flying saucer fans, coverup theorists, flying saucer cultists, conspiracy theories,* and *flying saucer devotees.* He appeared oblivious to the fact that Gallup polls have shown for more than 30 years that believers outnumber nonbelievers, and that the greater the education a person has, the more likely he or she is to believe that some UFOs are alien spacecraft. In fact, of engineers and scientists, two-thirds who express an opinion say flying saucers are real. And perhaps most telling was his reference to Walter Haut as being connected with the Roswell Museum, but never mentioning that Haut was the one who put out the first press release about the Roswell crash!

On July 29, 1995, the GAO released its long-awaited Roswell document search report (GAO/NSIAD-95-187 "Results of a Search for Records Concerning the 1947 Crash Near Roswell, New Mexico") to Congressman Schiff. Although Schiff could have held it for 30 days, he released it to the public later that same day with a press release which noted that numerous records of Roswell Army Air Field, which should have been kept, had been destroyed. According to the GAO report, these destroyed items included administrative records from March 1945 through December 1949, and outgoing messages from October 1946 through December 1949.

The GAO also included a separate two-page report to Congressman Schiff about the MJ-12 documents. The long and short of this special report is that the GAO made a number of inquiries to various archives and the Air Force concerning MJ-12, and—surprise! Nobody knew anything. The CIA "cooperated" with the GAO, doing a search of their files using only two keywords: *Project Mogul* and *Roswell!* (There must be dozens of other keywords they could have used, including *Corona, flying disc, flying saucer, crash,* etc.) A letter from the Department of Defense in the GAO report says that Colonel Weaver's report included all that they found. The FBI letter referenced their July 8, 1947 memo about Roswell, but said nary a word about the July 10 memo discussing a request from Brigadier General George Schulgen, Chief of the Requirements Intelligence Branch of Army Air Corps Intelligence, to the FBI requesting their assistance with regard to investigation of flying saucer reports. On that memo is this handwritten notation made five days later by J. Edgar Hoover: "I would do it but before agreeing to it we must insist upon full access to discs recovered. For instance in the Sw [or La—the handwriting is unclear] case the army grabbed it & would not let us have it for cursory examination." Surely this points to a recovered disc. Could *Sw* stand for Southwest? Or could *La* stand for Los Alamos?

In addition, the GAO reviewed only the FOIA files of the CIA, FBI, and NSA, rather than the entire files, as is borne out by one of the tables in the report. Surely the documents the GAO saw wouldn't have included highly classified materials! Based on past experience, these agencies should not be trusted to do their own searches. The GAO should have demanded that their staff gain access to the potentially useful files of these agencies.

So once again, absence of evidence was assumed to be evidence for absence. The GAO report fell victim to one of the basic false logic tricks of the debunkers. Although the GAO found no smoking guns, it is clear that the Air Force and other government agencies have played hardball about Roswell and MJ-12. Unless a congressional committee or some major media outfit has the courage and the resources to really dig into the subject, the public will be denied the truth about the cosmic Watergate.

THE MJ-12 DEBUNKERS

Ever since the publicity given to Kenneth Arnold's June 24, 1947 sighting of flying saucers, there have been people who have tried to prove that no sighting has ever been of an alien craft. Generally, their attacks have been based on three premises. First, all UFO sightings have prosaic explanations. Second, there is no evidence to support the notion of extraterrestrial visitors. Third, there is no government coverup about UFOs. Sometimes, a fourth premise is added: interstellar travel is impossible.

These debunkers seem to be serious in their beliefs. They have written over a dozen books and hundreds of articles buttressing their arguments. They make regular appearances on radio and television talk shows, provide testimony for learned panels, and publish white papers and their own periodicals. They claim to do serious research on the veracity of documents and witness reports. They spend so much time in this pursuit that their work must be legitimate, right?

Hardly. After years of locking horns with the naysayers, I have to admit to being somewhat perplexed by their attitudes. Perhaps it is their approach to research that is so confusing. Whereas the scientific method used by generations of research scientists is to collect all the data possible and then draw conclusions, the debunkers seem to take the opposite tack—decide on the conclusion, present data that agrees, and ignore data that does not agree. This slant is borne out by their minimal work in archives, the unfounded claims of fraud they make against ufologists, their restatement of theories and claims long ago discredited, and their problems when confronted with the facts.

Or maybe it is what they choose to ignore in making their pronouncements. I am sure that, because I am certain of the existence of alien UFOs, I make assumptions that I wouldn't make if I was not certain, and probably give more weight to some pieces of evidence rather than to others. However, my certainty is based on 38 years of investigation and the facts—such as the data in Project Blue Book Special Report 14, corroborated eyewitness accounts from reliable sources, physical traces, radar reports, and documents culled from endless hours in more than 15 archives. However, when you read the work of the debunkers, you generally do not find references to accepted legitimate sources such as Special Report 14. These people know about these works and how they point to the existence of extraterrestrial vehicles, but choose not to pass this knowledge on to their audience.

Or perhaps it is the emotional cast they have given the entire subject. Their publications are rife with wild charges against ufologists and UFO observers. They use highly charged terms to refer to their opponents—*UFO believers, buffs, flying saucer cultists, hoaxers,* and others. A poor way to deal with any subject.

Whatever the reasons for their actions, they seem to have captured the ear of the major media. This is sad, for poll after poll has established that the public overwhelmingly believes in the existence of extraterrestrial spacecraft.

Of the naysayers, Philip Klass (born 1919) has been the most persistent and the most influential. For decades senior avionics editor for the respected Washington magazine *Aviation Week and Space Technology,* his opinions and pronouncements receive great acceptance from the media. He has an impressive background, but has unfortunately fallen prey to the debunker's devil. Klass is often vituperative, and shows little predilection for true journalistic or scientific investigation about UFOs. He stands foursquare on the absolutely false premises that are the bedrock of debunker philosophy: every sighting has a prosaic explanation, and there is no coverup. He says that supposed abductees are either mentally disturbed or are publicity seekers. And his theories collapse when hard evidence is carefully considered.

He appears to have no qualms about using all the techniques of the propagandist: selective choice of data, name-calling, false reasoning, and misrepresentation. One of his favorite techniques in radio and TV battles is to distract the moderator with irrelevant sorties in order to avoid coming to grips with data that disproves his basic premises. "Why didn't Friedman apply for the Cutty Sark million-pound UFO award for evidence of an ET saucer?" Klass once asked on a Canadian TV show on which we both appeared. He was implying that I didn't really believe my own research. But what he didn't say, and what I pointed out, was that the Cutty Sark award was for an actual saucer or bona fide piece thereof, which I have never claimed to have, not simply documentary or eyewitness evidence.

Klass, since mid-1987, has been attacking the MJ-12 briefing document and the Cutler-Twining memo. A major venue for his attacks has been *The Skeptical Inquirer,* the periodical of the Committee for the Scientific Investigation of Claims of the Paranormal (CSICOP). Over and over, one finds in these writings false statements, character assassination, selective choice of data, and a seeming unwillingness to do adequate research.

The danger is that unless a reader knows about the subject, Klass's claims seem reasonable. For instance, in a June 1987 radio appearance about the MJ-12 briefing documents, Klass made his claim that Roscoe Hillenkoetter could not have been the briefing officer because he was away on sea duty from 1950 until 1956. Fortunately for that program's listeners, I was also on the show, and presented the evidence that Hillenkoetter certainly was back in the country by 1951.

Another example appeared in Klass's article "The MJ-12

Crashed-Saucer Documents" in *The Skeptical Inquirer* (Winter 1987-1988). He raised these two questions about the documents: "Why would the film [on which the documents appeared] be sent to Shandera, who has never published any papers on UFOs or crashed saucers and does not even consider himself a ufologist? How could the sender of the 35mm film even know that Shandera and Moore were friends and that the contents would find their way to Moore?" What an innocent reader would not know was that Shandera had been working and sharing information and contacts with Moore and me ever since we collaborated on the abortive 1980 UFO movie I discussed in Chapter 1. The insiders who contacted Moore (finally numbering 10 in all) knew very well that Moore and Shandera were working together and keeping me informed. And although Jaime had at the time never published any papers by himself, he has spent far more time at various archives than has Klass (despite the fact that Klass lives minutes away from the National Archives and the Library of Congress Manuscript Division).

Klass then comes to what he describes as "the most revealing substantive anomaly" in the briefing documents—the date format. Here is an opportunity to display the adequacy of Klass's research. As discussed in Chapter 4, Klass's complaint is that the format *18 November, 1952* and *01 August, 1950* (with the zero preceding the single-digit date) is an erroneous mixture of civil and military formats. Klass also claims that the zero was not used to precede a single-digit date until very recently: "Examination of numerous military and CIA documents written during the 1950s, 1960s, and 1970s shows the standard date format was to write: 1 August 1950."

Klass did not quantify the term *numerous,* and so the reader has no way of knowing how many military and CIA documents he checked. I suspect that he checked very few, for I have been able to find numerous examples of such documents with the "wrong" format in sources that are easily accessible to Klass. One was a letter from Hillenkoetter himself. Others show up in Tim Good's book *Above Top Secret* (page 446) and in the *Alsos Mission* by Colonel Boris T. Pash (pages 84 and 98). Perhaps most damning is a 1954 U.S. gov-

ernment document found by Bill Moore—Joint Army Navy Air
Publication (JANAP) 146 (C), which includes instructions to military personnel for reporting UFOs. And two different English
sources with extensive World War II military background made the
following comments to Tim Good, as reported in *Above Top Secret:*

> You raise the query that the prefix "0" as in "02 July 1947" was not
> used until modern computer technology was developed. I beg most
> strongly to differ. Certainly my experience in wartime in the Navy was
> that the "0" was a vital prefix whether in the date as in "02 July" or
> the hour as in "0300." I should think such methods were still used in
> NATO.
>
> NATO documents always used the "0" in front of single-date fig-
> ures in my day, but I do not know when it started.

In addition, there are numerous examples of the MJ-12 date format
in Ewen Montagu's fascinating book *The Man Who Never Was,*
an excellent account of the very effective World War II disinformation campaign intended to throw the Germans off the scent of
the Normandy invasion by placing bogus documents on a dead
body that was then "washed ashore" where the Germans could find
it. lThe declassified files of the Canadian Defence Research Board
also provide many other examples pre-1954, and English researcher
Nicholas Redfern has located numerous examples of various "
nonstandard" date formats, including the one in the briefing documents.

   Klass's other statements in this article, especially those about the
Truman-Forrestal memo, also reveal his poor scholarship. In discussing the likelihood that Vannevar Bush would be on MJ-12, he
states that Bush was "President of the Carnegie Foundation." First,
this statement makes it seem that Bush was involved with the char-
itable work done by that organization when in fact he was president
of the Carnegie Institution, which dealt with scientific research.
Second, Klass doesn't mention Bush's contemporaneous activities
with other organizations, especially the prewar NACA, the wartime

OSRD, and the postwar JRDB. Nor does he mention that Bush was the common person in the several organizations listed in General Twining's September 23, 1947 letter for receipt of UFO information. (This letter was, of course, dated the day before President Truman's special classified executive order creating MJ-12.)

The simple fact is that the formerly Top Secret Canadian memo of November 21, 1950 written by W. B. Smith and sent to me in the late 1970s by Canadian researcher Scott Foster, included a direct mention of Bush and a small group investigating the modus operandi of flying saucers. The memo also stated that "The matter is the most highly classified subject in the United States Government, rating higher even than the H-Bomb." Klass's response to this memo? A vicious attack on the late Smith, an award-winning Canadian engineer, as "crazy" in a debate with me on a Boston TV show.

Klass's second *Skeptical Inquirer* article, "The MJ-12 Papers: Part 2" (Spring 1988), contained so much baloney it should have been distributed by a delicatessen. Over and over he maintains what the main players in MJ-12 "logically" or "certainly" or "surely" would have done in hypothetical situations. You would think Klass had really gone all out to study these famous people. But as far as I know Klass had never been to the Eisenhower or Truman libraries, according to the archivists at both repositories, nor had he spent much time at the National Archives or Library of Congress Manuscript Division. Judging by what he says about the activities of the MJ-12 people, he hasn't even gone past a quick look at *Who's Who.* Some specific examples will illuminate his apparent lack of knowledge about the MJ-12 team.

Klass claims, with little supporting evidence, that people would have been chosen for a mythical MJ-12 because of the positions they held as of September 1947: "When they left these posts for other assignments or retired from government, their successors in those posts would logically have replaced them on MJ-12." This implies that the listing of MJ-12 members in the 1952 Eisenhower briefing is "out of date," as a number of these people had by that time switched jobs or left government. However, a much more intensive investigation of the people involved and of the Washington scene leads to the notion that the members would have been chosen for their skills, competence, background, and demonstrated capabilities, not for transitory titles. I have read many recommendations for government positions, including some from the MJ-12 people. The focus was always on capabilities, not job titles. World War II produced a host of people who, even when back in civilian jobs, served on government committees and task forces in Washington. The experience of Dr. Menzel jumps to mind.

Here is Klass's comment about Gordon Gray:

> Gordon Gray, who had become assistant secretary of the army about the time that MJ-12 allegedly was created, would have been a most unlikely member based on background and position. Gray was trained as a lawyer and had spent the previous ten years as publisher of two newspapers, and he did not hold a top-ranking Pentagon position. In mid-1949, Gray was named secretary of the Army, but he resigned April 12, 1950, to return to civilian life and was succeeded in that post by Frank Pace, Jr.

From this, you would think that Gray did his stint, went back to private life, and couldn't have been on such a powerful group as MJ-12. Similarly for Sidney Souers, about whom Klass says the following:

> Souers might have been a logical choice as an original member of MJ-12, because on September 26, 1947, he was named executive secretary of the president's newly created National Security Council. Souers, a naval reservist, had risen to the rank of rear admiral during World War II to become deputy chief of Naval Intelligence and played a role in organizing the then-new CIA. Souers retired from his NSC position in early 1950 to return to civilian life, but he, rather than his successor at NSC, is listed in late 1952 as an MJ-12 member.

The implication is that Souers was finished with Washington, and therefore his place on MJ-12 would have been taken by his NSC successor, James Lay. Klass makes similar remarks about other members listed in the briefing.

Unfortunately, it is not obvious to the unaware that Klass's evaluations are based on only the most superficial examination of the careers of these men. As discussed in Chapter 3, these were unique personalities whose activities on government panels and committees extended well beyond their publicized tenures in one or another office. When they moved on, they maintained their security clearances, their knowledge, their influence, and their ability to get things done discreetly. This would help maintain the need-to-know secrecy of the organization: instead of members changing each time someone new was appointed to a post (often a political consideration), only the person to whom the committee was accountable—the president—would be likely to change.

In a final misrepresentation, Klass claims that hard evidence of the MJ-12 briefing document's fraudulence can be found in the declassified December 10, 1948 Top Secret document "Analysis of Flying Object Incidents in the U.S." There is no such evidence at all in this document. It is clear that the Navy-Air Force group preparing it had been given specific guidelines for their work. Their primary objective was to investigate the possibility that some flying discs were of Soviet origin, perhaps constructed with the help of captured German scientists. There was no serious discussion of saucers having an extraterrestrial origin, and nothing about crashed saucers—which would have been Above Top Secret. This limited emphasis would not have been unusual for a classified task force. Many books about the CIA have stressed that there were often several groups set up completely independently to look at a particular problem and with no knowledge of the existence of the other groups. There is no reason to deny the possibility that the people who wrote the 1948 document had no need-to-know for Majestic-12 material.

These examples (there are many more) establish that, in denigrating UFOs in general and the MJ-12 briefing document in particular, Klass is basically whistling in the dark. The small amount of time he has spent in archives shows that he is essentially an armchair theorist, as are most debunkers. (On a 1991 Larry King show on which he appeared with Kevin Randle, Klass was forced to admit that he had not then spoken to any of the more than 90 Roswell eye-witnesses who we had located up to that time.) His minimal research, flawed logic, and propagandistic writing call into question the validity of his claims.

However, these considerations have never stopped Klass before, and will probably not in the future. The only way to overcome his brand of "scholarship" is to confront it with facts, as I have done. When Klass and I appeared together on the New York television program *People Are Talking* on March 14, 1988, 83 percent of phone respondents to a poll taken by the show said they believed UFOs are real. When an audience compares anti-UFO claims with pro-UFO facts side-by-side, the facts always win.

I was not surprised that Phil Klass attacked the MJ-12 documents almost from the first moment he heard about them. Obviously, if the documents are legitimate, then his basic position on UFOs would immediately be destroyed. I am sure that one of the reasons he never discusses Project Blue Book Special Report 14 is that he would have to admit that the Air Force says there are hundreds of UFO sightings that can't be explained. Besides, if a government agency admits that some UFOs are alien spacecraft, he would have to pay me $10,000 per the terms of an agreement we made many years ago.

However, another attack on MJ-12 came from another, and unexpected, quarter.

In 1991, Don Schmitt of the Center for UFO Studies (CUFOS) and Kevin Randle were publicizing their book *UFO Crash at Roswell*. I had shared a great deal of information with the two while they were working on the book, but when it came out I was surprised by the amount of misleading information it had. None of the many papers about Roswell that had been published in the proceedings of various Mutual UFO Network (MUFON) symposia were referenced. In the three pages of acknowledgments, there was no mention of the Fund for UFO Research, which had given the duo about $10,000 to help their research. (This is a princely sum for UFO research.) Bill Moore's major contributions to Roswell research were barely mentioned, although I was acknowledged well: "Stanton Friedman. Nuclear Physicist and UFO researcher, who first learned of the events at Roswell and through persistence was able to find the key witnesses that broke the story open." However, the treatment of Majestic-12 and the crash that occurred in the Plains of San Agustin was startlingly subjective.

At almost the same time as *UFO Crash at Roswell* was published, CUFOS issued "The Roswell Report: A Historical Perspective," a report that included a number of papers previously published in the organization's periodical *International UFO Reporter*. A 1988 paper of mine about MJ-12, "The MJ-12 Debunking Fiasco," was included; so was the anti-Majestic-12 paper by Joseph Nickell and John Fischer, "The Crashed Saucer Forgeries," although the two rebuttal pieces (one by Moore and one by me) which had originally accompanied the paper in the *Reporter* were not even referenced. CUFOS seemed to be taking an anti-Majestic-12 position, and the reason seemed to be testimony from an impeccable source, retired Air Force Brigadier General Arthur E. Exon, who had been commander of Wright-Patterson Air Force Base from August 1, 1964 through December 20, 1965.

I had first spoken with Exon in 1989 after he had been mentioned to me in a note from retired Colonel J. Bond Johnson, who had taken the widely circulated pictures in General Ramey's office on July 8, 1947 of the weather-balloon-and-radar-reflector debris that was the Army Air Force's first explanation of the Roswell wreckage. Johnson wrote me that Exon had told him quite openly that there were alien bodies at Wright-Patterson. He also indicated that it didn't appear that security was being enforced anymore on this matter. If what Johnson said was true, this was major news.

I had a long and friendly phone conversation with General Exon then. He made it very clear that Johnson had gone well beyond what he himself had said. He had heard scuttlebutt about bodies and wreckage, but had no firsthand knowledge of the subject. I sent him some background information and some of my papers and let it go at that.

Now, in the summer of 1991, Randle and Schmitt were claiming that Exon knew there was a control group (which they called "the unholy 13") for Roswell, knew who the members of that group were, and had direct firsthand involvement with the crashed saucer. They claimed that Exon told them the members of the control group included Stewart Symington, then Secretary of the Air Force; Carl Spaatz, first chief of staff of the Air Force; General Eisenhower, then Army chief of staff; General Ramey, head of the 8th Air Force; and others. None of the people they mentioned were on the MJ-12 briefing list.

The whole business sounded fishy. At the MUFON conference in Chicago in July 1991, a group of us from MUFON, CUFOS, and the Fund were talking about the possibility of congressional hearings and testimony behind closed doors. Since General Exon's testimony, if truthfully reported in *UFO Crash at Roswell*, would be very important, I asked Schmitt if he had sent a copy of that portion of the book to the general so he would be on record that it was accurate. If others approached him, he would not be able to deny having made the statements attributed to him. This is what Bill Moore had done with many witnesses before the publication of *The Roswell Incident*.

Don said that he had not sent Exon a copy of their version of his testimony. Looking at our stunned faces, he added, "And he hasn't been returning our calls."

Shaking this off, I then asked Don if he thought that the anthropologist, whose supposed testimony about bodies and wreckage and the military at the Corona site they touted so strongly, would be willing to testify behind closed doors. In the book, Randle and Schmitt noted that the man was concerned about losing government research contracts if he spoke out openly, strongly suggesting that he had a Ph.D. Surely, he would be an ideal eyewitness. Shock number two. Don said, "We don't know who he is. He was an anonymous phone caller."

I had had my doubts about Randle and Schmitt's book before,

and they were growing stronger. When I returned home from the conference, I wrote a detailed and generally negative review of the book for the *MUFON Journal.* The review, published in the September 1991 issue of the *Journal,* focused on the authors' negative slant on the Plains of San Agustin crash and what I perceived as their petty attitude toward many specific examples.

When I finished the review, I decided to give General Exon a call. I left him a message on his answering machine, and rather than ignoring me, a few days later he called me back. He had not seen Randle and Schmitt's book, and so I read him portions of his supposed testimony from the volume. He politely but firmly indicated that Randle and Schmitt had attributed considerably more to him than he had said. He had no firsthand involvement with Roswell, although he had heard lots of scuttlebutt from people he trusted. He had been at Wright Field in July 1947, when the Roswell wreckage had been brought there. He had heard stories while he was base commander (not even as commander did he have a need-to-know for all activities there) and also during a stint at the Pentagon. We had another enjoyable conversation, during which he gladly agreed to review my *Final Report on Operation Majestic 12.* I mailed him my report and copies of the pages from Randle and Schmitt's book on which he was mentioned.

Not wishing to burden the general unnecessarily, I waited a few weeks and then called and left another message. Once again, he returned the call promptly. He strongly approved of my MJ-12 report, and he reiterated his comments about Randle and Schmitt, adding that the names he had given them were those of high-level personnel he thought would know about what was happening, not of people he knew to be involved in a control group.

So now there were major elements of *UFO Crash at Roswell* that were suspect. And it seemed that every week brought more revelations from other sources of fabricated or misleading testimony, especially by Randle, in the book.

Randle and Schmitt's next book, *The Truth About the UFO Crash at Roswell* (1994), contained even more distortions and misrepresentations. In fact, a number of friends told me that parts of the book seemed like thinly veiled attacks on me! Included in the book was an appendix entitled "The Majestic 12 Hoax."

Soon after, at Randle's request, the Fund for UFO Research published a report by him (the work for this was not sponsored by the Fund) entitled *Conclusions on Operation Majestic 12*. I was clearly the target of the report, which included much of the material from the *Truth* appendix as well as the article "The Unholy Thirteen." This was an in-depth attack on the MJ-12 documents.

At first blush, *Conclusions* appears to be excellent investigative journalism. Nine of its 30 pages are given over to 103 footnotes and 92 references, and nine of the references are works I have written or coauthored. However, a careful review by somebody knowledgeable about the materials indicates that the paper is an almost textbook example of pseudoscientific propaganda.

Twenty-seven of the footnotes refer to personal communications or interviews which the reader cannot check. There are serious errors of omission and commission, false reasoning, and massive misrepresentation.

Randle quotes this 1991 statement of mine: "the simple fact of the matter is that Moore, Shandera, and I had already picked up on all the names of the list prior to receipt of the film (except for Dr. Donald Menzel) as a result of the many days spent in archival research begun a decade ago. . . . We had noted who was where in early July 1947, when the Roswell incident occurred." Randle then makes this outrageous claim: "In other words, Friedman was telling us that he along with Moore and Shandera had the knowledge to create the document . . . if that is what they had decided to do. The suggestion that no one could have invented the document without extensive research is accurate and Friedman was admitting they had done the research."

The obvious implication was that Jaime, Bill, and myself were the hoaxers! What Randle omitted, however, was a fair nod to my *Final Report on Operation Majestic 12* and its discussion of more than 30 items of information, some very subtle, in the MJ-12 documents which establish that the documents had to have been prepared by government insiders, not outsiders like Moore, Shandera, or myself. (See Appendix C.) Yes, our research on the *names* of the people (except Menzel) occurred before we received the film, but our research on the other details, including what we discovered about Menzel, could only have occurred after we got the film. Obviously, researching the MJ-12 people was only a small part of the information needed to evaluate the content of the documents.

Randle, it seems, would prefer to airbrush my research out of the picture entirely. Although I was the original investigator of the Roswell crash, was the first to locate and interview many of the key witnesses (including Jesse Marcel Sr., Walter Haut, Glenn Dennis, and others), and shared my research generously with Randle and Schmitt, in his later publications Randle has attempted to ignore my contributions. He scrapped the acknowledgment of my work from *UFO Crash at Roswell,* and omitted 29 of my 30 Roswell/MJ-12 papers in his list of sources in *The Truth About the UFO Crash at Roswell.* (He included more than 200 other references.) Instead, he leaned heavily on the pseudoscientific proclamations of Joseph Nickell, never mentioning that Nickell is a CSICOP Fellow. Though he often referenced Nickell and Fisher's paper "The Crashed Saucer Forgeries," he never mentioned the rebuttals by Moore and me which appeared in the very same issue of the *International UFO Reporter.*

Typical of the selective choice of data and a constant willingness to repeat without verification any argument against MJ-12 are the following:

- His discussion of the Truman-Forrestal memo. He does not mention that the date on the memo was typed by two typewriters, and the period after the date points to Van Bush's office as the place where it was typed. In addition, he refers to the order as an *Executive Order* or *EO* at least 15 times, using the initals SCEO only once, which implies that there is no difference between an Executive Order and a Special Classified Executive Order.

- Nickell and others have complained about the special classified executive order number 092447 being the date. As I found in a quiet but extensive research visit to the George C. Marshall Archives, the State Department normally used the date as part of filing nomenclature. This makes sense, since there would be few special classified executive orders. A date is a unique designation.

- His reliance on Nickell's work despite the fact that Nickell made the absurd claim in a letter in *International UFO Reporter* that he knew the date format for the briefing documents was wrong because it violated the government style manual! Anybody who spends serious time in archives with holdings of pre-1960 declassified material will note that the style manual is ignored in very limited distribution highly classified memos.

- His omission of Eisenhower's November 18, 1952 very-high-security briefing about national security matters at the Pentagon. Randle does mention Eisenhower's brief meeting with Truman on that day.

- His omission of my published comments about the membership of the MJ-12 group and his continued misrepresentation of General Exon's comments.

- His contention that the lack of exact titles for the military members of MJ-12 is a sign of fraud. Randle is upset by the use of generic military titles, such as Admiral instead of Rear Admiral. Neither General Exon, Colonel Jesse Marcel, Jr., nor several other military people with whom I spoke had any problem with the generic ranks. Randle is particularly upset by Hillenkoetter being referred to as Admiral rather than Rear Admiral. Randle doesn't seem to understand that a group with six military members and six civilians could not possibly make distinctions on the basis of military rank.

- His demand to see any letters signed by Hillenkoetter in which he includes the rank Admiral instead of Rear Admiral. Since Randle doesn't include the briefing document in his report, readers wouldn't know there are no signatures or even initials on the briefing, from Hillenkoetter or anyone else.

- His omission of linguistics expert Roger Wescott's conclusions supporting the legitimacy of the briefing document on the basis of Hillenkoetter's writing.

- His omission of the facts and research supporting the legitimacy of the Cutler-Twining memo, including Phil Klass's challenge to me about the typeface and the results of that challenge.

- His touting of unsubstantiated anti-Majestic comments by Air Force Colonel Richard Weaver, the man who authored the Air Force's preemptive strike against the General Accounting Office's attempt to locate Roswell-related documents.

- His nitpicking about certain mistakes in base names in the briefing document and assurances that such an important document wouldn't have had mistakes. All the air base names had been changed after the Air Force became an independent body in 1947. Neither Eisenhower nor Smith nor Hillenkoetter had been in the Air Force. What was important was the event. The briefing was not a public proclamation for a worldwide audience. It is marked "Eyes Only," so nobody but Eisenhower and the briefing officer would see it. Eisenhower was facing an entirely new career with a myriad of new duties, and had been in the United States only a few months in the preceding two years. He also had to plan a secret trip to Korea to end the war. He would be worried about proper base names?

Throughout *Conclusions*, Randle claims that information in the briefing document is wrong, basing his evaluation on the unsubstantiated claims of a new date and crash scenario at Roswell that he included in *Truth About the UFO Crash at Roswell*. According to Randle, the alien bodies were recovered soon after the crash on July 5 at a specific site 34 miles north of Roswell—far from the Foster ranch. However, as noted by Karl Pflock in his detailed and very extensive 1994 report *Roswell in Perspective* (available from the Fund for UFO Research), many of these claims as to a new scenario are without foundation.

I can personally testify to some of the misrepresentation. Randle claims that the testimony of Sergeant Pyles, a supposed firsthand witness to the crash, establishes a date, time, and location for the crash, as does a note in an event log of a Roswell Convent of a bright fireball between 11 and 11:30 P.M. on July 4. No texts are provided.

I spoke with Pyles (as did Pflock independently), who was very cooperative. Pyles stated to me that he couldn't pin down the date of his nighttime fireball observation much better than the first half of July 1947, he couldn't recall the direction it was traveling, and he certainly did not see a crash. There were no characteristics that would lead one to believe it was a vehicle and certainly none that back up a particular time, date, and location for a saucer crash. Apparently nothing in the convent entry would lead one to a vehicle crash location, either. But a time and date were noted which Randle focused on for his new scenario.

Randle ignores Mac Brazel's testimony, as noted in many contemporaneous newspapers, that there was a long delay between his discovery of the debris and his trip to Roswell to see Sheriff Wilcox on July 6. He also ignores the statement by mortician Glenn Dennis's nurse that the bodies smelled to high heaven and that the mortuary officer had noted that they had been out in the desert. Barbara Dugger, Sheriff Wilcox's granddaughter, told me she vaguely remembered hearing the crash site was "north of Roswell." That she had the impression it wasn't that far away is not proof of anything. There are very few main roads in and out of Roswell. "North of Roswell" covers a great deal of ground in New Mexico.

Much of Randle's new scenario depends on the word of a strange character named Frank J. Kaufmann, who is also listed as McKenzie and who Randle identified at another Chicago conference as Joseph Osborne. Kauffman/McKenzie/Osborne knew everything about everything. According to Randle, he claimed he had been assigned to watch a radar scope at White Sands for 24 straight hours, reporting directly to General Scanlon of the Air Defense Command. He was so clever he rigged up mirrors so he could watch from the latrine!

Randle provided no evidence that Kaufmann was knowledgeable

about radar, or even that he was in the military at that time. There were no Air Defense Command radars in New Mexico in 1947. General Scanlon was in the Air Defense Command, but he retired in February 1948, with his last job being Public Affairs Director at Mitchell Field on Long Island, New York, hardly a location from which to be in charge of radars seeking and monitoring flights of flying saucers in New Mexico. Finally, on June 30, 1995, Randle admitted to me that the absurd 24-hour duty came out of his imagination. Kaufmann had nothing to do with radar.

Randle also provided no backup or substantiation for the supposed eyewitness testimony as to how many alien bodies were recovered or the shape of the crashed craft. Kaufmann, who did appear on the television show *48 Hours*—probably wisely with his face blocked out—and on a Roswell special on British TV, would not even sign a notarized statement as to the truth of his claims. When I finally met with Kaufmann on July 3, 1995, thanks to the efforts of Don Schmitt, Kaufmann wouldn't allow me to record the conversation though both Schmitt and Randle were present.

During the conversation, he stated that he was in the military from 1941 to 1945. He claimed that after that he was in the "paramilitary," but gave no qualification of that term. He also told a very weird tale of being at White Sands when there was supposedly a huge flareup on the radar screen, indicating that a major explosion of some kind had occurred north of Roswell. He notified the Roswell base, and someone was sent north of town and saw a glowing something to the west. That person notified the base. Kaufmann rushed back the more than 100 miles, woke Colonel Blanchard and Major Marcel in the middle of the night, and then went with them cross-country to the crash site. There they found the alien bodies and crashed saucer. I asked why they wouldn't have waited until morning and a report from reconnaissance craft so they would have some idea what was out there. Kaufmann told me that there were no small planes on the base.

This story from Randle's major new source is simply not believable. First, radar experts tell me the only way to flood a screen with glare is for something to explode very close to the antenna. The supposed site was more than 100 miles away. (Balloon expert Dr. C. B. Moore also notes that the range of the radar was no more than 39 miles.) Second, the Roswell base did have small aircraft that could be used for reconnaissance. Third, the commander of an atomic bomb delivery outfit and his intelligence officer driving cross-country at night through terrain with gullies and arroyos and fences and rattlesnakes without foreknowledge of what might be there? Colonel Blanchard would have been derelict in his responsibility.

And if Marcel had already been to the crash site and had seen the crashed saucer and alien bodies, it doesn't sound reasonable that he would be sitting quietly eating lunch at the Officers Club the next day when he took the call from Sheriff Wilcox about strange wreckage brought in by rancher Brazel. If Marcel and Blanchard had been out to the crash site, it is more likely that they would already have been organizing a major recovery effort. Kaufman's entire story is at odds with Major Marcel's own recollection.

And so it goes for other "testimony" that Randle relies on. James Ragsdale was supposedly out in the boondocks at the Randle-Kaufmann site with his girlfriend when the crash occurred. However, Ragsdale insisted to me and others in Roswell that he was with his lady at a lovely wooded glade 53 miles west northwest of Roswell, rather than in the desolate treeless area 34 miles north of Roswell, where Randle places the crash and where no Lothario would take a girlfriend. And the testimony of Frankie Rowe, whose father was a fireman who supposedly went to the Randle crash site and who herself supposedly played with a piece of wreckage at the firehouse, also has no substantiation. According to a former Roswell city councilman, the Roswell fire department, which employed Rowe's father, didn't make treks 30 miles out of town.

Although Philip Klass has worked hard at trying to debunk UFOs for several decades and Kevin Randle has been trying to debunk the MJ-12 documents for several years, the most popular debunker, in terms of worldwide coverage, has been Carl Sagan. As one of the

world's best-known scientists, Carl has probably done more to pop-
ularize science in general and the Search for Extra-Terrestrial
Intelligence (SETI) than anyone. His *Cosmos* TV series has been
shown in many countries. The book *Cosmos* was a major bestseller,
and he has published a number of other bestselling books which
often discuss life in the universe. His occasional articles in *Parade*
magazine are read by upwards of 80 million people. He has appeared
on a wide range of TV shows, and has pontificated about UFOs on
shows as various as the *Tonight Show, 48 Hours, Nova,* a Larry King
special on UFOs in 1994, and many others.

Now, Carl and I were classmates at the University of Chicago
from 1953 to 1956, where we were both physics majors. In fact, we
are the same age, and we agree on many things, scientific or not. But
as far as UFOs go, he just hasn't been getting things right.

Some people have wondered why Sagan, who has pushed so hard
to search the reaches of space for intelligent life, would have a problem with the idea of alien visitations. Carl claims that there are very
likely more than a million civilizations in our galaxy, and that some
are emitting radio waves that radiotelescopes can detect if we look
hard enough. But he claims that since there is no evidence that any
UFOs are extraterrestrial spacecraft, no one from any of these advanced civilizations is coming here.

Sagan, and SETI supporters in general, never discuss the scientific evidence that some UFOs are extraterrestrial craft. In the many
articles and TV appearances where Carl has discussed UFOs, he has
consistently misrepresented or ignored the facts. For instance, in his
latest book, *The Demon Haunted World: Science as a Candle in the
Dark,* Carl takes on the MJ-12 documents. He states:

> . . . an envelope containing a canister of exposed but undeveloped film
> was thrust into the home mail slot of a film producer, Jaime Shandera,
> interested in UFOs and government coverup—remarkably just as he
> was about to go out and have lunch with the author of a book on al-
> leged events in Roswell, New Mexico. When developed it "proved to
> be" page after page of a classified eyes only executive order dated 24

September, 1947, in which president Harry S. Truman seemingly established a committee of twelve scientists and government officials .
. . tantalizing references to appendices about the nature of the aliens
. . . but the appendices were not included in the mysterious film.

Sagan writes that "The Air Force says the document is bogus," and
that "UFO expert Philip J. Klass and others find lexicographic and typographic inconsistencies that suggest that the whole thing is a hoax."

These statements contain obvious errors of fact: Truman's memo
to Forrestal was, of course, only one page of the Eisenhower briefing document. Sagan takes a belittling tone toward Jaime Shandera
and the MJ-12 documents: Klass is a "UFO expert," whereas
Shandera is merely a "film producer . . . interested in UFOs." Sagan
feels it is "remarkable" that the film was delivered just before Jaime
went to lunch with an unnamed author who wrote about "alleged"
events. He leaves out that the author was Bill Moore, whom Jaime
often met for lunch; and the book was *The Roswell Incident*, the
events in which were attested to by more than 100 eyewitnesses.

Throughout the book, Sagan stresses the need for objective skepticism and relevant evidence while decrying appeals to authority.
However, he accepts the Air Force's pronouncement without mentioning that they made it but never provided any backup. And he accepts Klass's pronouncements without mentioning the outcome of
the typographic challenge over the Cutler-Twining memo—which
certainly puts Klass's credentials as an expert in doubt.

Then Sagan equates MJ-12 with a fairy tale: "Where the
MJ-12 documents are most vulnerable and suspect is exactly on the
question of provenance—the evidence miraculously dropped on a
doorstep like something out of a fairy story, perhaps 'The Shoemaker
and the Elves.'"

As I have established, there was nothing miraculous about how
the evidence arrived. The film came in the regular mail, delivered by
the mail carrier upon his appointed rounds. Whether the documents
are valid or not, they must have been created by an insider, and Jaime
and Bill had been having conversations with insiders (including

Richard Doty of the OSI) for years before Jaime got the film.

Sagan says "A coverup to keep knowledge of extraterrestrial life or alien abductions almost wholly secret for 45 years, with hundreds if not thousands of government employees privy to it, is a remarkable notion." Why is it remarkable? The Manhattan Project involved more than 50,000 people. At least 10,000 people knew we had broken the German and Japanese codes during World War II. And thousands were involved in the secret development of the Stealth bomber.

In discussing the idea of a government coverup, he comments:

> Certainly government secrets are routinely kept, even secrets of substantial general interest. But the ostensible point of such secrecy is to protect the country and its citizens. Here though it's different. The alleged conspiracy of those with security clearances is to keep from the citizens knowledge of a continuing alien assault on the human species.

Any serious researcher recognizes that the major value of UFO wreckage and detailed scientific observations of flight characteristics is the technological advances they demonstrate. Thus, the government would feel that these must be kept secret lest the technology fall into the hands of the country's enemies, which would obviously endanger the country and its citizens.

Carl also gives an incomplete account of the NSA and their UFO documents: "So a more or less typical intercept released by NSA in response to an FOIA request will be a third of a page blacked out, a fragment of a line saying 'reported a UFO at low altitude,' followed by two thirds of a page blacked out. The NSA's position is that releasing the rest of the page would potentially compromise sources and methods."

The complete truth is that there are no "typical" intercepts released by NSA, at least in regard to UFOs. The NSA has *never* released any portion of any page of its 156 UFO documents, even to the federal judge who ordered them to search for the documents.

Another illustration of Carl's misrepresentations about UFOs is this statement in *The Demon Haunted World:* "There are reliably reported cases that are unexotic, and exotic cases that are unreliable. There are no cases—despite well over a million UFO reports since 1947—in which something so strange that it could only be an extraterrestrial spacecraft is reported so reliably that misapprehension, hoax, or hallucination can be reliably excluded."

That the truth is exactly the opposite is borne out by the Air Force's own Project Blue Book Special Report 14. This report, which evaluated 3,201 UFO sightings, categorized the sightings as "knowns," "unknowns," and "insufficient information." *Unknown* was defined as "Those reports of sightings wherein the description of the object and its maneuvers could not be fitted to the pattern of any known object or phenomenon." It also rated the quality of each sighting, from "excellent" to "poor." The number of unknowns— 689—represented 21.5 percent of all the sightings evaluated. And of the 308 sightings considered "excellent," more than 35 percent— 108—were deemed to be unknowns. The better the quality of the sighting, the more likely it is to be listed as "unknown." Clearly, there are many reliably reported "exotic" cases.

But why denigrate a scientist who has done so much to bring science to the masses? Surely Sagan deserves better treatment than Klass and Randle, who do not have Sagan's scientific credentials.

That is precisely the point. The public trusts Sagan; they believe what he says. About UFOs, however, what he says is far from the whole truth. But since he consistently avoids dealing with the substantial scientific evidence and doesn't even reference it in his works, the public is denied the truth.

A prime example of this is his treatment of the 1961 abduction case of Betty and Barney Hill. Their story was well depicted in John Fuller's 1966 book *The Interrupted Journey.* The Hills, a respected couple, were returning to their home in New Hampshire from Montreal when they saw a strange light in the sky. They remembered watching it through binoculars as it followed them, then zoomed ahead of their car and hovered in the air approximately 200 yards ahead of them. They recalled Barney getting out of the car to get a better look, and Betty screaming at him to get back in the car. They remembered driving away from the scene and going home.

Curious about the experience and wanting to find an explanation, a few days later, Betty obtained a book about UFOs by NICAP director Donald Keyhoe. At the back NICAP's address was given as a place to send a report. She wrote a letter to NICAP about their experience, and a month later was interviewed by a NICAP investigator. When he went over the case systematically, it became obvious that they had gotten home two hours later than they should have. The investigator suggested that they be hypnotized to find out what happened in those two hours. Betty, who was a social worker, checked with a psychologist colleague who told her not to worry; their memories would probably return if they waited a while.

So they waited. Over the next two years, both had unexplained physical and psychological complaints. Barney developed ulcers that resisted medical treatment. Betty had recurring dreams of being captured by strange beings. His doctor suggested that they see Dr. Benjamin Simon, a psychotherapist, who used medical hypnosis in weekly sessions for several months to help the Hills independently recreate their missing two hours on board the flying saucer.

Carl met once with the Hills, and once with Dr. Simon. He discussed the Hills in *Cosmos* (both the book and the TV series), in a *Parade* article in March 1993, and in *The Demon Haunted World.* In the latter, he states that "Betty spotted a bright initially starlike UFO that seemed to follow them," and "Because Barney feared it might harm them, they left the main highway for narrow mountain roads, arriving home two hours later than they'd expected." (There is no basis for this claim about the mountain roads.) And finally, "The experience prompted Betty to read a book that described spaceships from other worlds; their occupants were little men who sometimes abducted humans."

Carl didn't mention that the craft had followed the Hills, had swooped ahead of their car, and then had hovered in front of them. He didn't mention that Barney got out of the car and walked toward the craft, nor that both Hills observed through binoculars what they described as an object the size of an airliner. And he didn't mention that in 1961, there were no books that described aliens who abducted humans. (In fact, Sagan himself calls the Hill case "the first alien abduction story in the modern genre.")

It is a shame, since in *The Demon Haunted World,* Sagan enjoins scientists and educators to "Encourage substantive debate on the evidence by knowledgeable proponents of all points of view." However, when the subject is UFOs, Carl almost never appears in venues where a knowledgeable critic can confront him. For instance, for Larry King's October 1, 1994 UFO special, Kevin Randle and I appeared live; Sagan appeared only in taped segments. Since Carl once again made false claims about lack of evidence for extraterrestrial spacecraft, about a month later I sent him a letter formally challenging him to a debate about UFOs. Correspondence went back and forth; Carl never said no, but he never said yes. (He then became seriously ill, and I dropped the matter.) It appears to me that he has no desire to take on scientists who are knowledgeable about UFOs.

Many people have asked me why Carl has been so stridently, unscientifically negative about UFOs. Despite all his references to obscure texts about demons, he doesn't refer to the many excellent UFO papers presented by scientists in various forums—including the July 29, 1968 Congressional hearings and the 1969 session of the American Association for the Advancement of Science, to both of which Carl contributed papers. (He even edited the proceedings of the latter.) Although Carl is an astronomer, he doesn't reference the work of J. Allen Hynek, the astronomer who for 20 years was the scientific consultant for Project Blue Book.

Others have suggested that he is fulfilling the role that Donald Menzel seems to have originated—sort of a government rent-a-skeptic. This explanation doesn't sit well with me: Sagan has far more often been at odds with the government—about nuclear testing, for example—than Menzel ever was. In addition, Menzel was in the military for many years, and Sagan was never in the service.

For decades, Carl has been one of the major champions of SETI as the way to investigate alien life. If aliens are visiting earth, abducting earthlings, and occasionally crashing their vehicles, what is the point of spending billions of dollars on a massive array of radiotelescopes trying to detect faint radio waves from advanced civilizations within the galaxy? Has Carl been putting his credibility on the wrong horse all these years?

Enough. The more debunkers say about UFOs and MJ-12, the more holes appear in their arguments. As more details come out, as more eyewitnesses surface, as more corroboration for the existence of alien craft on earth is produced, the debunkers' version of events is stretched thinner and thinner. You have to wonder how much longer this can go on without the fabric shredding altogether.

In the meantime, for new members of the audience, here is my "top ten" list of debunker principles of logic, gleaned from many years of contact with them:

1. What the public doesn't know, don't tell them.
2. Don't bother me with all the facts.
3. Absence of evidence is evidence of absence.
4. Select the data that matches your conclusions.
5. If at first a scenario supporting your theory crumbles under the weight of the facts, try, try again to prop up your theory with another scenario, then another, then another.
6. Hearsay testimony is acceptable if it supports you, but unacceptable if it supports the other guy.
7. It is important to be right.
8. Loudly proclaim the strength of your testimony.
9. Pepper your publications with references to as many personal (i.e., unverifiable) interviews as possible.
10. Don't mention references that don't support your theory. The public won't know the difference.

NEW MJ-12 DOCUMENTS

In late 1992, out of the blue, three new Majestic-12 documents were received by Tim Cooper, a California researcher.

Tim had become interested in Roswell and MJ-12, and tried to learn as much as he could about crashed saucers in New Mexico. He had been talking to a number of retired military personnel who were living near him and who had been heavily involved in highly classified matters back in the 1940s. His own father, while running the printing department at Alamogordo Army Air Field, had apparently been asked to print a long, highly classified document dealing with at least one crashed saucer and alien bodies. His father always refused to give many details. We had a number of telephone conversations, and Tim eventually passed on copies of the documents he had received.

The appearance of the documents was exciting because they were the first Majestic-related documents to surface since the Cutler-Twining memo in 1985. If they were genuine, they would buttress the validity of the original Operation Majestic-12 documents—among other details, they cross-referenced Special Classified Executive Order 092447 and had similar security markings. In some ways, however, they were too perfect. Once again, we would have to do much quiet and careful research before going public with the documents. It was a good thing we did.

The first document was extremely poorly reproduced, and Tim was initially reluctant to pass it on for fear he would be accused of forging it. Several members of the Fund for UFO Research, including myself, Rob and Susan Swiatek, Fred Whiting, Don Berliner, and Bruce Maccabee combined to salvage the message. It was supposedly from Roscoe Hillenkoetter, and was headed only *MEMO-RANDUM FOR THE PRESIDENT.* Centered at the top and bottom were the security markings *TOP SECRET/MAJIC EYES ONLY.* In the upper right corner were the date, *February 1948,* and what appears to be a reference number, *092447.* The memo read as follows (material in brackets are our best approximations):

Subject: "Majic"

I have heard that you seldom see the Army summaries of "Majic" material. For some time, the last two months in particular, I have had our intelligence lia[ison] organization concentrating on a [possi]ble presentation on "Majic" for my use as well as for the other officials concerned, particularly yourself. A highly specialized organization is [now engaged in the very] neccessary [sic] process of seperating [sic] the wheat [from the chaff and] correlating the items with past information in order that I may be able to quickly and intelligently evaluate the [importance] of the product.

Recently I have had these summaries [bound in a] Black Book both for convenience of [reading] and for greater [security] in handling. Sometimes two or three of these booklets are [gotten] out in a single day. I think they contain all of the worthwhile information culled from the tremendous mass of material now available and that are accumulated each twenty-four hours. The recent discovery of the machines has added a tremendous [amount] of such material and will continue to give us a great deal from day to day. The problem is how to avoid being [buried under] the mass of information, and I think the present arrangements satisfactorily meets that difficulty.

I am attaching two of the [current] booklets which I hope you will glance through in order to familiarize yourself with the manner in which the information is presented. I will send these booklets each week to you direct at the White House.

/S/

R. H. Hillenkoetter

Rear Admiral, USN

Director of Central Intelligence

In the lower left corner was a list of organizations to receive carbon copies, including NSC, JCS, USAFOSI, SAG/USAF, ONI, and G2 USA. In the lower right corner, under Hillenkoetter's closing, was a stamped *APPROVED* followed by a handwritten *Harry* and the handwritten initials *V.B.*

The Director of Central Intelligence sending the President possibly 10 or 15 books of "Majic" information a week? You would think that we would run right out and start tracking leads. Not so. We started by posing some questions to ourselves. If a group were running tests on a crashed flying saucer, the results would be pretty technical stuff. Why would the President be interested in such material? Wouldn't he be more concerned with the global implications of the results? The books were supposedly to be sent to the President direct. Why? What would he do with them after he looked at them? And how could the President have the time to read even the summaries?

Yet, there *were* the appropriate security markings, and the *092447* that matched the date on the Truman-Forrestal memo. At least initially, this document had to go in the gray basket—neither positively authentic nor definitely fraudulent.

Several weeks later, Tim sent me two more documents. One was a TOP SECRET/MAJIC Eyes Only memo to President Truman from General George Marshall, dated September 25, 1947:

Ref: 'MAJIC'	Cryptographic security does not apply
EO 092447	Handle as TOP SECRET correspondence per
MJ-12 Rpt	Par 44-G and 53-A AR 380-5
19 SEP '47	

Dr. Lloyd Berkner

Dr. Detlev Bronk

Dr. Vannevar Bush

James Forrestal

Dr. Gordon Gray

Adm. Roscoe Hillenkoetter

Dr. Jerome Hunsaker

Dr. Donald Menzel

Gen. Robert Montague

Gen. Walter Smith

Adm. Sidney Souers

Gen. Nathan Twining

Gen. Hoyt Vandenberg   Robert Cutler

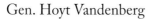

(L-R) Stanton Friedman, William Moore, and Jaime Shandera
at June 1987 UFO conference in Burbank, California.

Gen. Roger Ramey (R),
commander of the 8th Air Force
in 1947, shown with
Gen. Curtis LeMay during
World War II.

Col. William Blanchard,
commander of the 509th
Composite Bomb Wing
and Roswell Army Air Field
in 1947.

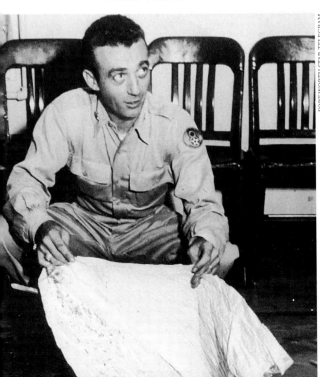

Maj. Jesse Marcel, Sr.
shown with phony
wreckage which Air
Force claimed was from
Roswell crash site.

U.S. AIR FORCE

Walter Haut, Roswell
Army Air Field
public information
officer in 1947.

U.S. AIR FORCE

Dr. Jesse Marcel, Jr.

Stanton Friedman (R) with Phillip Klass (L) at a debate in the late 1970s at Trinity University in San Antonio, Texas.

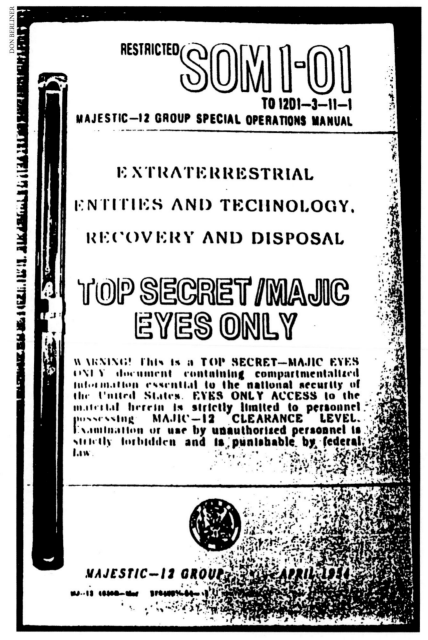

RESTRICTED

SOM 1-01

TO 12D1–3–11–1

MAJESTIC–12 GROUP SPECIAL OPERATIONS MANUAL

EXTRATERRESTRIAL

ENTITIES AND TECHNOLOGY,

RECOVERY AND DISPOSAL

TOP SECRET/MAJIC
EYES ONLY

WARNING! This is a TOP SECRET—MAJIC EYES ONLY document containing compartmentalized information essential to the national security of the United States. EYES ONLY ACCESS to the material herein is strictly limited to personnel possessing MAJIC—12 CLEARANCE LEVEL. Examination or use by unauthorized personnel is strictly forbidden and is punishable by federal law.

MAJESTIC—12 GROUP   APRIL 1954

Cover page of the first copy of the Majestic-12 Group Special Operations Manual—a photocopy of a photocopy that Don Berliner made from the prints he developed from film he received.

The memo itself read as follows:

MEMORANDUM FOR THE PRESIDENT

The following letter from Secretary Marshall to the President was dictated to me this morning over the secret telephone:

"Dear Mr. President:

"I understand General Twining is presenting his report to you at noontime today. It seems to me mandatory that we treat Twining's report top secret and that no indication to its contents be divulged to the public. This will allow us time to review our policy in the light of the report.

"If you agree, I suggest Twining be informed by you accordingly.

"If questioned, you might state a cover summary of the report be issued until careful consideration has been given it by the various chiefs of staff and department heads of the Government concerned.

Faithfully yours,

G.C. MARSHALL

The memo had a second closing and a signature, of a "C. H. Humelsine, Executive Secretary," of whom I was not familiar. The initials were run together with the last name—*CHHumelsine.*At the bottom was a handwritten "I agree" and the initials *HST.* The other document was a Top Secret Eyes Only directive to General Twining. This memo had no typed-in date, but at the bottom was a scrawled "Approved Harry Truman July 9, 1947." The memo read:

DIRECTIVE TO LIEUTENANT GENERAL TWINING

You will proceed to the White Sands Proving Ground Command Center without delay for the purpose of making an appraisal of the reported unidentified objects being kept there. Part of your mission there will deal with the military, political and psychological situations—current and projected. In the course of your survey you will maintain liaison with the military officials in the area.

In making your appraisal it is desired that you proceed with de-

tachment from any opinions of feelings expresed by personnel involved which do not conform to sound reasoning with regard to the
possible outcome. In presenting the findings of your mission you
should endeavor to state as concisely as possible your estimate of the
character, extent, and probable consequences in the event that assistance is not given.

When your mission in New Mexico is completed you will proceed on a brief trip to the Sandia AEC facility to make an appraisal of
the situation there, also of the reaction by the Los Alamos people involved. Before going to White Sands you will communicate with
General Eisenhower to ascertain whether he desires you to proceed
via Kirtland AAF.

You will take with you such experts, technicians, scientists and assistants as you deem necessary to the effectiveness of your mission.

These two documents we could do some checking on. I made
preliminary phone calls to researcher Dennis Bilger, a long-time contact at the Truman Library, and to the Marshall Foundation, with
which I had had contact earlier about the date format in correspondence between General Walter Smith and General Marshall. I was
informed that Truman, if confronted with something as significant as
the recovery of crashed flying saucers in New Mexico, would have
very likely consulted Marshall, then Secretary of State.

According to many sources, Truman considered Marshall the
outstanding living American. Marshall certainly knew all the top
military people, since he had been Army chief of staff during World
War II. Though he turned 65 on December 31, 1945, the work that
he is justifiably most famous for—the Marshall Plan and the rebuilding of Europe—was still ahead of him. He was Truman's
Secretary of State from January 1947 to January 1949, and then
Secretary of Defense from September 1950 to September 1951.

Bilger made two encouraging remarks. He told me that C. H.
Humelsine had worked for Marshall at the State Department, and
that the Truman Library had various documents with the handwritten "Approved Harry Truman" or similar notation at the bottom.

However, he also noted that no meeting was listed between Truman and Twining for September 25 or 26, 1947.

As it turned out, this last was not a negative. I knew (and Bilger later reconfirmed) that Truman often had meetings that were not listed on his official calendar. Although I couldn't get confirmation from Truman's calendar, I did have the flight log for General Twining, which had been declassified for me at the Library of Congress Manuscript Division when I was checking on the dates of the attachments in the original MJ-12 documents. I also had the copy of his pilot's flight log. In the pilot's log, there was a roundtrip from Dayton (home of Wright Field) to Washington on September 18 and 19, 1947, which corresponds to the listing "Preliminary Analytical Report" (Attachment D) noted in the Eisenhower briefing document. But there was no flight listed to Washington for September 25, and the pilot was definitely off somewhere else. However, when I checked Twining's own log, I discovered that he himself had flown a complete roundtrip from Dayton to Washington on September 26.

So Twining did go to Washington, but on September 26. That was a very busy time at the White House—the first meeting of the National Security Council was held on that very day, involving Truman, Forrestal, Souers, and Hillenkoetter, among others. When Marshall dictated his note to Humelsine, he might have been operating under preliminary information that the meeting would be on September 25. Or perhaps Humelsine made a mistake. (I have a copy of a memo from Secretary Forrestal about his meeting with Truman and Vannevar Bush on September 24, 1947 in which Forrestal refers to the date as September 25.)

There were other positive signs. From the Marshall Library, I learned that C. H. Humelsine was Carlisle Hubbard Humelsine (1915-1989). He was not a typewriting, dictation-taking secretary, but an executive in the State Department who had worked for Marshall during the war. He later served for many years as president of the Colonial Williamsburg Foundation, and was chairman of the board of the National Trust for Historic Preservation.

As for the directive to General Twining, I had long since noted that Twining had flown from Dayton to Alamogordo on July 7, 1947. He had spent a full work week in New Mexico, visiting White Sands, Sandia, and Kirtland and supposedly making a "routine" inspection of Alamogordo Army Air Field. This was actually no routine inspection, since there was no advance planning for it, no PR pictures were taken, and the team was too high-powered for a regular inspection. In addition, the Air Materiel Command group at Alamogordo actually staged a launch of a weather balloon with a radar reflector on July 9 for the press so that they could claim loudly that this was the explanation of the flying saucer reports . . . which made little sense except as disinformation. And although the handwritten date of July 9 on the Twining directive seems to be contradictory, I have often seen documents with different dates on them for preparation, receipt, approval, and so on. In addition, I had located a letter indicating that Twining had canceled a long-planned trip to Boeing in Seattle "because of a very important and sudden matter that developed here."

In the back of my mind, though, was the nagging suspicion that the documents, or at least some of them, might be too good to be true. The original MJ-12 documents had long ago been publicized, and so the dates, people involved, and security markings on the documents were well known. It just seemed like too many elements were matching up. Two of the new documents, for example, make reference to *092447* and *MAJIC*. The memo from Hillenkoetter clearly puts him in charge, which would jibe with the reference to him as *MJ-1* in the briefing document. The security markings on the directive to Twining—written before the Truman-Forrestal memo establishing Majestic 12—is TOP SECRET/Eyes Only, whereas the later Hillenkoetter and Marshall memos are both TOP SECRET/MAJIC Eyes Only. The directive to Twining instructs him as to what to do at places we know he visited. The initials VB certainly suggest high involvement of Vannevar Bush, which was already strongly indicated. None other than Twining's pilot had already noted to Don Berliner and I that he saw Twining and Bush together often.

There were seeming contradictions that would have to be resolved as well:

- Why did Marshall use the secret telephone to dictate his note to Truman instead of just calling in a secretary?
- If Twining made a presentation on September 19 to the MJ-12 group and/or the president, why would he then fly a round trip by himself just a week later to make another presentation to the president?
- Why did the Marshall memo refer to AR (Army Regulation) 380-5? Was this just window dressing? Did Paragraphs 44-G and 53-A mean anything in 1947? AR 380-5 is mentioned in Air Intelligence Report 100-203-79, *Analysis of Flying Object Incidents in the U.S.*, dated December 10, 1948. This report is one of very few formerly Top Secret UFO documents which have been released. It is well known amongst serious UFO researchers, such as the members of CAUS, some of whom have been attacking the MJ-12 documents for years. Since the report doesn't discuss extraterrestrial spacecraft but focuses on foreign technology, some debunkers claim that it somehow proves that no UFOs are alien spacecraft. Could this be a sting operation by the anti-UFO crowd to get us to tout the document and then show they had faked it?
- RH has a rubber stamped *APPROVED* below which is handwritten *Harry* and *VB*. Did President Truman ever sign anything *Harry*?

With expense money provided by the Fund for UFO Research, I went to Washington and then on to the Marshall Archives in Lexington, Virginia in order to puzzle out as many details as possible by finding false clues, "facts" inconsistent with reality, and details not before known to anybody on the outside.

The Marshall Foundation had sent me a 164-page Guide to the George C. Marshall Papers, and they informed me that Marshall biographer Dr. Forrest Pogue was probably still alive and living in the Arlington, Virginia area near Washington. They also mentioned that a Sergeant Heffner, who had been Marshall's aide for eleven years, also lived in Virginia and that some of Marshall's office secretaries were still alive. I arranged to visit Dr. Pogue, and spoke on the phone with Heffner and two secretaries.

I determined that not only did the Foundation have the more than 255 archive boxes and other materials listed in the guide I received before the visit, but, of very much more utility, an unlisted collection of almost 1 million pages of Marshall-era files from the State Department, Defense Department, and other agencies which had been reviewed and declassified at the National Archives by Dr. Pogue and others. Thankfully, summaries of each document in this batch of papers, cross-referenced by name, were kept on 5" x 8" file cards contained in filing cabinets. There was a three-inch stack of cards under *Forrestal*, for example. None of the other fourteen archives I have visited have anything approaching this cross-reference file.

The documents themselves are kept in filing cabinets full of five-sided (open top) manila file holders. Since there are no longer any classified materials at the center, I was permitted to go right into the vault and dig out the documents I had noted on the file cards. The documents were ordered with a fairly elaborate numerical scheme.

As I was familiarizing myself with the numerical scheme, I realized that the system included dates as part of the key numbers. For instance, document 710.J/3-2548 was an item dated March 25, 1948; document 710.J/4-648 was dated April 6, 1948. The September 24, 1947 Truman-Forrestal memo is referred to in the 1952 briefing and in the newer documents as Special Classified Executive Order 092447. Thus, at least one major branch of the U.S. government uses a similar date format for referral or filing purposes.

Although the Marshall Archive was a joy to use, getting the full cooperation and assistance of the Marshall Foundation was not so easy. I had to convince Foundation historian Dr. Larry Bland, who was at first very skeptical, that there was indeed a cosmic Watergate. What seemed to have the most impact was the story of the legal battle over the CIA and NSA UFO documents. When I showed him the mostly blacked-out NSA affidavit about their documents and the blacked-out CIA documents, he was won over.

After Bland looked at those documents and my MJ-12 report, he was very helpful. He remarked that he, an historian, would not have been able to fake the MJ-12 documents because of the many details included. He could find the correct stationery and an appropriate typewriter, but there would have been virtually no way for him to discover all of the inside information required to fake the documents.

As a result of these fortuitous events, my trip to Virginia was remarkably productive, and I was able to go far in judging the authenticity of the new MJ-12 documents.

Dr. Pogue, though 80 years old and slowly losing his eyesight, was very vigorous of mind and memory and most cordial. He could find no reason to dismiss either the Marshall-Truman memo or the directive to Twining. Before I even showed him the documents, he assured me that Truman often signed his initials vigorously at the bottom of memos, and that he remembered Truman signing off on various documents. He knew a lot about Humelsine, including his work for Marshall during the war and his later work at the Colonial Williamsburg Foundation. He confirmed that Humelsine was much more than a paper-pushing clerk.

Pogue had received a Ph.D. in history before enlisting during World War II, and was actually at the Normandy landing on D-Day +2. Earlier, he had been a code clerk with a high-level Crypto clearance, giving him access to coded and decoded Top Secret messages. He had been asked to work on the official histories of a number of Army groups. After the war he spent a year in Europe as a civilian interviewing many military leaders as well as lower-level people. (General Marshall had refused to write his memoirs, but did respond to questions asked by Pogue in many interviews.) He had letters of introduction from Eisenhower and Marshall. His ability to evaluate the validity of Top Secret documents was vastly superior to that of a number of armchair historians, who have trouble believing that secrets can be kept for decades. However, Pogue, who had been in the military and had had a very-high-security clearance, had no problem at all with the notion of major secrets being kept.

Dr. Pogue took a lively interest in my MJ-12 report and my methodology. He agreed that formats in highly classified, pre-FOIA documents did not follow any style guide. He volunteered that General Marshall was a stickler about editing subordinates' memos, making every effort to keep the wording simple and clear. He could write like a bureaucrat, but didn't like to. Of course, much of what Marshall signed off on had been prepared by others, so style is not a final arbiter on legitimacy.

That Pogue could find nothing obviously fraudulent with the documents did not prove they were valid. However, it was comforting that such a well-informed expert on General Marshall felt that they could be authentic.

At the Marshall Library, I learned a number of other facts that helped me evaluate the new documents:

When going through the 5" x 8" filing cards, I found occasional notations such as "signed Approved, Harry Truman [date]." I dug out a number of these documents and copied them and also received some examples from the Truman Library. (At one time, the Truman's director, Dr. Zobrist, wrote to me that although he had stated they had such examples, none had been found.) These approvals vary in format both for the order, the wording, and the date format. Truman did sign off on various documents using wording like that on the ones Tim had sent me.

In early September 1947, Truman went to Brazil for a major international conference. He and his family returned home on a Navy ship, and they were not yet back at the White House on September 19, 1947. File copies of communiques between Rio de Janiero and Washington establish this, and Margaret Truman also talks about the trip in one of her books about her father. Thus, Truman could not have attended General Twining's briefing on September 19 noted in the original MJ-12 document, and Twining would have had to return to Washington later to brief him.

Marshall was in attendance as head of the U.S. delegation to the United Nations in New York City starting September 21, 1947 and lasting for several days. He was not in Washington on September 25.

Thus, the use of the secret telephone to dictate the memo to Humelsine makes sense. Scramblers were already in wide use; for instance, Roosevelt and Churchill had used them often for their phone conversations during the war.

Humelsine worked for Chief of Staff Marshall at the Pentagon from 1941 to 1945. According to one article about Humelsine, his first major assignment from Marshall was to reorganize the handling of secret military communications between Marshall and military commands around the world. Soon he was in charge of this communications effort. Marshall had a reputation for not tolerating incompetence. Humelsine would certainly have been familiar with Army Regulation 380-5, which deals at great length with protection of classified documents.

(Don Berliner, with the help of Larry Bryant at the Pentagon Library, found a 1946 version of AR 380-5 containing the relevant paragraphs 44-G and 53-A. In a much later version which I found in the government documents section of the University of New Brunswick Library, the regulation was different, having only fourteen sections. Military installations normally destroy old versions of regulations when they receive new versions. Thus, if someone was trying to forge the letter from Marshall, not only would he need to know Marshall's whereabouts on that day, but he would have to be familiar with Army regulations *in 1947.*)

In both Humelsine's *Who's Who* entry and in his handwritten background file at the Marshall Foundation, the term *Executive Secretary* is used. Nowhere else was this title used in reference to Humelsine. His official titles were Deputy Under Secretary of State and Assistant Secretary of State. What forger would have known about Humelsine's little-used title?

While Humelsine achieved a considerable reputation for his work at Williamsburg, being on the boards of many projects, and being awarded four honorary degrees, his name is certainly not well known these days for his work at the State Department or with Marshall. (He actually assisted Marshall at the Malta, Yalta, and Potsdam conferences that helped shape the postwar world.) One

wonders how many modern-day ufologists or even government people would have recognized his name. Indeed, one of Marshall's secretaries from his Department of Defense days didn't recognize
Humelsine's name.

The Marshall Foundation had a folder of information on
Humelsine which made it possible for me to locate his two daughters
and his widow. I called Mrs. Humelsine and then sent her a copy of
the Marshall memo so she could authenticate her husband's unusual
signature. The run-together initials didn't match any of the big signatures of his that I found in a quick look at his file, although all of
these occurred in important letters on fancy stationery when he was
head of Williamsburg. On the phone, Mrs. Humelsine, who was very
alert, remarked that her husband usually ran the CHH together in
his signature. Upon later contact, she and her daughter agreed that
the signature was indeed his.

Mrs. Humelsine also indicated that her husband had Marshall's
full trust, and that Carlisle had actually established a large group of
secretaries at the State Department at Marshall's request, since
Marshall liked how that form of organization worked for him during
the war. She also noted that on some occasions her husband acted
as a courier taking classified items to the White House for Marshall.

I knew that all classified documents accepted at the White
House or any other classified installation are receipted, and I had
seen some receipt lists at the Eisenhower Library. Perhaps the
Humelsine memo had been receipted and was listed at the Truman
Library. I checked with Dennis Bilger, but he was unable to find any
White House receipts for classified documents for 1947. He did
however forward Truman's phone logs for September 25 and 26,
1947, and there is an entry for Humelsine at 4:42 P.M. on September
26. Bilger also told me that the library did have various items, especially personal notes to old friends, which were signed simply *Harry.*

During this trip, I also got back in touch with George Elsey in
Washington, who was well known to Dr. Pogue, and sent him a copy
of the new documents seeking his comments. He had worked for
Roosevelt and then Truman in the White House, had a high-level

clearance, and had responded three years before to my questions as to whether he could find anything wrong with the original MJ-12 documents and the Cutler-Twining memo. He could find no problems.

I had learned to be very careful in how I posed questions to people like Elsey. If he had known about Majestic-12 as a program whose very existence was classified, he would not have been able to tell me anything useful in response to direct questions. I didn't ask him if he thought the documents were genuine; rather, I asked if he saw anything about the documents that would lead him to believe they were fraudulent. This was a question he could answer, having handled thousands of classified documents at the White House. His answer was no; there was nothing to make him think they were fraudulent.

Since Elsey knew almost all the listed MJ-12 members, I asked if there was any reason to think that Truman would not have appointed any of them to such an important group, if it had been real. Again the answer was no; there was no question in his mind that these were all people who Truman trusted. Since he knew James Lay and Robert Cutler, I asked if there was any reason to think that Lay would not have prepared a simple administrative memo for Cutler if Cutler was out of the country. Again Elsey said no, and noted that the two men worked very closely together. Finally, I asked about the possibility of Bush and/or Forrestal preparing a memo for Truman's signature. Elsey noted that perhaps 90 percent of what a president signs is prepared by someone else, and that Truman certainly trusted those two.

Because Mr. Elsey had been so forthright the first time around, I sent him the Humelsine and Twining memos and sought his opinion. On February 11, 1993, he wrote:

In response to the questions posed in your letter of 5 February:

(1) From the appearance of the photo-copies, I have no reason at all to doubt the authenticity of the directive to General Twining approved by President Truman and dated July 9, 1947 and the Memorandum for the President of September 25, 1947 from Carlisle Humelsine.

(2) As to who prepared the directive to Twining, the style of language convinces me that it was prepared in the War Department. It is definitely not phrased in terms that President Truman would have used nor would any of the White House staff employed such stilted military praseology. I have no way of surmising which office in the War Department might have been involved.

(3) As for my knowledge as to whether President Truman had off the record meetings, of course he did—as have Presidents before and after. They were customarily held right in the Oval Office—as secure a place as any in the country. Occasionally, for one reason or another, a meeting might be held in the family quarters of the mansion or some other room in the mansion—as, for example, the meeting referred to by Robert Cutler in the 7/13/53 memo you include in your document. There is no need for a President to leave the White House; secrecy was and is easy to maintain there and is impossible to maintain anyplace else. Moving a President involves complicated logistics with an unbelievable number of persons involved.

(4) You are quite right in assuming "somebody always knew where to reach the president . . . ." Scores of people know—Secret Service, his Press staff, his national security advisor, those involved in making the travel arrangements, etc etc. I was associated with the Truman White House in one capacity or another throughout the administration, as a relatively junior staff member, and there was never a day in the nearly eight years that I did not know where the President was and how to reach him should occasion arise.

Obviously, the letter doesn't prove the documents are genuine, but I know of no one better qualified than Elsey to appraise them as hoaxes.

I had planned a follow-up trip to the Truman and Eisenhower libraries seeking more documents that might have been added to their collections or been declassified when another bunch of documents arrived from Tim Cooper!

Several of these documents also looked too good to be true. One, which was a terrible reproduction, was ostensibly a long letter to Humelsine from General Marshall dated September 27, 1947. Typed on it were "TOP SECRET/Eyes Only" and "For Mr. Humelsine's eyes only." It began "My Dear Carl," and referred to "MAJIC military communications" being sent to Humelsine.

I sent the letter to Dr. Bland at the Marshall Foundation. He immediately recognized it as a retyped and slightly reworded version of a well-known letter from Marshall to Republican presidential candidate Thomas Dewey during the 1944 campaign. Dewey had been trying to make an issue out of the Pearl Harbor attack by raising questions as to how much the top command knew via document interception that might have prevented the surprise attack. Marshall on his own was trying to keep Dewey from saying too much in public that might lead the Japanese to worry about their codes having been compromised, and noted one incident that caused the Japanese to change their codes. It was a delicate time in the war—the Allies had recently landed at Normandy and were fighting their way through France. Since the Japanese ambassador to Germany was sending coded information about German plans back to Japan, the Allied command simply could not afford a slip that would make the Japanese change their codes.

With this unambiguous fraud as background, I became convinced that several other items were retyped and slightly changed versions of old memos or letters. For example, one document dealt with supposed travels to New Mexico of "Archbishop" Spellman in the summer of 1947, during which he would be protected by the military. By checking the *New York Times Index*, I determined that Spellman was clearly in New York during the summer, did not travel to New Mexico, and had already been named a Cardinal. During the war, however, he had traveled to the European theater, quietly and with military protection.

I also concluded that the March 1948 Hillenkoetter memo—the first document that Tim Cooper had sent to me—was really a doctored version of a memo that would have been sent to President Roosevelt during World War II. It just made no sense that President

Truman would want to see loads of notebooks containing technical data about flying saucers. However, it made perfect sense that President Roosevelt would want to see summaries of decoded Japanese military messages—which were done as part of a very classified project whose code name was *MAGIC*.

If the original Majestic-12 documents are genuine, as clearly appears to be the case, the person who risked so much in sending that roll of film in 1984 must have been feeling terribly frustrated. Nine years were gone, and there were no truly solid results from the revelation. The original documents were still being attacked, and the government agencies involved continued to stonewall. The source couldn't go public without revealing his identity and the fact that he probably broke several laws by distributing highly classified material to uncleared persons. The debunkers seemed to be holding the upper hand. Perhaps the documents that Tim Cooper received showed that the source was still alive, still trying to get the truth out.

A year later, a new breakthrough confirmed this hope.

THE MAJESTIC-12
OPERATIONS MANUAL

In December 1994, I learned of what is perhaps the mother of all Majestic-12 documents! I was on the phone with Don Berliner, who is a member of the board of the Fund for UFO Research, when Don let slip that he had received another MJ-12 document in March. Just as a decade before Jaime Shandera had received the original MJ-12 documents on a roll of film in the mail in a manila envelope with no return address, so did Don receive this new material.

The roll of 35mm film had been mailed from Wisconsin, but without a return address. At first, Don thought nothing of the matter, since he had recently come back from the huge Experimental Aircraft Show in Oshkosh, Wisconsin, where he had shot many rolls of film. He presumed that he had left a roll of film behind and someone from the show had sent it on to him.

Only when he had the film developed did he realize that he had black-and-white pictures of a document, not of aircraft. The first frame was the cover page of a report entitled *Majestic-12 Group Special Operations Manual: Extraterrestrial Entities and Technology, Recovery and Disposal.* It was marked TOP SECRET/MAJIC Eyes Only, and was dated April 1954. The report outlined how to secure, package, ship, and store artifacts and extraterrestrial biological entities from recovered alien flying saucers! The contents page indicated that the original manual contained six chapters, four appendixes, 30 pages of text, and a section of photographs. Unfortunately, not all of the pages of the manual had been photographed.

There were 22 images on the roll of film, each showing a hand holding a different page of a document apparently held together by an Accobinder. Don had a trustworthy associate print 5" x 7" prints of each frame. On the back of each page was a security warning:

WARNING! This is a TOP SECRET—MAJIC EYES ONLY document containing compartmentalized information essential to the national security of the United States. EYES ONLY ACCESS to the material herein is strictly limited to personnel possessing MAJIC-12 CLEARANCE LEVEL. Examination or use by unauthorized personnel is strictly forbidden and is punishable by federal law.

Removal of any page(s) from this document for examination by authorized persons requires written authorization from the MJ-12 OPNAC OPERATIONS OFFICER. Reproduction in any form or the taking of written or transcribed notes is strictly forbidden.

Don had made a few people aware of the document, including the General Accounting Office, which at that time was in the midst of trying to find government records about the Roswell event. The GAO apparently submitted a copy to the Air Force. However, neither the Air Force, in their official attack on Roswell in September 1994, nor the GAO, in its report of July 28, 1995, mentioned the manual.

If this manual proves to be genuine (research on it is ongoing), then it is truly dynamite. It corroborates information found in the Eisenhower briefing and certain other MJ-12 documents. For example, one section of the manual, titled "History of the Group," includes this statement referring to the Truman-Forrestal memo: "Operation Majestic-12 was established by special classified presidential order on 24 September 1947 at the recommendation of Secretary of Defense James V. Forrestal and Dr. Vannevar Bush, Chairman of the Joint Research and Development Board."

As information about this find has become public, a number of people have leaped to the conclusion that the document is fraudulent, seemingly just on the basis of a quick review of the poor-quality photocopies of the prints and their presumption that there was never any Majestic-12 group. But those of us who have dug into the subject have concluded that none of the objections yet raised are substantive. Some new, very-high-quality 8" x 10" prints clearly indicate that the photographer had done a much better job than had originally seemed to be the case, and we have been able to read just about every word in the manual.

There are a number of ways that the manual is being checked for validity. For instance, page 28 of the manual is a list of references. Don went to the Army archives at Carlyle Barracks, Pennsylvania and talked to some oldtimers, who found copies of some of the unclassified documents referenced in the manual. The particular editions listed were accurate and appropriate for pre-April 1954.

At my request, Don sent me a set of photocopies of photocopies of the prints done two to a page. I began focusing on the facts given in the manual that could be independently checked. For example, Paragraph 17 is a table listing facilities to which artifacts should be sent. Were these facilities in operation at the time? As to the rest of the manual, were there anachronisms with regard to other manuals? Were the instructions for packaging both wreckage and biological specimens reasonable?

A number of obvious questions came to my mind when I received the copies. For example, if the person who took the pictures had enough time to shoot more than 20 pages, why didn't he take apart the Accobinder, lay the pages flat, and get much better quality by using two hands to hold the camera? The Eisenhower briefing document had clearly been laid flat on a kind of jig using the punched holes so that focus would only have to be set once. The copies Don had sent me were very poor quality, and parts of many of the pages were obscured. Why wasn't the focus better? Was the focus deliberately poor? Who took the pictures? Where? When? Why?

And why was page 30 missing from the film? According to the

table of contents, this was the listing of MAJIC personnel. Did this mean that when the pictures were taken, some of the personnel were still alive? The Eisenhower briefing document film had been received about three months after the death of the last surviving member of the original MJ-12 group.

Another obvious concern was the mention of "downed satellites" on page 8 as one of several acceptable "Deceptive Statements" to distribute to help provide a cover. Considering that the first Sputnik wasn't launched until 1957, was this a goof by a forger? I dug out some pre-1954 books about space flight and checked back issues of the *Readers' Guide to Periodical Literature* for uses of the term *satellite*. I found several articles that used the term for a manufactured object in orbit around the earth prior to April 1954. There had also been an active program led by Clyde Tombaugh, who had discovered Pluto as a very young amateur astronomer in 1930, to search for artificial satellites near earth.

And the manual used the term *UFOB*, instead of *UFO*, for *unidentified flying object*. I checked some old government documents and found that in 1954, *UFOB* was used, even though it was out of favor within a short time.

With Don's permission, I shared a copy of what he sent with Dr. Robert Wood, who had recently retired after more than 40 years as a scientist and project manager for McDonnell Douglas in California. Bob had a high-level professional interest in UFOs and advanced technology dating back to the 1960s and had given lectures on UFOs to several organizations. He is one of a handful of professional people interested in UFOs whom I trust completely: excellent technical background, sound judgment, very knowledgeable about UFOs and high security. I hoped that Bob, because of past efforts on high-security programs, could check on the appropriateness of the security warning and other markings. We discussed the document at length.

Bob then did something truly special. Using his computer, he matched the typefaces in the manual and tried to read every portion of the available pages. Don had better 8" x 10" prints made from some of the negatives and used a magnifying glass to determine what some of the words were. With a lot of effort, Don and Bob were finally able to decipher just about every square inch of the pages.

In addition, Bob and a colleague, who also had long experience with highly classified reports, each found somebody knowledgeable about the Government Printing Office and made some sense out of the little numbers on the bottom of the pages. Everything they found was consistent with a typeset GPO document of that era. For instance, although Bob's digitally-typeset version of the manual is very professional-looking, there are subtle differences between it and the original typesetting, which was done mechanically. In other words, although someone could create this document on a computer, and even use the same typeface and typesize, there would be telltale signs that the pages were not mechanically set.

Why would a manual such as this even exist? From the wording of the manual, it is obvious that it would have been circulated more widely than the other MJ-12 documents that have been found, strongly implying that more crashes were occurring. As Don Berliner explained in a July 1989 paper he had given at a MUFON conference, the government would have to have a set of wreckage handling procedures. Without a standard operating procedure, there would be too much risk of information leaking out inadvertently, as occurred in 1947 directly after the Roswell crash. Attempts to duplicate alien technology and understand alien biology would require careful handling of wreckage and specimens and prompt action to prevent both publicity and recovery by others.

Various government agencies have had special retrieval teams whose activities and identification have been kept very low profile for decades. One recently published article in a scientific journal noted that there were seven different teams ready to take action in case of a nuclear accident, the loss of nuclear-weapons-related materials, and so on. Trucks and airplanes with nuclear weapons, spent fuel, and other classified cargoes crisscross the country regularly. Terrorists and spies seek such materials. Vehicles do crash. Highly classified, and

sometimes highly radioactive, portions of satellites sometimes survive reentry into the atmosphere and fall to earth. Both sides in the
cold war were desperate to recover these in secret.

Most of the members of rapid response teams have other jobs, but
are ready to go anywhere at a moment's notice. When portions of the
Soviet Cosmos 954 satellite came down in January 1978, sprinkling
many chunks of radioactive debris from its nuclear reactor across a
large area in northern Canada, response teams were in action quickly.

A highly classified Stealth aircraft, about whose existence the
public had not yet been apprised, crashed near Bakersfield,
California a number of years ago. Security teams were in place very
quickly, keeping people away from the crash site. They were followed
by collection, packaging, and clean-up teams. These groups made
sure that all the wreckage was recovered and that the ground was
treated so that no one would be able to recover a piece of the high-
technology skin of the vehicle. Civilians unfortunate enough to be
caught up in the security web were made to sign silence agreements
ending with the phrase "upon penalty of death" according to a witness who very quietly spoke to me about it after a lecture.

Following is some of the text of the manual, as determined by Dr.
Wood, Don Berliner, and others. Words that could not be made out
from the photographs, or that were illegible, are bracketed. Note that
Chapter 6 ends in midsentence; besides the list of references
(Appendix I), this was the last page of the manual that was received.

A detailed proposal to validate this document by investigating its
internal references, the appropriateness of the procedures enumer-
ated, the relationship to the other MJ-12 documents, and the occur-
rences of any possible anachronisms has been made by myself, Dr.
Wood, Dr. Bruce Maccabee, and another researcher, and it awaits
funding. Based upon past experience, authentication will be no easy
task, as the results must be solid enough to withstand the onslaught
of both debunkers and a government that denies the existence of
alien craft.

RESTRICTED

SOM1-01

TO 12D1—3—11—1

MAJESTIC—12 GROUP SPECIAL OPERATIONS MANUAL

EXTRATERRESTRIAL ENTITIES AND TECHNOLOGY, RECOVERY AND DISPOSAL

TOP SECRET/MAJIC EYES ONLY

WARNING! This is a TOP SECRET—MAJIC EYES ONLY document containing compartmentalized information essential to the national security of the United States. EYES ONLY ACCESS to the material herein is strictly limited to personnel possessing MAJIC—12 CLEARANCE LEVEL. Examination or use by unauthorized personnel is strictly forbidden and is punishable by federal law.

MAJESTIC—12 GROUP • APRIL 1954

MJ—12 4838BMAN   270435[1]-54-1

This unclassified copy is for research purposes. Rev 3; 2/28/95; Helvetica headers, Times text

TOP SECRET/MAJIC EYES ONLY

SOM—01

Special Operations Manual   MAJESTIC—12 GROUP
No. 1-01   Washington 25, D.C., *7 April 1954*

EXTRATERRESTRIAL ENTITIES AND TECHNOLOGY RECOVERY AND DISPOSAL

CHAPTER 1
OPERATION MAJESTIC—12

Section I. PROJECT PURPOSE AND GOALS

1.   Scope

This manual has been prepared especially for Majestic—12 units. Its purpose is to present all aspects of Majestic—12 so authorized personnel will have a better understanding of the goals of the Group, be able to more expertly deal with Unidentified Flying Objects, Extraterrestrial Technology and Entities, and increase the efficiency of future operations.

2.   General

MJ—12 takes the subject of the UFOBs, Extraterrestrial Technology and Extraterrestrial Biological Entities very seriously and considers the entire subject to be a matter of the very highest national security. For that reason everything relating to the subject has been assigned the very highest security classification. Three main points will be covered in this section.

a. The general aspects of MJ—12 to clear up any misconceptions that anyone may have.

b. The importance of the operation.

c. The need for absolute secrecy in all phases of operation.

3.   Security Classification

All information relating to MJ—12 has been classified MAJIC EYES ONLY and carries a security level 2 points above that of Top Secret. The reason for this has to do with the consequences that may arise not only from the impact upon the public should the existence of such matters become general knowledge, but also the danger of having such advanced technology as has been recovered by the Air Force fall into the hands of unfriendly foreign powers. No information is released to the public press and the official government position is that no special group such as MJ—12 exists.

4.   History of the Group

Operation Majestic-12 was established by special classified presidential order on 24 September 1947 at the recommendation of Secretary of Defense James V. Forrestal and Dr. Vannevar Bush, Chairman of the Joint Research and Development Board. Operations are carried out under a Top Secret Research and Development—Intelligence Group directly responsible only to the President of the United States. The goals of the MJ-12 Group are as follows:

a. The recovery for scientific study of all materials and devices of a foreign or extraterrestrial manufacture that may become available. Such material and devices will be recovered by any and all means deemed necessary by the Group.

b. The recovery for scientific study of all entities and remains of entities not of terrestrial origin which may become available though independent action by those entities or by misfortune or military action.

c. The establishment and administration of Special Teams to accomplish the above operations.

   d. The establishment and administration of special secure facilities located at secret locations within the continental borders of the United States for the receiving, processing, analysis, and scientific study of any and all material and entities classified as being of extraterrestrial origin by the Group of the Special Teams.

   e. Establishment and administration of covert operation to be carried out in concert with Central Intelligence to effect the recovery for the United States of extraterrestrial technology and entities which may come down inside the territory of or fall into the possession of foreign powers.

   f. The establishment and maintenance of absolute top secrecy concerning all the above operations.

5.   Current Situation

   It is considered as far as the current situation is concerned, that there are few indications that these objects and their builders pose a direct threat to the security of the United States, despite the uncertainty as to their ultimate motives in coming here. Certainly the technology possessed by these beings far surpasses anything known to modern science, yet their presence here seems to be benign, and they seem to be avoiding contact with our species, at least for the present. Several dead entities have been recovered along with a substantial amount of wreckage and devices from downed craft, all of which are now under study at various locations. No attempt has been made by extaterrestrial entities either to contact authorities or to recover their dead counterparts of the downed craft, even though one of the crashes was the result of direct military action. The greatest threat at this time arises from the acquisition and study of such advanced technology by foreign powers unfriendly to the United States. It is for this reason that the recovery and study of this type of material by the United States has been given such a high priority.

TOP SECRET/MAJIC EYES ONLY

CHAPTER 2
INTRODUCTION

Section I. GENERAL

6. Scope

a. This operations manual is published for the information and guidance of all concerned. It contains information on determination, documentation, collection, and disposition of debris, devices, craft, and occupants of such craft as defined as Extraterrestrial Technology or Extraterrestrial Biological Entities (EBEs) in Section II of this chapter.

b. Appendix I contains a list of current references, including technical manuals and other available publications applicable to these operations.

c. Appendix II contains a list of personnel who comprise the Majestic-12 Group.

7. Forms and Records.

Forms used for reporting operation are listed in Appendix Ia.

Section II. DEFINITION AND DATA

8. General

Extraterrestrial Technology is defined as follows:

a. Aircraft identified as not manufactured in the United States or any terrestrial foreign powers, including experimental military or civilian aircraft. Aircraft in this category are generally known as Unidentified Flying Objects, or UFOBs. Such aircraft may appear as one of several shapes and configurations and exhibit extraordinary flight characteristics.

b. Objects and devices of unknown origin or function, manufactured by processes or of materials not consistent with current technology or scientific knowledge.

c. Wreckage of any aircraft thought to be of extraterrestrial manufacture or origin. Such wreckage may be the results of accidents or military action.

d. Materials that exhibit unusual or extraordinary characteristics not consistent with current technology or scientific knowledge.

Extraterrestrial Biological Entities (EBEs) are described as:

a. Creatures, humanoid or otherwise, whose evolutionary processes responsible for their development are demonstrably different from those postulated or observed in homo sapiens.

9. Description of Craft

Documented extraterrestrial craft (UFOBs) are classified in one of four categories based on general shape, as follows:

a. Elliptical, or disc shape. This type of craft is of a metallic construction and dull aluminum in color. They have the appearance of two pie-pans or shallow dishes pressed together and may have a raised dome on the top or bottom. No seams or joints are visible on the surface, giving the impression of one-piece construction. Discs are estimated from 50-300 feet in diameter and the thickness is approximately 15 per cent of the diameter, not including the dome, which is 30 per cent of the disc diameter and extends another 4-6 feet above the main body of the disc. The dome may or may not include windows or ports, and ports are present around the lower rim of the disc in some instances. Most disc-shaped craft are equipped with lights on the top and bottom, and also around the rim. These lights are not visible when the craft is at rest or not functioning. There are generally no visible antenna or projections. Landing gear consists of three extendible legs ending in circular landing pads. When fully extended this landing gear supports the main body 2-3 feet above the surface at the lowest point. A rectangular hatch is located along the equator or on the lower surface of the disk.

b. Fuselage or cigar shape. Documented reports of this type of craft are extremely rare. Air Force radar reports indicate they are approximately 2 thousand feet long and 95 feet thick, and apparently they do not operate in the lower atmosphere. Very little information is available on the performance of these craft, but rader reports have indicated speeds in excess of 7,000 miles per hour. They do not appear to engage in the violent and erratic maneuvers associated with the smaller types.

c. Ovoid or circular shape. This type of craft is described as being shaped like an ice cream cone, being rounded at the large end and tapering to a near-point at the other end. They are approximately 30-40 feet long and the thick end diameter is approximately 20 per cent of the length. There is an extremely bright light at the pointed end, and this craft usually travels point down. They can appear to be any shape from round to cylindrical, depending upon the angle of observation. Often sightings of this type of craft are elliptical craft seen at an inclined angle or edge-on.

d. Airfoil or triangular shape. This craft is believed to be new technology due to the rarity and recency of the observations. Radar indicated an isosceles triangle profile, the longest side being nearly 300 feet in length. Little is known about the performance of these craft due to the rarity of good sightings, but they are believed capable of high speeds and abrupt maneuvers similar to or exceeding the performance attributed to types "a" and "c".

10. Description of Extraterrestrial Biological Entities (EBEs)

Examination of remains recovered from wreckage of UFOBs indicates that Extraterrestrial Biological Entities may be classified into two distinct categories as follows:

a. EBE Type I. These entities are humanoid and might be mistaken for human beings of the Oriental race if seen from a distance. They are bi-pedal, 5-5 feet 4 inches in height and weigh 80-100 pounds. Proportionally they are similar to humans, although the cranium is somewhat larger and more rounded. The skin is a pale, chalky-yellow in color, thick, and slightly pebbled in appearance. The eyes are small, wide-set, almond-shaped, with brownish-black irises with very large pupils. The whites of the eyes are not like that of humans, but have a pale gray cast. The ears are small and not low on the skull. The nose is thin and long, and the mouth is wider than in humans, and nearly lip-less. There is no apparent facial hair and very little body hair, that being very fine and confined to the underarm and the groin area. The body is thin and without apparent body fat, but the muscles are well-developed. The hands are small, with four long digits but no opposable thumb. The outside digit is jointed in a manner as to be nearly opposable, and there is no webbing between the finger as in humans. The legs are slightly but noticeably bowed, and the feet are somewhat splayed and proportionally large.

MJ—12 4838B   5

TOP SECRET/MAJIC EYES ONLY

b. Type II. These entities are humanoid but differ from Type I in many respects. They are bi-pedal, 3 feet 5 inches-4 feet 2 inches in height and weigh 25-50 pounds. Proportionally, the head is much larger than humans or Type I EBEs, the cranium being much larger and elongated. The eyes are very large, slanted, and nearly wrap around the side of the skull. They are black with no whites showing. There is no noticeable brow ridge, and the skull has a slight peak that runs over the crown. The nose consists of two small slits which sit high above the slit-like mouth. There are no external ears. The skin is a pale bluish-gray color, being somewhat darker on the back of the creature, and is very smooth and fine-celled. There is no hair on either the face or the body, and these creatures do not appear to be mammalian. The arms are long in proportion to the legs, and the hands have three long, tapering fingers and a thumb which is nearly as long as the fingers. The second finger is thicker than the others, but not as long as the index finger. The feet are small and narrow, and four toes are joined together with a membrane.

It is not definitely known where either type of creature originated, but it seems certain that they did not evolve on earth. It is further evident, although not certain, that they may have originated on two different planets.

11. Description of Extraterrestrial Technology

The following information is from preliminary analysis reports of wreckage collected from crash sites of extraterrestrial craft 1947-1953, excerpts from which are quoted verbatim to provide guidance as to the type of characteristics of material that might be encountered in future recovery operations.

a. Initial analysis of the debris from the crash site seems to indicate that the debris is that of an extraterrestrial craft which exploded from within and came into contact with the ground with great force, completely destroying the craft. The volume of matter indicates that the craft was approximately the size of a medium aircraft, although the weight of the debris indicates that the craft was extremely light for its size.

b. Metallurgical analysis of the bulk of the debris recovered indicates that the samples are not composed of any materials currently known to Terrestrial science.

c. The material tested possesses great strength and resistance to heat in proportion to its weight and size, being stronger by far than any materials used in military or civilian aircraft at present.

d. Much of the material, having the appearance of aluminum foil or aluminum-magnesium sheeting, displays none of the characteristics of either metal, resembling instead some kind of unknown plastic-like material.

e. Solid structures and substantial beams having a distinct similarity in appearance to very dense grain-free wood, was very light in weight and possesses tensile and compression strength not obtainable by any means known to modern industry.

f. None of the material tested displayed measurable magnetic characteristics or residual radiation.

g. Several samples were engraved or embossed with marks and patterns. These patterns were not readily identifiable and attempts to decipher their meaning has been largely unsuccessful.

h. Examination of several apparent mechanical devices, gears, etc. revealed little or nothing of their functions or methods of manufacture.

TOP SECRET/MAJIC EYES ONLY

TOP SECRET/MAJIC EYES ONLY

CHAPTER 3

RECOVERY OPERATIONS

Section I. SECURITY

12. Press Blackout

Great care must be taken to preserve the security of any location where Extraterrestrial Technology might be retrievable for scientific study. Extreme measures must be taken to protect and preserve any material or craft from discovery, examination, or removal by civilian agencies or individuals of the general public. It is therefore recommended that a total press blackout be initiated whenever possible. If this course of action should not prove feasible, the following cover stories are suggested for release to the press. The officer in charge will act quickly to select the cover story that best fits the situation. It should be remembered when selecting a cover story that official policy regarding UFOBs is that they do not exist.

a. Official Denial. The most desirable response would be that nothing unusual has occurred. By stating that the government has no knowledge of the event, further investigation by the public press may be forestalled.

b. Discredit Witnesses. If at all possible, witnesses will be held incommunicado until the extent of their knowledge and involvement can be determined. Witnesses will be discouraged from talking about what they have seen, and intimidation may be necessary to ensure their cooperation. If witnesses have already contacted the press, it will be necessary to discredit their stories. This can best be done by the assertion that they have either misinterpreted natural events, are the victims of hysteria or hallucinations, or are the perpetrators of hoaxes.

c. Deceptive Statements. It may become necessary to issue false statements to preserve the security of the site. Meteors, downed satellites, weather balloons, and military aircraft are all acceptable alternatives, although in the case of the downed military aircraft statement care should be exercised not to suggest that the aircraft might be experimental or secret, as this might arouse more curiosity of both the American and the foreign press. Statement issues concerning contamination of the area due to toxic spills from trucks or railroad tankers can also serve to keep unauthorized or undesirable personnel away from the area.

13. Secure the Area

The area must be secured as rapidly as possible to keep unauthorized personnel from infiltrating the site. The officer in charge will set up a perimeter and establish a command post inside the perimeter. Personnel allowed on the site will be kept to the absolute minimum necessary to prepare the craft or debris for transport, and will consist of Military Security Teams.

Local authorities may be pressed into service as traffic and crowd control. *Under no circumstances* will local official or law enforcement personnel be allowed inside the perimeter and all necessary precautions should be taken to ensure that they do not interfere with the operation.

a. Perimeter. It is desirable that sufficient military personnel be utilized to set up a perimeter around the site large enough to keep both unauthorized personnel and the

TOP SECRET/MAJIC EYES ONLY
REPRODUCTION IN ANY FORM IS FORBIDDEN BY FEDERAL LAW

perimeter personnel from seeing the site. Once the site is contained, regular patrols will be set up along the perimeter to ensure complete security, and electronic surveillance will be utilized to augment the patrols. Perimeter personnel will be equipped with hand communication and automatic weapons with live ammunition. Personnel working at the site will carry sidearms. No unauthorized personnel will be allowed into the secured area.

b. Command Post. Ideally, the command post should be as close to the site as is practical to efficiently coordinate operations. As soon as the command post is operational, contact with the Majestic—12 Group will be established via secure communications.

c. Area Sweep. The site and the surrounding area will be cleared of all unauthorized personnel. Witnesses will be debriefed and detained for further evaluation by MJ—12. *Under no circumstances* will witnesses be released from custody until their stories have been evaluated by MJ—12 and they have been thoroughly debriefed.

d. Situation Evaluation. A preliminary evaluation of the situation will be completed and a preliminary report prepared. The MJ—12 Group will then be briefed on the situation at the earliest possible opportunity. The MJ—12 Group will then make a determination as to whether or not a MJ—12 RED TEAM or OPNAC Team will be dispatched to the area.

Section II. TECHNOLOGY RECOVERY

14. Removal and Transport

As soon as communication is established, removal and transport of all material will commence under order of MJ—12.

a. Documentation. If the situation permits, care should be taken to document the area with photographs before anything is moved. The area will be checked for radiation and other toxic agents. If the area cannot be kept secure for an extended period of time, all material must be packed and transported as quickly as possible to the nearest secure military facility. This will be accomplished by covered transport using little-traveled roads wherever possible.

b. Complete or Functional Craft. Craft are to be approached with extreme caution if they appear functional, as serious injury may result from exposure to radiation and electrical discharges. If the craft is functioning, but appears to be abandoned, it may be approached only by specially trained MJ—12 RED TEAM personnel wearing protective clothing. Any craft that appears to be functioning should also be left to MJ—12 RED TEAM disposal. Complete craft and parts of crafts too large to be transported by covered transport will be disassembled, if this can be accomplished easily and quickly. If they must be transported whole, or on open flatbed trailers, they will be covered in such a manner as to camouflage their shape.

c. Extraterrestrial Biological Entities. EBEs must be removed to a top security facility as quickly as possible. Great care should be taken to prevent possible contamination by alien biological agents. Dead EBEs should be packed in ice at the earliest opportunity to preserve tissues. Should live EBEs be encountered, they should be taken into custody and removed to a top security facility by ambulance. Every effort should be taken to ensure the EBEs survival. Personnel involvement with EBEs alive or dead must be kept to an absolute minimum. (See Chapter 5 for more detailed instruction on dealing with EBEs.)'

15. Cleansing the Area

Once all material has been removed from the central area, the surrounding area will be thoroughly inspected to make sure that all traces of Extraterrestrial Technology have been removed. In the case of a crash, the surrounding area will be thoroughly gone over several times to ensure that nothing has been overlooked. The search area involved may vary depending on local conditions, at the discretion of the officer in charge. When the officer in charge is satisfied that no further evidence of the event remains at the site, it may be evacuated.

16. Special or Unusual Circumstances

The possibility exists that extraterrestrial craft may land or crash in heavily populated areas, where security cannot be maintained effectively. Large segments of the population and the public press may witness these craft. Contingency Plan MJ-1949-04P/78 (TOP SECRET * EYES ONLY) should be held in readiness should the need to make a public disclosure become necessary.

17. Extraterrestrial Technology *(See Table on next page)*

Figure 2. MJ Form 1—007

TOP SECRET/MAJIC EYES ONLY
REPRODUCTION IN ANY FORM IS FORBIDDEN BY FEDERAL LAW

17. Extraterrestrial Technology Classification Table

No.	Item	Description or condition	MJ—12 Code	Receiving Facility
1	Aircraft	Intactact, operational, or semi-intact aircraft of Extraterrestrial design and manufacture.	UA-002-6	Area 51 S-4
2	Intact device	Any mechanical or electroic device or machine which appears to be undamaged and functional.	ID-301-F	Area 51 S-4
3	Damaged device	Any mechanical or electronic device or machine which appears to be damaged but mostly complete.	DD-303N	Area 51 S-4
4	Powerplant	Devices and machines or fragments which are possible propulsion units, fuel and associated control devices and panels.	PD-40-8G	Area 51 S-4
5	Identified fragments	Fragments composed of elements or materials easily recognized as known to current science and technology, i.e., aluminum, magnesium, plastic, etc.	IF-101-K	Area 51 S-4
6	Unidentified fragments	Fragments composed of elements or materials not known to current science and technology and which exhibits unusual or extraordinary characteristics.	UF-103-M	Area 51 S-4
7	Supplies and provisions	Non-mechanical or non-electronic materials of a support nature such as clothing, personal belongings, organic ingestibles, etc.	SP-331	Blue Lab WP-61
8	Living entity*	Living non-human organisms in apparent good or reasonable health.	EBE-010	OPNAC BBS-01
9	Non-living entity	Deceased non-human organisms or portions of organisms, organic remains and other suspect matter.	EBE-XO	Blue Lab WP-61
10	Media	Printed matter, electronic recordings, maps, charts, photographs and film.	MM-54A	Building 21 KB-88
11	Weapons	Any device or portion of a device thought to be offensive or defensive weaponry.	WW-010	Area 51 S-4

Living entity must be contained in total pending arrival of OPNAC personnel

MJ—12 4838B

18. Packaging and Packing Data

a. Domestic Shipment. Individual items are tagged and wrapped in a moisture-vaporproof barrier and heat sealed. They are then placed in a corrugated fiberboard box. The voids within the box are packed thoroughly with a neutral cellulose wadding to prevent movement of the items. The box closure is sealed with gummed Kraft tape. MJ Form 1-007 is placed in a sealed manila envelope marked "MAJIC—12 ACCESS ONLY" and is firmly taped to the top of the box. The box is then cushioned at each corner and at the top and bottom with fiberboard inserts and is placed within a large corrugated fiberboard box. The entire outer box closure is sealed with gummed Kraft tape. A label is affixed to the outer box bearing the following information: destination, shipping code number, and the warning, "MAJIC—12 ACCESS ONLY."

b. Overseas Shipment. Items are packaged as described above except that a dessicant and humidity indicator are included within the inner corrugated fiberboard box. Next, the box is wrapped in a moisture-vaporproof barrier and heat sealed. Then, packaged items are placed within a second waterproof carton sealed with waterproof tape. This second carton is marked "MAJIC—12 ACCESS ONLY" on all sides and is placed within a water-grease-proof lined wooden shipping container. The lining is sealed with waterproof tape and the wooden shipping container is screwed shut. The shipping container is reinforced further by nailing two [3/4]-inch metal caps about 8 inches from each end. Shipping information is then stenciled on the surface of the wooden shipping container.

Note. The packaging and packing procedure detailed above applies to non-organic items only. Data for handling, packaging, packing, and shipping of organic matter and non-living entities is provided in Chapter 5, Section II of this manual.

CHAPTER 4

RECEIVING AND HANDLING

Section I. HANDLING UPON RECEIPT OF MATERIAL

20. Uncrating, Unpacking, and Checking

(fig. 3)

Note. The uncrating, unpacking, and checking procedure for containers marked "MAJIC—12 ACCESS ONLY" will be carried out by personnel with MJ—12 clearance. Containers marked in this manner will be placed in storage in a top security area until such time as authorized personnel are available for these procedures.

a. Be very careful when uncrating and unpacking the material. Avoid thrusting tools into the interior of the shipping container. Do not damage the packaging materials any more than is absolutely necessary to remove the specimens; these materials may be required for future packaging. Store the interior packaging material within the shipping container. When uncrating and unpacking the specimens, follow the procedure given in (1) through (11) below:

(1) Unpack the specimens in a top security area to prevent access of unauthorized personnel.

(2) Cut the metal wires with a suitable cutting tool, or twist them with pliers until the straps crystallize and break.

(3) Remove screws from the top of the shipping container with a screw driver.

(4) Cut the tape and seals of the case liner so that the waterproof paper will be damaged as little as possible.

(5) Lift out the packaged specimens from the wooden case.

(6) Cut the tape which seals the top flaps of the outer cartons; be careful not to damage the cartons.

(7) Cut the barrier along the top heat sealed seam and carefully remove the inner carton.

(8) Remove the sealed manila envelope from the top of the inner carton.

(9) Open the inner carton and remove the fiberboard inserts, dessicant, and humidity indicator.

(10) Lift out the heat sealed packaging containing the specimens; arrange them in an orderly manner for inspection.

(11) Place all packaging material in the shipping container for use in future repacking.

[In place here is Figure 3—a diagram showing how to package non-organic extraterrestrial specimens.]

b. Thoroughly check all items against the shipping documents. Carefully inspect all items for possible damage during shipping or handling. Sort the items according to classification number in preparation for transfer to the designated Laboratory or department. Laboratory or department personnel are responsible for transporting items to the designated areas. This will be accomplished as quickly as possible by covered transport escorted by security personnel.

CHAPTER 5

EXTRATERRESTRIAL BIOLOGICAL ENTITIES

Section I. LIVING ORGANISMS

21. Scope

a. This section deals with encounters with living Extraterrestrial Biological Entities (EBEs). Such encounters fall under the jurisdiction of MJ-12 OPNAC BBS—01 and will be dealt with by this special unit only. This section details the responsibilities of persons or units making the initial contact.

22. General

Any encounter with entities known to be of extraterrestrial origin is to be considered to be a matter of national security and therefore classified TOP SECRET. Under no circumstance is the general public or the public press to learn of the existence of these entities. The official government policy is that such creatures do not exist, and that no agency of the federal government is now engaged in any study of extraterrestrials or their artifacts. Any deviation from this stated policy is absolutely forbidden.

23. Encounters

Encounters with EBEs may be classified according to one of the following categories:

a. Encounters initiated by EBEs. Possible contact may take place as a result of overtures by the entities themselves. In these instances it is anticipated that encounters will take place at military installations or other obscure locations selected by mutual agreement. Such meeting would have the advantage of being limited to personnel with appropriate clearance, away from public scrutiny. Although it is not considered very probable, there also exists the possibility that EBEs may land in public places without prior notice. In this case the OPNAC Team will formulate cover stories for the press and prepare briefings for the President and the Chiefs of Staff.

b. Encounters as the result of downed craft. Contact with survivors of accidents or craft downed by natural events or military action may occur with little or no warning. In these cases, it is important that the initial contact be limited to military personnel to preserve security. Civilian witnesses to the area will be detained and debriefed by MJ-12. Contact with EBEs by military personnel not having MJ-12 or OPNAC clearance is to be strictly limited to action necessary to ensure the availability of the EBEs for study by the OPNAC Team.

24. Isolation and Custody

a. EBEs will be detained by whatever means are necessary and removed to a secure location as soon as possible. Precautions will be taken by personnel coming in contact with EBEs to minimize the risk of disease as a result of contamination by unknown organisms. If the entities are wearing space suits or breathing apparatus of some kind, care should be exercised to prevent damage to these devices. While all efforts should be taken to assure the well-being of the EBEs, they must be isolated from any contact with unauthorized personnel. While it is not clear what provisions or amenities might be required by non-human entities, they should be provided if possible. The officer in charge of the operation will make these determinations, since no guidelines now exist to cover this area.

b. Injured or wounded entities will be treated by medical personnel assigned to the OPNAC Team. If the team medical personnel are not immediately available, First Aid will be administered by Medical Corps personnel at the initial site. Since little is known about EBE biological functions, aid will be confined to the stopping of bleeding, bandaging of wounds and splinting of broken limbs. No medications of any kind are to be administered as the effect of terrestrial medications on non-human biological systems are impossible to predict. As soon as the injuries are considered stabilized, the EBEs will be moved by closed ambulance or other suitable conveyance to a secure location.

c. In dealing with any living Extraterrestrial Biological Entity, security is of paramount importance. All other considerations are secondary. Although it is preferable to maintain the physical well-being of any entity, the loss of EBE life is considered acceptable if conditions or delays to preserve that life in any way compromises the security of the operations.

d. Once the OPNAC Team has taken custody of the EBEs, their care and transportation to designated facilities become the responsibility of OPNAC personnel. Every cooperation will be extended to the team in carrying out duties. OPNAC Team personnel will be given TOP PRIORITY at all times regardless of their apparent rank or status. No person has the authority to interfere with the OPNAC Team in the performance of its duties by special direction of the President of the United States.

Section II. NON-LIVING ORGANISMS

25. Scope

Ideally, retrieval for scientific study of cadavers and other biological remains will be carried out by medical personnel familiar with this type of procedure. Because of security considerations, such collection may need to be done by non-medical personnel. This section will provide guidance for retrieval, preservation, and removal of cadavers and remains in the field.

26. Retrieval and Preservation

a. The degree of decomposition of organic remains will vary depending on the length of time the remains have been lying in the open unprotected and may be accelerated by both local weather conditions and action by predators. Therefore, biological specimens will be removed from the crash site as quickly as possible to preserve the remains in as good a condition as possible. A photographic record will be made of all remains before they are removed from the site.

b. Personnel involved in this type of operation will take all reasonable precautions to minimize physical contact with the cadavers or remains being retrieved. Surgical gloves should be worn or, if they are not available, wool or leather gloves may be worn provided they are collected for decontamination immediately after use. Shovels and entrenching tools may be employed to handle remains provided caution is exercised to be certain no damage is done to the remains. Remains will be touched with bare hands only if no other means of moving them can be found. All personnel and equipment involved in recovery operations will undergo decontamination procedures immediately after those operations are [sic] have been completed.

MJ—12 4838B   14

TOP SECRET/MAJIC EYES ONLY

c. Remains will be preserved against further decomposition as equipment and conditions permit. Cadavers and remains will be bagged or securely wrapped in waterproof coverings. Tarpaulins or foul weather gear may be used for this purpose if necessary. Remains will be refrigerated or packed with ice if available. All remains will be tagged or labeled and the time and date recorded. Wrapped remains will be placed on stretchers or in sealed containers for immediate removal to a secure facility.

d. Small detached pieces and material scraped from solid surfaces will be put in jars or other small capped containers if available. Containers will be clearly marked as to their contents and the time and date recorded. Containers will be refrigerated or packed with ice as soon as possible and removed to a secure facility.

[In place here is Figure 4—diagrams of the various types of extraterrestrial craft discussed in the text.]

TOP SECRET/MAJIC EYES ONLY
REPRODUCTION IN ANY FORM IS FORBIDDEN BY FEDERAL LAW

CHAPTER 6
GUIDE TO UFO IDENTIFICATION

Section I. UFOB GUIDE

27. Follow-up Investigations

A UFOB report is worthy of follow-up investigation when it contains information to suggest that positive identification with a well-known phenomenon may be made or when it characterizes an unusual phenomenon. The report should suggest almost immediately, largely by the coherency and clarity of the data, that there is something of identification and/or scientific value. In general, reports which should be given consideration are those which involve several reliable observers, together or separately, and which concern sighting of greater duration than one quarter minute. Exceptions should be made to this when circumstances attending the report are considered to be extraordinary. Special attention should be given to reports which give promise to a "fix" on the position and those reports involving unusual trajectories.

28. Rules of Thumb

Each UFOB case should be judged individually but there are a number of "rules of thumb," under each of the following headings, which should prove helpful for determining the necessity for follow-up investigation.

a. Duration of Sighting. When the duration of a sighting is less than 15 seconds, the probabilities are great that it is not worthy of follow-up. As a word of caution, howerver, should a large number of individual observers report an unusual sighting of a few seconds duration, it should not be dismissed.

b. Number of Persons Reporting the Sighting. Short duration sightings by single individuals are seldom worthy of follow-up. Two or three competent independent observations carry the weight of 10 or more simultaneous individual observations. As an example, 25 people at one spot may observe a strange light in the sky. This, however, has less weight than two reliable people observing the same light from different locations. In the latter case a position-fix is indicated.

c. Distance from Location of Sightings to Nearest Field Unit. Reports which meet the preliminary criterion stated above should all be investigated if their occurrence is in the immediate operating vicinity of the squadron concerned. For reports involving greater distances, follow-up necessity might be judged as being inversely proportional to the square of the distances concerned. For example, an occurrence 150 miles away might be con-

APPENDIX I
REFERENCES

There is some writing here   No. 4, AB

---

1. [Applicable] Regulations

-4   Military security (Safeguarding Security Information.

Maintenance Supplies and Equipment, Maintenance Responsiblities and Shop Operation.

2. Supply

xx 725-405-5   Preparation and Submission of Requisitions for Supplies.

3. Other Publications

XX 219-20-3   Index of Training Manuals.

XX 310-20-4   Index of Technical Manuals, Technical Regulations, Technical Bulletins, Supply Bulletin, Lubrications Orders, and Modification Work Orders.

XX310-20-5   Index of Administrative Publications.

XX310-20-7   Index of Tables of Organization and Equipment, Reduction Tables, Tables of Organization, Tables of Equipment, Type Tables of Distribution and Tables of Allowance.

4. Test Equipment References

TM 11—664   Theory and Use of Electronic Test Equipment.

5. Photographic References

TM 11—404A   Photographic Print Processing Unit AN/TFQ-9.

TM 11—405   Processing Equipment PH—406.

TM 11—401   Elements of Signal Photography.

TM 11—2363   Darkroom PH—392.

10

SCOPE OF THE MAJESTIC-12 ACTIVITY

A thoughtful reader would have recognized by now that the few documents relating to Majestic-12 discussed in this book are surely only the tiny tip of the iceberg. Somewhere there is a huge number of documents done under the auspices of Majestic-12 and whatever successor groups there may be. Just think of the paperwork necessary for the recovery operations discussed in the Special Operations Manual!

If you have difficulty believing that undertakings involving huge quantities of data and many thousands of people can be kept secret for years, two World War II examples prove that it can be done: the Manhattan Project and the breaking of the German and Japanese secret codes.

The Manhattan Project involved more than 50,000 people between 1942 and 1945 and the creation of huge new installations at Oak Ridge, Tennessee; Hanford, Washington; Los Alamos, New Mexico; and other places. The cost of the project has been estimated at $2 billion in 1940s dollars—or about $20 billion in today's dollars.

Breaking the enemy codes and the subsequent interception, decoding, and distribution of messages involved, according to an estimate by Robin Wink, a Yale professor, at least 10,000 people. Yet there was no unclassified word about this in public view until 25 years after the war was over.

Both of these comparatively short-term projects produced a huge amount of paperwork. If in 1947, an organization was established to recover and investigate material from extraterrestrial vehicles, then all the many groups participating in one way or another in the analysis and evaluation of the specimens, the transmission of information from each group to a few compartmented special offices, and the interpretation of what it all means from a technological, military, political, social, economic, and religious standpoint, would have produced a veritable mountain of paperwork.

Between 1956 and 1970, I worked on a number of fairly large classified (not black budget) research and development programs. In 1958, the Aircraft Nuclear Propulsion program at General Electric was spending more than $100 million a year and employed about 3,500 people. Almost everything we did was classified Secret Restricted Data as mandated by the Atomic Energy Act of 1954. We published internally classified documents in the tens of thousands. Some of these documents were updated in format and style and were distributed to professionals at other installations who were involved in the ANP program; for example, Oak Ridge National Laboratory, General Dynamics in Fort Worth, Pratt and Whitney Aircraft in Connecticut, and others. Every time we did a series of experiments, classified technical reports had to be written. Every time plans were made for an experiment, reports had to be written. Paper was just a natural part of the system.

All classified documents had to be accounted for. When you left the company, if you couldn't locate and return all the documents you had signed out, you were in deep, deep trouble. Each scientist or engineer might have two or three large filing cabinets stuffed with these documents, and some had a good many more.

Of course, none of this material made it out to the public at the time, although some was declassified after the program was canceled in 1961. A couple of people have suggested to me that there must be serious morale problems among professionals working in isolation on highly classified projects. This, quite frankly, is nonsense. It is very exciting and satisfying to work on leading-edge technology where you have the finest equipment, outstanding colleagues, and a chance to make a real contribution, even if you can't publish in the open scientific literature. Academics may think in terms of publish or perish. Nonacademic scientists and engineers get their satisfaction from accomplishment.

We used code words in our work, whose use was gradually changed as they became compromised. For example, when I began work at GE, the term *lithium hydride*—a compound of hydrogen and lithium which has very attractive nuclear properties even though it's a pain in the neck to formulate into large chunks—was classified. It was not classified because of our program, which concerned radiation shielding material, but because combinations of hydrogen and lithium play a role in building hydrogen bombs. By changing isotope ratios—using the right isotopes of hydrogen and the right isotopes of lithium—you get a material that produces the fusion portion of the hydrogen bombs that were made. So any facilities that manufactured and tested segments of lithium hydride, for any purpose, were classified.

As I recall, the code name for lithium hydride was *black salt*. Pretty soon, you could use the term *lithium hydride,* but you couldn't say what its use was. Next, you could say it was used for radiation shielding purposes, but you couldn't say which project it was being used for.

Classification people often went overboard in their zeal to protect security. One classification officer thought that soon we would find a magic material that could be painted on and would absorb all radiation. Therefore, all radiation shielding work had to be highly classified. As a matter of fact, there were unclassified charts of various compounds with certain classified materials left off. These materials would have been identifiable by any enlightened reviewer, who probably could figure out that their absence was a tip-off that we were using them for our classified work. This is a bit too subtle for some classification officers.

As soon as you start spending money on extensive experimentation and testing, you produce reports: test data, preliminary reports, final reports, summary reports, quarterly reports, annual reports. Projects are littered with paper. For an operation such as Majestic-12, clearly numerous tests would have been done to try to determine the characteristics of the materials that were found, reproduce those materials, and test them against other materials. As new analytical techniques became available, new tests would have been run.

This drawn-out process of testing is not understood by most people. I once met somebody who claimed to have a small piece of the Roswell saucer. First he was willing to have it analyzed by an outstanding test laboratory, as long as he could be there to ensure that the small piece he had would not be destroyed or stolen. He didn't want any publicity. Robert Wood and I were able to line up a testing lab with the assurance that his name wouldn't be revealed, although we each met him separately. We stressed that a whole host of tests would have to be run because it would not be easy to determine that something was not produced on earth. The man stalled. Finally his lawyer got in on the act.

I met with the lawyer, and we had a pleasant lunch. He said, "My client really doesn't want to get involved. He's fearful that he will be identified and then perhaps eliminated by the government. What he'd like is to get a simple test done that shows this is an extraterrestrial material, and then sell this to someone. Obviously, whoever had that data would put the aluminum and steel industries out of business."

I agreed that an extraordinarily strong, lightweight material is of obvious economic value, but explained that it wasn't easy to determine that something was not of terrestrial origin. It was very likely made of elements that are found here, but put together in a different way using special techniques, perhaps under special circumstances. Furthermore, knowing that something isn't a conventional alloy doesn't prove that it isn't used in some very highly classified program, such as a vital component in nuclear weapons, Star Wars, laser weapons systems, and so on. Those alloys aren't known to the general run of technical people.

Furthermore, proving that a material is of extraterrestrial origin and has special properties not only doesn't allow you to duplicate it, but also clearly doesn't establish economic viability. Material that costs $500 a pound to produce will not find immediate acceptance by automobile or airplane or rocket manufacturers. There is no way that any test would ensure that anybody would want to purchase the material, except for souvenir value.

I argued in vain. Finally I asked, "How much do you think he wants for the material?" The lawyer answered, casually, "Oh, $15 million."

We've never seen the material, but that's not even the point. Showing that something is, for example, ten times as strong as any other known element at a temperature of 1500° doesn't tell you how to duplicate it. That takes years of research and development, and billions of dollars.

Some people have suggested that alien craft would be made of materials composed of elements that we don't know about here on earth. A great deal of attention has been given to a man named Robert Scott Lazar, who claims to be a physicist and to have discovered the motive force for flying saucers—which requires something he calls "element 115." Almost all matter in our world is composed of elements with atomic numbers 1 through 92, from hydrogen to uranium. (The atomic number of an element is the number of protons and electrons in one atom of the element.) The Manhattan Project produced plutonium, which is element 94, and a whole host of higher-than-uranium atomic number (transuranic) elements. Every couple of years some new ones are discovered, updating the Periodic Chart of Elements to the low hundreds. These transuranic elements normally have several special characteristics:

- They have very short half-lives, existing on the average for perhaps a millionth of a second.
- Only very small numbers of these atoms are produced despite enormous effort to produce them with huge accelerators.

- They are all radioactive in one way or another, which means they decay rapidly. All elements above 90, including uranium, are radioactive. Uranium has a half-life measured in millions of years. Depending on the isotope, plutonium's half-life can be 27,000 years. Cobalt 60, which is used for medical purposes, has a half-life of 5.3 years. This is a relatively long life, and large amounts can be accumulated by exposing certain cobalt isotopes in reactors.

Lazar at one time claimed that his project had over 500 pounds of element 115, which he said wasn't radioactive and had an incredible potential energy production rate. But there is no way to accumulate so much of such a short half-life material. He also claimed that he had stolen some element 115. Such material would certainly have been as accountable as fully enriched uranium or weapons-grade plutonium. Private citizens are simply not able to steal any.

There are a number of other problems with Lazar's claims, including apparently bogus statements—which I checked—that he has made about his education and work history at Los Alamos National Laboratory and the mysterious Area 51 near Las Vegas. His proposed propulsion system involving element 115 sounds wonderful, but collapses on close examination. The point remains—and this has been borne out by our trips to the moon, tests on meteorites that have hit the earth, and especially by analysis of light from distant stars—that materials found other places in the universe are going to be composed of the same elements as those we have found here. It would be up to the scientists connected to Majestic-12 to determine *how* the elements were combined to create the materials that have been described to us by eyewitnesses.

The Operation Majestic-12 leaders would have been well aware of the rapidly improving analytical capabilities of scientists. In the 1950s, for example, there were nuclear reactor systems proposed which used liquid sodium, a metallic element that is a very good heat transfer agent, as the reactor coolant instead of water. Liquid sodium can remove much more heat from the reactor per unit time and at lower pressure than can water. However, researchers found that they couldn't predict corrosion of the piping no matter how many tests they ran.

The answer—it depended on the amount of oxygen in the sodium—was found only after equipment was developed that could measure sodium abundances in parts per million. We couldn't measure oxygen in sodium that accurately at the beginning of the development effort, so we didn't know then how to be sure of preventing corrosion. But as the analytical techniques improved, scientists could learn more about the process and determine corrosion-controlling techniques.

In biology, there are a whole host of biochemical compounds in the human body for which we couldn't analyze 50 years ago, and genes that we didn't even dream of analyzing 50 years ago. So the Majestic-12 scientific leaders like Bush, Bronk, Berkner, Menzel, and Hunsaker would have been sure that, in time, improvements would be made. This would mean that the initial samples, both biological and metallurgical, would have to be preserved and eventually reanalyzed.

Thus, in a number of labs around the country there would have been tests done, reports written, people involved, who may not even have known what their work was a part of, but who were doing significant, step-by-step work to understand and eventually duplicate this entirely new collection of technologies.

Some people have asked why, if we earthlings have recovered the wreckage of at least two very advanced flying saucers in New Mexico in 1947, that technology hasn't shown up yet in our own products. In response, I have to say that I think it has shown up. As a matter of fact, I think we can look at a couple of specific examples of relevant technology originating with flying saucers and being moved from the secret world to the outside world by Majestic-12 members.

Vannevar Bush and his associates were completely familiar with all the major high-technology, high-security laboratories in the country in 1947 as the result of all the projects carried out by the OSRD. Specimens would be sent under security to each lab without identification as to the source of the material—it could have been obtained by spies, or from German or Russian laboratories investigated in Europe.

At one lab, the charge might be to determine the composition of the sample. After running a battery of tests, the lead scientist might report, "I don't know where you obtained this material, but it is a combination of two elements, samarium and cobalt. I have no idea why those two materials would be combined."

"Are you sure?"

"Yes, I checked three times. It is samarium and cobalt."

"Thanks."

The samples then would have been sent out to other labs to determine physical properties such as strength at high temperature, electrical and magnetic properties, and so on.

"I don't know what this is or its origin, but it has the highest magnetic moment of any material I have ever measured. It would make a great permanent magnet."

"Thanks."

Next, a fabricating lab would work hard to determine the best way to combine the proper proportions of samarium and cobalt to make permanent magnets. The saucer propulsion secret would not have been determined, but there would be a real technological advance. I mean *real* advances: manufacturers of portable stereos are major users of samarium-cobalt materials.

I used to use this example in my talks since samarium-cobalt permanent magnets were for many years the best available. Then while preparing a weekly science commentary I did for six years at the Canadian Broadcasting Company radio station in Fredericton, I read about new and improved permanent magnets made of iron, boron, and neodymium. Buried in the article was the comment that the old samarium-cobalt technology was developed at Wright Air Development Center in Ohio—located at the old Wright Field. I laughed out loud, thinking, "I bet that technology was stimulated by investigation of a piece of a flying saucer."

A much more speculative example would be the development of the transistor by Bell Labs, one of the world's finest scientific research and development facilities. Bell had for many years close ties with Sandia National Laboratory in Albuquerque (one of the trio of high-security U.S. nuclear weapons labs), and did a lot of highly classified electronics research during the war. The official birthdate for the transistor is given as December 23, 1947, although the announcement of its discovery wasn't actually made until mid-1948 because of the patenting process, journal article submission, and so on. The first transistor was a very simple sort of device.

The team that worked on the transistor included three very well-established scientists. Normally when a new idea is being investigated, a senior scientist works with a junior one. It is very unlikely that three top scientists would be assigned to a single project unless someone knew that if the secret could be unlocked, the results might be very exciting indeed. Sandia, of course, is very close to the New Mexico crash sites, and there is evidence that wreckage from the crashes was investigated there.

The single most important aspect that makes a new development project more likely to succeed (or less likely to be canceled) is knowing that the desired objective can be achieved. For example, Soviet scientists pushing to develop the atomic bomb after World War II knew for certain that atomic bombs could be made to work, since five had been exploded by the United states by the end of 1946. German scientists working on the bomb during World War II did not know for sure such a weapon could be built, especially in time to help win the war. Hence, the German research and development focus was on making better missiles such as the V-2 rather than on the atomic bomb.

This does not mean we have learned either how to duplicate flying saucer propulsion techniques or how to copy the technique economically. The development of industries to make new materials and products based on the extraterrestrial specimens is not easy. New machines and new processes have to be invented. Materials might have to be molded at higher pressures than ever imagined, or in a vacuum. How do you contain materials that need to be poured at very high temperatures—probably above the melting point of the available containers for those materials? It could take decades to duplicate the simplest specimens of extraterrestrial material. This isn't to say that progress wouldn't be made in many areas, but it would be slow. There would have to be quantum leaps in other areas of our knowledge before we would be able to duplicate the vehicle, let alone the propulsion system.

Consider what would happen if you gave Christopher Columbus a modern nuclear submarine in 1492, and said, "Chris, money is no object. Build me three more of these babies." A mighty tall order—and not just because nuclear power was unknown. Electricity was unknown. The internal combustion engine was unknown. Even the steam engine was more than 200 years in the future. The scientific principles governing the skin of the ship, its propulsion, its power source, and its instrumentation did not exist in his world. Even the vessel's purpose might be suspect. Travel below the waves? Why?

Here's another example closer to our time. Suppose you gave a digital wristwatch, costing about $15, to the smartest people around in 1940. Could they have duplicated it from scratch? Not the slightest chance. They would have known it was a watch. They would have known it was battery-powered. But they would have had to create the whole science of solid-state electronics before they could even begin to analyze the computer chip that runs the watch.

But these great pioneers would have given it their best try. And step by step, they would build a path that others would follow straight to the future.

THE "ALIEN AUTOPSY" FILM

After almost four decades of intensive UFO research, I am not easily surprised by new UFO stories. But on January 14, 1995, I received a phone call that truly shocked and excited me. It was from an English colleague with whom I had spent time a decade before during a speaking tour in England. He stated that the day before, Friday the 13th, the well-known rock musician Reg Presley (no relation to Elvis) had said on network TV that he knew of fifteen 10-minute reels of silent, black-and-white 16mm motion picture film showing the autopsy of alien bodies recovered near Roswell in 1947!

Presley's primary interest was in crop circles, of which there had been very many in the UK over the past several years. After a long conversation with my friend about the TV report, I decided that my best bet was to contact people in the UK who might be able to put me in touch with Presley. I called Dan Silver of London's Value Added Talent, a booking agency that arranges concerts and tours by rock groups. We had previously talked about a lecture tour.

Dan was able to get Reg's phone number, and Reg and I had a long, friendly conversation during which he said that the film was in the possession of Ray Santilli of Merlin Productions, who supposedly had obtained it from a former military cameraman who had shot the footage himself and somehow managed to keep a copy. Reg had seen only a little of the film.

Reg put me in touch with Santilli, and our first phone conversation was very cordial. He claimed he had done two years' research about Roswell to establish the validity of the cameraman and his footage, although this was the first time he had heard my name and he was unfamiliar with the MJ-12 documents. Plans were afoot to make a BBC documentary movie using the footage, Ray said, and he wasn't worried about government agents giving him a hard time. He said he had "boxes" of paperwork from the cameraman proving that he was who he said he was and where he said he was in 1947.

When Ray mentioned that there were recognizable people in the film, I immediately thought of the copy of the base yearbook that I had. I also knew the faces of the prominent scientists of the time, or I could get their pictures. Name tags and vehicle license plates could be read. I asked Ray if he had recognized anybody in the film.

"How about President Truman?" he responded.

"Is he in the film?"

"Yes, he is, and we have established that he was indeed in Dallas at the time of the autopsy."

"Dallas?" Strange.

"Yes. Hasn't anybody mentioned Dallas to you?"

"No, but the headquarters of the 8th Air Force was in Fort Worth, not too far away," I mused. "Did you check with the Truman Library?"

"Yes."

Why would Truman want to go see the aliens himself? He trusted his advisors. If Forrestal, Bush, and Marshall told him there were bodies and wreckage of a crashed saucer, I couldn't imagine Truman wanting to get involved, what with all the logistic problems of keeping it secret.

Ray also told me that his company had originally spoken to the cameraman about some footage he had shot of Elvis Presley in Ohio in the 1950s when he was just starting out. After they reviewed that footage, which Ray admired, the cameraman said he had something else that he might be willing to sell. And that's when he mentioned the footage of the autopsy.

Ray's story was that, supposedly, the cameraman always processed his own film, and so the cameraman was able to make a copy for himself. The cameraman was supposedly now in his eighties and had sold the film only because he wanted to buy a wedding present for his granddaughter. I told him that if he would give me the cameraman's name, I would be happy to look it up in confidence in my copy of the Operation Crossroads yearbook of 1946, which has pictures of many cameraman who helped film the explosions of nuclear weapons at Bikini atoll in 1946 by the 509th Bomb Group.

All the cameramen involved in Crossroads had to have high-level security clearances, which would also be required to film alien bodies, and they had to be known to the 509th. If Ray's man was listed in the yearbook, it would be a strong indication of his legitimacy. Ray declined to give me the name.

I wanted to see the film. If it was genuine, it was clearly of extraordinary importance—the smoking gun that would break the case wide open. If it was fraudulent, all my work on Roswell might come crashing down on my head. The debunkers would claim, "The film is a fraud, and therefore Roswell is a fraud." Although an irrational claim, rationality has never guided the press and the debunkers in their attacks against UFOs.

Dan Silver made an appointment to see Ray. Ray canceled that date, accepted another, canceled again, and then canceled a third appointment before seeing Dan. He didn't seem at all interested in having anybody knowledgeable about Roswell review the footage. In the meantime, I checked with Dennis Bilger at the Truman Library and found that, according to their records, Truman was in neither Texas nor New Mexico between June and October 1947. This does not mean that somehow Truman didn't fit in a secret trip to the Southwest then, but it's highly unlikely, considering how many people would have to know about even a "secret" trip by the president. In addition, this was the time when the military was undergoing its major reorganization, the National Security Council was established, the Marshall Plan was going into effect, and the cold war was heating up. But it was clear that Ray had not obtained confirmation of a Truman presence in Dallas from the Truman Library. What else was he stretching the truth about?

During March, there was a great deal of media talk in England and across the Internet about the footage. Philip Mantle of the British UFO Research Association (BUFORA) had said that Ray would show the footage at the association's conference in Sheffield in August. That seemed to imply acceptance of the footage by BUFORA. All sorts of faxes and letters were rushing back and forth, partly because of rivalries between various UK UFO groups. The idea of actual film of an alien autopsy and saucer wreckage was catching the fancy of people around the world, and publicity about the footage was starting to take off.

On March 29, Dan invited me to come to Birmingham, England to be on a Central TV talk show discussing the footage, with Ray possibly in attendance. It was short notice, for the show was scheduled for March 31, but Dan came up with a low-fare option for the sudden trip, Central TV said come ahead, and I jumped at the opportunity.

When I got to Birmingham and talked to the show's producer, he laughed when I told him about Ray not having come across my name in two years of research. The producer had found many references to me in an hour-and-a-half of effort.

As it turned out, Ray didn't show up. Several UK debunkers were in the live audience, as well as a debunking astronomer who was with me on stage. This man knew nothing about UFOs, New Mexico, how security works, or classified development programs. It was a battle royal. Also in the audience were Mantle and his long-time opponent, Graham Birdsall from Leeds, who publishes *UFO Magazine*, which has a worldwide circulation of approximately 50,000. Despite their rivalry, they both stood up for UFOs. Solicitor Harry Harris was also present on the pro-UFO side. Mantle has been more or less inclined to accept the footage, which Santilli had mentioned—but had not shown—to him almost two years before. Birdsall is convinced it is all a scam to make money. (It has been claimed on the Internet that Santilli and associates paid the cameraman at least $100,000 for the footage.)

Amidst other media interviews that Dan Silver set up for me, I managed to see Ray Santilli at his office. It is a small place, and has no sign on the door. Before we could talk, Ray hustled me out to a coffee shop. He said the cameraman had been married to the same woman for more than 50 years and was living in Orlando, Florida. (He has told others that they were living in Cleveland and Cincinnati.) He claimed that the wife was the dominant partner in the marriage, but didn't know about the money for the film. (Giving a big gift to a granddaughter without your spouse finding out? Someone in the family would tell.) Naturally Ray didn't show me the film.

When I boarded the plane back to Canada, I was pretty frustrated. The trip was not without its positives, but I didn't get any of the answers I had been seeking. Soon after I got home, I heard that the footage was going to be shown on May 5 to a bunch of media types for the purpose of getting someone to pay for the rights to show it on television. I prepared a challenge to Ray to back up his claims with facts.

The footage was shown at the London Museum with no introduction, no explanations or background, and no question-and-answer session afterward. (Dan Silver was there, and he distributed my challenge to many of the attendees.) The immediate reactions to the footage bordered on pandemonium. Some viewers claimed—with no follow-up research—that the footage was fraudulent because of various anachronisms; for example, a coiled phone cord shown in the film was supposedly not made until after 1947. (Western Electric later told me that the production of such a cord started in 1937.) Others said the autopsy looked real. Meanwhile, Ray was negotiating with TV networks all over the world who wanted to broadcast the film and were willing to pay lots of money for the privilege.

Fox Network was the leading candidate to take the prize; Robert Kiviat, a producer of UFO segments for various TV shows, even set up a separate company—Kiviat-Greene Productions—to develop the property. However, Ray was again being difficult. He canceled a meeting with top executives at the last minute and made various promises about access to the cameraman that he didn't keep. I had made an offer, on behalf of the For the People Network, which included a large fee and royalties on sales, contingent on my acceptance of the footage as genuine and access to the cameraman. Ray didn't acknowledge the offer, although he referred to it later (without the conditions) as though I was saying the film was genuine.

In June, I had another chance to talk to Ray. Dan Silver had arranged a lecture in London, and he and I and Ray and an associate met in a hotel lounge. Ray was perturbed, and insisted I had said the film was fraudulent. (What I had said was that I had found no reason to think it was genuine, which means I hadn't been given sufficient evidence.) I gave Ray a copy of my 1995 MUFON paper *Roswell Revisited,* in which I called into question Ray's motives, indicating that Ray seemed to be in this strictly for the money and didn't care whether or not the film was genuine. (Ray had himself said he wasn't a researcher and was only interested in the money.) This upset Ray and his associate. I also mentioned that I had called the Truman Library to ask about Truman's trips in 1947 and was told that he did not visit Texas or New Mexico between June and October of that year. Ray responded that Truman's Southwest trip was made in conjunction with his trip to Ottawa in June. Unfortunately, the meeting turned acrimonious, and once again we were disappointed in our quest.

Returning home again, I checked the *New York Times Index* and called the Truman Library once more and found out that Truman *did* make a very public trip to Ottawa around June 10; by train, at that. He spoke to the Canadian Parliament and was in full public view. Since Ottawa is 450 miles north of Washington and Dallas is 1,100 miles southwest, there seems little credible connection between the two sites.

Since I had made no headway with Santilli, I called Kiviat, who had bought the rights to the film. We had a number of conversations about bringing together an interdisciplinary group in Roswell to review the footage and be interviewed about it. Kiviat told me that I was "their man on Roswell," and that the goal of this project was the truth.

As the weeks went by, dates and places were changed. Finally, Kiviat asked me to go down to Washington, D.C., in early August 1995 to review the footage with Bruce Maccabee, who is experienced in film analysis. That was a good start, I thought, because I have known and respected Bruce as a colleague and friend for more than two decades. However, there was no mention of the interdisciplinary team—no pathologists or doctors, no cameramen, no film makers.

I was in Washington for three days. I spent most of one day with Bruce at his home carefully reviewing about 20 minutes of footage that Kiviat provided. The tape included a segment showing pieces of girders inscribed with what apparently were ancient Greek letters. These girders looked nothing at all like the lightweight I-beams with strange lavender symbols described by the Marcels. But there were some very interesting panels on the girders which had handholds for six-fingered hands. These would not have been cheap to manufacture.

Not surprisingly, President Truman was nowhere to be seen. There was no second autopsy of a similar being, without a gash on the right thigh, which others had said was on the tape. One story is that Santilli sold this to a collector to make some quick money. There was no saucer on the ground with a crane ready to haul it away as described by others. There was no sheet of paper with MJ-12 member Detlev Bronk's name plainly visible on it, as had been claimed.

The amount of footage was also much different. Originally, Santilli had claimed there were fifteen 10-minute reels. Then the story was fourteen 7-minute reels. Then it became twenty-two 3-minute reels, but several had film that couldn't be used. (Spring-wound Bell and Howell Filmo cameras used the latter 100-foot reels of film.)

People knowledgeable about the movie business indicated that many oldtimers almost routinely ran off extra copies of the stuff they filmed. But keeping extra copies of a highly classified film? It would seem extremely unusual that somebody with a clearance would blatantly violate security, or even be allowed to walk away with that many film cans, especially in 1947. Other explanations have been proposed: one that the cameraman had processed and shipped off to the government the bulk of the footage, but that he kept the reels requiring special processing for later processing. When he asked the government to get them, they never responded.

Experienced oldtime cameramen did say that the lack of image sharpness in close shots is because the Filmo camera did not have through-the-lens viewing. Focus could be set only from the front of those cameras, making focusing on closeups difficult.

Santilli had told me that Kodak had definitely dated the film from 1947, but that question has been debated much since. Many people said they were quoting the cameraman's answers to a variety of questions, but later had to admit that they were only going by what Santilli said. This is highly suspect, since Ray changed dates and crash locations and the homebase for the cameraman with aplomb, seemingly responding to details in various publications about Roswell. Both Fox and Channel 4 (London), which was making its documentary for showing in England, claimed they would interview the cameraman, but when both shows were aired on August 28, neither network had done so. In fact, I have yet to see any evidence that this cameraman is alive and, as discussed below, have very serious factual reasons for my skepticism.

The bodies in the film looked nothing like any aliens described to me by either Roswell eyewitnesses or abductees. None of the witnesses I interviewed mentioned aliens with six fingers, but there they were on each hand in the film. (The right hand of the alien in the film seemed to have been chopped off, and so might have been placed there from another body.) Each foot also had six toes. John Carpenter, a psychiatric social worker trained at the Menninger Clinic, confirms this analysis. He has worked on more than 130 alien abduction cases, and none of his witnesses have mentioned six fingers and only one said five. Almost all had said four long fingers, as the Roswell and San Agustin witnesses had.

The day after reviewing the tape, I spent the evening being interviewed below the Lincoln Memorial with the Washington Monument in the background to prove we were in Washington. Every few minutes, we had to stop as airliners passed overhead. Earlier that day, the crew had interviewed world-famous forensic pathologist Dr. Cyril Wecht, but I couldn't talk to him. Since researcher Linda Howe had mentioned that someone had said that the beings in the film were female earthlings with a genetic defect known as Turner's Syndrome, I called around and found a geneticist, located the Turner Syndrome Society, and attempted to get educated quickly. I continued my research along these lines after I returned home. The more I learned, the better the Turner's Syndrome explanation seemed.

The one-hour Fox special *Alien Autopsy: Fact or Fiction* was well put together, but was weak in several aspects. None of the long interview with Dr. Maccabee was used. A very short segment of my interview was used completely out of context. Many minutes were given over to a detective talking about trying to find the cameraman. All he wound up with was a trip to Florida to see someone in a Denny's restaurant who claimed he had been at a bar in Florida and heard someone say he had been at Roswell when the saucer crashed. I am absolutely certain many Army Air Force men who served at Roswell in 1947 eventually retired to Florida. (Both Counter-Intelligence Corps officer Rickett and General DuBose were living in Florida when I met with them.) No evidence of a cameraman was found.

The tearful, yet totally unsubstantiated testimony of Frankie Rowe was portrayed without any hint that there are many reasons to reject it. Her father was a fireman who supposedly saw the crashed saucer and alien bodies some 30 miles north of Roswell because of the fire that the crash caused. However, a former Roswell fire chief and a city councilman say trucks rarely, if ever, went out that far. And that a state police officer would bring a piece of wreckage from a highly classified crash site and show it to his buddies at the firehouse where Frankie was allowed to play with it, as maintained in the special, makes no sense to me in a state where national security was such a big issue.

Much of the show focused on trying to set up an either/or situation—either the footage was a hoax or it was of an actual alien autopsy. Many outstanding Hollywood special effects people pointed out that it would have been very difficult and expensive to fake such a gory autopsy. Certainly the organs didn't look like earthling ones, though body proportions were very earthling. However, the footage is not continuous, so we don't know what took place while the camera wasn't running.

There are two other, more important, problems with the footage. First, there was absolutely nothing in the film that linked it to Roswell, the Plains of San Agustin, alien spacecraft, or a crashed flying saucer. Second, there are other options. It could have been a real autopsy of a real earthling with a genetic defect such as Turner's Syndrome. The body seemed to be short, definitely female, but with no breasts; with unusual earlobes, a wide chest, and what seemed to be a somewhat webbed neck; i.e., more skin at the bottom than at the top. These characteristics, plus the unusual palate, the angle of the elbow, the length of the cranial bones, and others, all suggest Turner's. The eyes were large, but not like those described so often for aliens. There was a dark flap lifted off the eyes by the surgeons, but it apparently was not actually attached. Eyewitnesses have generally described the aliens as having holes for noses and ears rather than an almost normal human nose and real ear flaps, as shown in the footage.

The people shown conducting the autopsy did not seem to be taking any extraordinary, or even scientific, measures. Pathologists examining obviously alien life form and not making measurements, not weighing organs, not examining carefully? It is hard for me to believe.

I was further shocked by the segment featuring Dr. Wecht, who said that his first thought was that these bodies were those of Turner's Syndrome patients, but that survival of these patients into the teens "would have been rare." Having done my homework on

Turner's Syndrome—I spoke with a doctor who sees many TS patients, the parent of a young lady who has the condition, and have heard of a TS patient who is over 90 years old—I knew that this is simply not true. Most fetuses with the genetic defect, which includes the absence of an X chromosome and therefore only afflicts women, do not come to term. But one in about 2,500 live female births have the syndrome. Without growth hormone, they are almost always short, with an average height for hundreds of adults of 4'6". With estrogen and other hormones, secondary sexual characteristics can develop. Though most would otherwise be sterile, a number of TS women have given birth as a result of artificial practices. The disease does not kill at an early age despite a wide variety of related symptoms such as misplaced or horseshoe kidneys, certain heart defects, diabetes, hearing problems, and others.

I do have a grudging admiration for the way in which Ray Santilli has managed to manipulate ufologists and the media and make a load of money without solid backup for any of his stories. As of October 1, 1995, the cameraman's story and name have been changed. The location and date of the crash, despite always being associated with the Roswell events, have been changed to near Socorro, New Mexico, and late May or very early June. Other rumors include the notion that the cameraman actually has died and his son is making claims based on his diaries. Supposedly, the cameraman told Santilli that he was flown from Washington to Wright Field to Roswell, and then driven overland the 170 miles to Socorro. (Why this route, when Alamogordo, White Sands, Kirtland, and Sandia are much closer to Socorro than Roswell?) Yet because of the high ratings that TV shows featuring portions of the footage had around the world, the autopsy's bubble will not be burst for some time.

Those who do not know the truth seem to be blissful in their ignorance. One downer for me was to review loads of submissions about the footage on various computer networks. The percentage of garbage was awfully high. For instance, two of the comments after I got back from England were that I had both seen the footage and

had demonstrated that Truman was in Dallas at the time of the autopsy. Both were false.

And through the disinformation highway, order forms for the
raw Santilli footage—initially at $60 apiece—traveled around the
world. Even though the form carried four disclaimers—Santilli guaranteed nothing—many orders for the video were taken. I am sure
that once people saw the specials on Fox TV in the United States and
on UK Channel 4 that orders leaped.

Other people have done real research on aspects of the story as
well. First, it was determined that Kodak had not positively identified the film as from the 1947 time period. To be able to accurately
date the film by analysis of its composition would require Kodak to
have at least 50 full-width frames (less than three-seconds' worth)
showing actual scenes, not just from the leader. Several times, Santilli
promised to provide this from the original film, but he never did.
Then he claimed that he no longer had access to the actual footage,
which was supposedly being kept by his financial backer, Voelker
Spielberg, in a European vault.

A French researcher named Nicholas Maillard has really dug
into the various cameraman stories. Santilli had quietly told me and
others that the cameraman's name was Jack Barnett. Maillard located
a quote in *Elvis Presley from A to Z* stating that a Jack Barnett had
filmed Elvis for the first time in Cleveland in 1955. However, the
owner of the rights to that footage was a famous disc jockey named
Bill Randle who worked in both New York and Cleveland and was
the first to play Elvis records outside the South. Randle went on to
get a Ph.D. in history and then became a successful lawyer. He sold
the rights to the film to Santilli in 1992. He had indeed known Jack
Barnett.

However, Barnett, who was a well-known cameraman for Fox
Movietone News and later for NBC, died in 1967 in Chicago.
Although he was a war correspondent in Europe during World War
II, he was never in the military, according to both his death certifi-
cate and obituary information that I managed to obtain. Apparently
he did know Eisenhower and Truman.

Maillard also checked on the name later attributed to the cameraman—Jack Barrett. His military service ended in December 1945. He was not a motion picture cameraman though he did take some stills. He was in the movie industry as a grip for Columbia Pictures for 35 years, but he died in Los Angeles in August 1995. Interestingly, a graphologist to whom Maillard submitted Barrett's signature along with copies of the labels from some of the purported film cans indicated that the writing on the labels could have been Barrett's. Had the autopsy footage been stored in some Hollywood vault, perhaps from some science fiction film? After this, a new name for the cameraman—Bennett—was put forth.

Many special effects experts have been asked about the footage. In one survey, eight of nine said that the body in it was manufactured. One outfit, Truly Dangerous, even published more than 20 pages of instructions on how to make the body shown in the footage.

I spoke with Richard Doty, the former Air Force OSI agent. He said he had seen the film in the early 1980s and even then it was known not to be of aliens.

Bill Moore had an interesting suggestion in the September 1995 issue of *Saucer Smear,* a UFO gossip sheet published every month by Jim Moseley:

> The story I get is that there was a remote village in Brazil wherein quite a number of these cases [of Turner's Syndrome] had developed. The footage reportedly depicts scenes of actual autopsies performed upon two unfortunate victims around 1960 . . . shot opportunistically by some B grade sci-fi film outfit with the vague intention of somehow using it as the centerpiece of a feature film at some later date. . . .

This doesn't explain what might be a real film dating of 1947, but is as good an explanation as any.

My current position on the footage is that I believe it is possibly that of a genuine autopsy of an abnormal earthling, probably one with Turner's Syndrome. Alternatively, it might be a special effects triumph. But I can find no reason to relate it to crashed saucers or alien bodies in New Mexico in 1947. Although it has been exploited by Ray Santilli, I don't think he was responsible for creating it.

One positive result of all the discussion has been that far more people are thinking about UFOs and are willing to express themselves than had been the case just a couple of years ago. It's like the old Hollywood line—"I don't care what you say about me, just spell my name right."

At last count, parts of the footage have been seen in at least 36 countries. Because of the high ratings in Argentina, a major company there decided to publish a book about Roswell in Spanish. Dan Silver managed to book me for a series of seven lectures in England and a debate at the historic Oxford University Debate Union in October 1995. The question before the house: "This house believes that intelligent alien life has visited Planet Earth." My partner on the affirmative side was British solicitor Harry Harris, who played several audiotapes dealing with abduction cases. I presented a series of slides to cover major studies.

Our opponents included a pair of students who spoke very cleverly and humorously, but who gave no factual evidence, and a writer named Peter Brookesmith. He had written clever articles about UFOs, but he focused on quotes from contactees and tabloid stories while ignoring the data I presented. There was a packed house, and at the end a vote of the club members was taken to decide the winner. The result: Aye, 207; Nay, 140. Sixty percent of the Oxford Debating Society agreed with Harry and myself.

This vote was of special importance to me because I had found in the course of doing 40 interviews and seven lectures in England that the audiences and interviewers, though certainly friendly, were woefully uninformed about the scientific side of the UFO question. The results at the Debate Union confirm for me that, when presented with the facts, people will come down on the side of the truth.

12

THE BOTTOM LINE

I have approached reaching a conclusion about the Majestic-12 documents from three different directions. First, I have critically examined the available documents in comparison with other highly classified documents, with the kinds of papers I have seen at 15 archives, and those I handled myself in industry. I have consulted with a number of trusted professional colleagues, some of whom have spent decades working under security with a wide variety of documents. I have directly confronted the arguments of anti-MJ-12 writers rather than ignore them, and I have been honest about the questions we cannot yet answer.

Second, I have tried to take advantage of my more than 17 years of investigation of the Roswell incident and my more than 35 years of investigation of the cosmic Watergate. The seminal events of 1947 cannot be examined out of context. That agencies of the U.S. government have been withholding data about extraterrestrial flying saucers seen all over the world, in the sky and on the ground, by eye and with radar, is as certain as that the sun will rise tomorrow. That secrets can be kept from the public is also an absolute certainty.

Third, I have examined the behavior of the aliens, so far as we know it, and of the government, based on what little we have been able to observe, by putting myself in the shoes of each to come up with a behavioral approach to the actions of both groups and the impact that those actions might have on the public. Although I am not a psychologist or psychiatrist, I have interacted with all kinds of people in all kinds of places as a result of my more than 700 lectures, hundreds of classroom appearances and informal discussions, and many hundreds of media appearances, many of them on call-in radio shows. Since I almost always provide an address to which people can write for more information, I also receive a great deal of mail.

I am convinced that the documents, when carefully and objectively examined, lead to the conclusion that there indeed was an Operation Majestic-12. All of the Top Secret/MAJIC documents that have been discovered so far are old ones, the most recent being the Standard Operating Manual, which dates back to 1954. Of course I would like access to more recent documents. As a scientist who took great joy in working on leading-edge technology, I would like to know far more about what has been learned under the auspices of the Majestic-12 group and its successors. What are the origins of our visitors, their mode of propulsion, their motivation? Have official government representatives been dealing directly with aliens? Have we learned what the aliens know about our origins, the local galactic neighborhood association, the world of the mind and spirit?

When I read my first book about UFOs in 1958, my focus was on hard data. That was my role in life—dealing with technical questions associated with the design, evaluation, and testing of radiation shielding materials. I was heavy into exciting experiments with expensive and exotic materials at specialized facilities. The goal was to synthesize a mountain of data to determine what it all meant in practical terms.

Having found the very exciting privately published version of Project Blue Book Special Report 14 in about 1961, the challenge was the same: evaluation and interpretation of a mountain of data. The report had over 240 tables, maps, and charts covering a wide

variety of aspects of the UFO phenomenon. There were quality evaluations and categorizations of more than 3,000 sightings. There were
cross-comparisons between the knowns and the unknowns. There
were tables showing the size, color, velocity, and other characteristics of all the UFOs. I was in data heaven.

Although I still discuss the very important and exciting Special
Report 14 in all my lectures, that data is no longer my focus. Most
people have no trouble accepting the notion that humans are not
alone in the universe, that aliens are visiting, and that our governments are not telling all they know. In fact, as the polls show and my
personal experiences attest, the greater a person's education, the more
likely he is to accept flying saucer reality. What people really want
to know are the answers to the *why* questions.

1. Why have government agencies such as Majestic-12, the CIA,
   Defense Intelligence Agency, NSA, Air Force, etc., been covering up the UFO data mountain?
2. Why would aliens come here?
3. What difference does it make to us that flying saucers are visiting
   and that there was an official investigatory group reporting only
   to the president?<

Many years ago it was widely proclaimed that the reason the government wouldn't tell us about flying saucers was fear of panic.
Supposedly this was a legitimate fear, based upon the numbers of
people who supposedly took seriously Orson Welles's 1938 radio
broadcast of H. G. Wells's *War of the Worlds.*

I think references to the broadcast are red herrings. If it had been
about an actual invasion, with extraterrestrials destroying everyone
and everything in their path, panic would have been justified. But
as far as we can tell, aliens are not coming here to slash and burn. A
much more probable radio announcement would be that a delegation
of extraterrestrials would be landing to discuss trade, sharing of technology, and wisdom about the universe. Would there be large-scale
panic over that? I think not.

My feeling of history is that governments usually act out of their own self-interest, or at least what they believe to be their own self-interest. *National security* is one of the favorite buzz words of our time for politicians and bureaucrats who want to keep secrets from the public. But over the years, conditions change. Is a national security matter of 50 years ago still a national security matter today?

In 1947, the U.S. government may not have had any choice but to cover up the crashes in New Mexico. The world was in a terrible mess. It was a mere two years after the end of the most devastating war in history. Anywhere from 40 million to 70 million people were killed, the majority of them civilians. More than 1,600 cities were flattened, entire regions were blasted, and the world economy was shattered. Food, clothing, and shelter were in very short supply in many countries. The only countries spared were those in the Western Hemisphere, and the United States was far and away the foremost political, military, and economic power of the world.

After fighting a desperate war to defeat the greatest threat the world had ever experienced, could the U.S. government come out and say, "We thought you would like to know that our skies are being invaded by alien spacecraft whose origin and purpose we do not know. They have been observed near our most secret facilities in New Mexico, Tennessee, Washington, and elsewhere. Their technology is far beyond our own. We cannot stop them from entering our airspace. If they have evil intentions, we cannot defend against them." This message could not possibly be sent.

Such an announcement would have shook the world and might have stopped the postwar rebuilding in its tracks. In addition, if it had been revealed that the U.S. government was in possession of at least two flying discs and their crews, this would have told the Soviet Union, then building its military capabilities as rapidly as it could, that here was military technology which, if understood, could put them in the driver's seat.

Thus, it seems to me that another primary reason for the coverup is military secrecy. The U.S. had in its possession vehicles (or wreckage thereof) with the ability to fly at extremely high speed with incredible maneuverability and very little noise, and the ability to land and take off from areas little larger than themselves. They could literally fly circles around anything we had and would make wonderful weapons delivery and defense systems. Certainly no conventional systems under development at the time could duplicate these capabilities or defend against them. This would be of great military benefit to whomever could understand the secrets.

Thus the initial coverup makes sense. But why continue it to the modern era? There are several cogent, but not overwhelming, arguments.

1. Contrary to what debunkers say, it might take decades or centuries, not merely a few years, to be able to understand, duplicate, and economically mass produce the new technology revealed by the wreckage of the flying discs. Rule 1 for security is that you can't tell your friends anything without also telling your enemies. Opening the files would give competitors access to the new technology.

2. Although the cold war is over, we still have enemies around the world. A constant worry would be penetration of the research work by enemy spies and fear that they might discover the mode of propulsion or other new weapons technologies based on their own crashed saucer recoveries before we did. We don't want them to know we know they know.

3. If the public learned that other intelligent life was actually coming to our planet, many of our social institutions would be disrupted. Probably church attendance would increase tremendously, as would psychiatric admissions, and the stock market would go down. Perhaps most important from a political viewpoint, younger members of society, especially those who grew up with the space program, would push for a new view of ourselves. Instead of thinking of ourselves as Americans, Canadians, Peruvians, French, or Chinese, they would start to think of themselves as earthlings.

As idyllic as this sounds, I know of no government that wants its citizens to owe their primary allegiance to the planet instead of to the nation. (Look at the problems the UN has.) Nationalism is really the only game in town. The biggest fear of anybody in power, whether mayor, governor, or president, is losing that power. National governments do *not* want their subjects to have a planetwide orientation.

4. Certain religious groups would be very disturbed by any announcement that humans are not alone, even though this is presumed to be true by many Eastern religions, the Mormons, and others. Certain Christian fundamentalist sects have made public announcements that earthlings are the only intelligent life in the universe—let us hope they are wrong—and that this UFO stuff is the work of the devil. (I frequently hear this view on call-in shows.) These same people have been for years supporting the conservative politicians who, at least for the moment, hold the whip hand in American government at all levels. They could be left up a religious creek without a paddle if it were widely known that aliens—in all probability more advanced than us—were visiting.

Other religions might have problems with the theological implications of extraterrestrial life. For example, for over 1,000 years, the Catholic Church has been against the notion of reincarnation, which is an important idea for many religions. Any advanced civilization would investigate biology as well as the physical sciences. Doing so would mean gaining understanding of genetics and aging. This would lead to controlling disease and aging, suggesting that their members would live proportionately much longer than earthlings. And they would certainly investigate the world of the mind and spirit. Suppose they long ago recognized the kind of information that indicates reincarnation does occur, as discussed by psychiatrist Brian Weiss in two outstanding books: *Many Lives, Many Masters* and *Through Time into Healing.* If our government has learned about such work, they might well be disposed to withhold it in the interest of preserving the Church, a major influence on the lives and behavior of hundreds of millions of earthlings. You can't just take away an article of faith without replacing it with something else.

5. There might well be economic discombobulation brought about by even the mildest announcement of the most peaceful of alien visitations. Many thoughtful people, including the captains of economy, would undoubtedly feel that, since alien technology is so

far beyond ours, there would soon be new methods of energy production, ground transport, air transport, communications, medicine, computers, and other systems. But which of the old buggy whip manufacturers would build the new systems and which would fade into oblivion? Uncertainty is the enemy of the stock market.

We need look no farther than Eastern Europe to see what happens when there is sudden, large-scale economic upheaval. When the Berlin Wall came down it was widely believed that with freedom, democracy, and capitalism, everything would soon be splendid for the peoples of the old Soviet Empire. What they have found instead is increased crime, corruption, inflation, and loss of opportunity. We earthlings don't seem to be very good at handling large-scale economic changes without bloodshed.

6. The government may know things about the aliens that are truly terrible. Aliens eat earthlings. Aliens kidnap them to distant planets. Earthlings are sexual fodder for aliens to use. Earth is due to be destroyed. We are the booby prize in some celestial lottery.

Those with very-high-level security clearances and access to such terrible secrets may well believe that, since they know more than the public does, they must make the choices for us ignorant beings. This runs counter to democracy, wherein educated voters make rational decisions about their elected representatives.

A major assumption of all these arguments is that, when confronted with the truth, the public will do the wrong thing—panic, withdraw all their savings, sell their stocks, desert the churches, what have you. What our governments must recognize is that people will more often than not do the *right* thing when presented with correct information. They will not panic. They will do their best to survive. But they may not support the old authorities as they used to.

I have on occasion been asked pointblank if I really think the public should be told the truth. There is an obvious downside to the revelation of technical data related to flying saucers—the technology could be used for new weapons systems or some other form of coercion. I don't think that all the information should be put on the table. However, I believe humans need to know that we are being visited. In the long run, I think we will use the revelations for correct purposes.

I am convinced that our future is inextricably tied with the exploration of other planetary bodies and interactions with more advanced civilizations in our local galactic neighborhood. Our future is not limited by earth's resources, but by a failure to see that other worlds are in reach. I am not advocating the exploitation of new worlds a la the Spanish conquistadors and more recent plunderers. But despite crashes, explosions, failed missions, and variable funding, humans have continued to probe the skies and our reach is steadily becoming longer.

Part of my own faith in the public's ability to handle whatever it is our governments know comes from my own assessment of what spacefaring civilizations are like. Despite the vision of galactic battle shown in the *Star Wars* trilogy and other popular myths, I believe that space travelers will ultimately be peaceful. It seems to me that advancing technology means control of new and more powerful energy sources. As we have moved from human power to animal power to water power to steam, oil, electric, and nuclear power, we are learning that we must either learn to live at peace with our neighbors or be destroyed by the power available in our new sources of energy. Any civilization that has advanced enough to travel across space—meaning any civilization that is far beyond ours—has undoubtedly learned to live at peace with their neighbors—anybody they can reach—because of the immense power available in the energy sources they must be using.

This does not mean I believe aliens are necessarily coming here to "help" us—a common theme in sci-fi literature. So if they're not here to destroy us, and they're not here to help us, why are they here?

The question is a fair one, if somewhat egocentric. The first thing to consider is that the galactic neighborhood is not as big as some researchers make it out to be. Those seeking radio signals from distant civilizations often act as though visitors would have to come from other galaxies millions of light years away, and that they would be using the dumb old chemical rockets we are stuck with now. If that were the case, of course no one would be visiting. That would be like having to go from Canada to Australia to get a loaf of bread.

But this point of view is not the truth. There are about 1,000 stars within our local galactic neighborhood, meaning the region within 54 light years of earth—a mere walk down the block by galactic standards. According to an excellent study done by Terence Dickinson, one of North America's finest astronomy writers, 46 of those stars are very similar to our sun. Amongst astronomers, there seems to be a general consensus that sunlike stars are likely to have planets.

As Dickinson has pointed out, the star pair Zeta 1 and Zeta 2 Reticuli, in the southern sky constellation Reticulum (the Net) only 37 light years away from us, are sunlike stars about 100 times closer to each other than the sun is to our nearest stellar neighbor. They are also about 1 billion years older than the sun. A civilization that had a billion-year head start on us will certainly know things that we can't even dream of. Our own limited science has shown that nuclear fusion rockets can provide thrust far in excess of that provided by chemical rockets, and so interstellar travel may be as easy for other civilizations now as nonstop flight across the ocean is for us today. (Remember that less than 70 years ago, many people considered Charles Lindbergh to be crazy, or at least eccentric, to attempt to fly nonstop across the Atlantic Ocean. In 1995, about 10 million people made the trip.)

Once the travel is easy, the number of reasons for making the trip rapidly increases. From the aliens' point of view, they might have as many reasons for traveling here as we have for visiting San Francisco or London. Maybe the visitors are broadcasters with a weekly show called *Bloopers in the Boondocks*. Maybe they are graduate students doing theses on the development of primitive societies. Maybe we are somebody's colony, perhaps the Devil's Island of the interstellar neighborhood, which is how Georgia and Australia were founded. The original settlers might have been the bad boys and girls of the neighborhood, and that is why we are so nasty to each other. Or maybe the earth is the honeymoon capital of the neighborhood or the place with the best fishing and hunting. Advanced civilizations must have time for leisure, too.

There is one reason I believe that would be incumbent on any advanced civilizations—namely that they are concerned with their own security and survival. Thus, they have to pay attention to all the primitive societies in the neighborhood, and especially close attention to those showing signs of venturing beyond ancestral boundaries.

Earthlings had been showing signs of accelerating technological growth for some decades prior to World War II. The air was polluted with easily measured products of industrial development from mining and smelting, from large-scale agriculture, from power plants, and from electromagnetic radiation. The pace jumped during the early 1940s. By the end of the war, it would be perfectly clear to any alien observers that this primitive society, whose major activity seemed to be tribal warfare, would within about 100 years—a short time by cosmic measures—be turning starward. There were three obvious indicators:

- Powerful rockets such as the V-2
- Nuclear weapons
- Powerful electromagnetic devices such as those used for advanced radar systems

Combining these three technologies with the will to progress would lead to star travel. If you were an alien, would you wish to have these people, for whom every new frontier seemed to become a new place to battle, move out without some advance warning? I doubt it.

I don't believe it is coincidence that the first crash of flying saucers occurred in southeastern New Mexico, the only place on the globe in 1947 where all three of these technologies could be monitored. The first atomic explosion took place at Trinity Site at the White Sands Missile Range. All American firings of captured German V-2 rockets took place at White Sands as well. In addition, our best radar systems were being used there to track the rockets, which often went astray.

In other words, I believe that the aliens are here primarily for their own purposes, one of which is to make sure that our brand of "friendship" is not visited upon other civilizations in the neighborhood. If we can't get our act together, they will keep us from leaving.

I also believe that the members of Operation Majestic-12, a very impressive group, would have come to similar conclusions, especially in view of their remarkable contributions during World War II. They were all aware that the Germans were far ahead of the Allies in technology at the beginning of the war. They knew the United States could never again be protected by the oceans in time of general war. They would have done everything possible to study advanced alien technology and keep our enemies from beating us to the punch which that technology might represent.

However, the cold war now being over, it's time for planetary discussion as to what it means to be part of a galactic neighborhood. International conferences should be convened, perhaps through the United Nations, to evaluate the religious, economic, military, political, and philosophical implications of our situation with regard to extraterrestrial visitors. I hope we can soon qualify for admission to the cosmic kindergarten—or at least the preschool. I am sure space will be the place in the future. My own personal goal is to help move earthlings down this path. The current members of Operation Majestic-12 (or whatever it is now called) must have the courage to do the same.

APPENDIX A

SECRET

MAJESTIC-12
BRIEFING DOCUMENT

TOP SECRET / MAJIC
EYES ONLY
NATIONAL SECURITY INFORMATION

· · · · · · · · · · · · ·
· TOP SECRET ·
· · · · · · · · · · · · ·

001

EYES ONLY   COPY ONE OF ONE.

BRIEFING DOCUMENT: OPERATION MAJESTIC 12

PREPARED FOR PRESIDENT-ELECT DWIGHT D. EISENHOWER: (EYES ONLY)

18 NOVEMBER, 1952

WARNING! This is a TOP SECRET - EYES ONLY document containing
compartmentalized information essential to the national security
of the United States. EYES ONLY ACCESS to the material herein
is strictly limited to those possessing Majestic-12 clearance
level. Reproduction in any form or the taking of written or
mechanically transcribed notes is strictly forbidden.

· · · · · · · · · · · · ·
· TOP SECRET ·
· · · · · · · · · · · · ·

TOP SECRET / MAJIC

EYES ONLY   EYES ONLY   T52-EXEMPT (E)

00

TOP SECRET / MAJIC
EYES ONLY
* TOP SECRET *
....

EYES ONLY

COPY <u>ONE</u> OF <u>ONE</u>.

SUBJECT: OPERATION MAJESTIC-12 PRELIMINARY BRIEFING FOR
PRESIDENT-ELECT EISENHOWER.

DOCUMENT PREPARED 18 NOVEMBER, 1952.

BRIEFING OFFICER: ADM. ROSCOE H. HILLENKOETTER (MJ-1)

NOTE: This document has been prepared as a preliminary briefing
only. It should be regarded as introductory to a full operations
briefing intended to follow.

* * * * * *

OPERATION MAJESTIC-12 is a TOP SECRET Research and Development/
Intelligence operation responsible directly and only to the
President of the United States. Operations of the project are
carried out under control of the Majestic-12 (Majic-12) Group
which was established by special classified executive order of
President Truman on 24 September, 1947, upon recommendation by
Dr. Vannevar Bush and Secretary James Forrestal. (See Attachment
"A".) Members of the Majestic-12 Group were designated as follows:

       Adm. Roscoe H. Hillenkoetter
       Dr. Vannevar Bush
       Secy. James V. Forrestal*
       Gen. Nathan F. Twining
       Gen. Hoyt S. Vandenberg
       Dr. Detlev Bronk
       Dr. Jerome Hunsaker
       Mr. Sidney W. Souers
       Mr. Gordon Gray
       Dr. Donald Menzel
       Gen. Robert M. Montague
       Dr. Lloyd V. Berkner

The death of Secretary Forrestal on 22 May, 1949, created
a vacancy which remained unfilled until 01 August, 1950, upon
which date Gen. Walter B. Smith was designated as permanent
replacement.

....
* TOP SECRET *
....

TOP SECRET / MAJIC

EYES ONLY

EYES ONLY

T52-EXEMPT (E)

EYES ONLY   COPY ONE OF ONE.

On 24 June, 1947, a civilian pilot flying over the Cascade
Mountains in the State of Washington observed nine flying
disc-shaped aircraft traveling in formation at a high rate
of speed. Although this was not the first known sighting
of such objects, it was the first to gain widespread attention
in the public media. Hundreds of reports of sightings of
similar objects followed. Many of these came from highly
credible military and civilian sources. These reports resulted in independent efforts by several different elements
of the military to ascertain the nature and purpose of these
objects in the interests of national defense. A number of
witnesses were interviewed and there were several unsuccessful
attempts to utilize aircraft in efforts to pursue reported
discs in flight. Public reaction bordered on near hysteria
at times.

In spite of these efforts, little of substance was learned
about the objects until a local rancher reported that one
had crashed in a remote region of New Mexico located approximately seventy-five miles northwest of Roswell Army Air
Base (now Walker Field).

On 07 July, 1947, a secret operation was begun to assure
recovery of the wreckage of this object for scientific study.
During the course of this operation, aerial reconnaissance
discovered that four small human-like beings had apparently
ejected from the craft at some point before it exploded.
These had fallen to earth about two miles east of the wreckage
site. All four were dead and badly decomposed due to action
by predators and exposure to the elements during the approximately one week time period which had elapsed before their
discovery. A special scientific team took charge of removing
these bodies for study. (See Attachment "C".) The wreckage
of the craft was also removed to several different locations.
(See Attachment "B".) Civilian and military witnesses in
the area were debriefed, and news reporters were given the
effective cover story that the object had been a misguided
weather research balloon.

TOP SECRET / MAJIC
EYES ONLY
• • • • • • • • • • • •
• TOP SECRET •
• • • • • • • • • • • •

A-4

004

COPY <u>ONE</u> OF <u>ONE</u>.

<u>EYES ONLY</u>

A covert analytical effort organized by Gen. Twining and
Dr. Bush acting on the direct orders of the President, resulted in a preliminary concensus (19 September, 1947) that
the disc was most likely a short range reconnaissance craft.
This conclusion was based for the most part on the craft's
size and the apparent lack of any identifiable provisioning.
(See Attachment "D".) A similar analysis of the four dead
occupants was arranged by Dr. Bronk. It was the tentative
conclusion of this group (30 November, 1947) that although
these creatures are human-like in appearance, the biological
and evolutionary processes responsible for their development
has apparently been quite different from those observed or
postulated in homo-sapiens. Dr. Bronk's team has suggested
the term "Extra-terrestrial Biological Entities", or "EBEs",
be adopted as the standard term of reference for these
creatures until such time as a more definitive designation
can be agreed upon.

Since it is virtually certain that these craft do not originate in any country on earth, considerable speculation has
centered around what their point of origin might be and how
they get here. Mars was and remains a possibility, although
some scientists, most notably Dr. Menzel, consider it more
likely that we are dealing with beings from another solar
system entirely.

Numerous examples of what appear to be a form of writing
were found in the wreckage. Efforts to decipher these have
remained largely unsuccessful. (See Attachment "E".)
Equally unsuccessful have been efforts to determine the
method of propulsion or the nature or method of transmission
of the power source involved. Research along these lines
has been complicated by the complete absence of identifiable
wings, propellers, jets, or other conventional methods of
propulsion and guidance, as well as a total lack of metallic
wiring, vacuum tubes, or similar recognizable electronic
components. (See Attachment "F".) It is assumed that the
propulsion unit was completely destroyed by the explosion
which caused the crash.

• • • • • • • • • • • • •
• TOP SECRET •
• • • • • • • • • • • • •

<u>EYES ONLY</u> TOP SECRET / MAJIC
EYES ONLY

T52-EXEMPT (E)

004

TOP SECRET / MAJIC
EYES ONLY

005

•••••••••••••
• TOP SECRET •
•••••••••••••

A need for as much additional information as possible about
these craft, their performance characteristics and their
purpose led to the undertaking known as U.S. Air Force Project
SIGN in December, 1947. In order to preserve security, liason
between SIGN and Majestic-12 was limited to two individuals
within the Intelligence Division of Air Materiel Command whose
role was to pass along certain types of information through
channels. SIGN evolved into Project GRUDGE in December, 1948.
The operation is currently being conducted under the code name
BLUE BOOK, with liason maintained through the Air Force officer
who is head of the project.

On 06 December, 1950, a second object, probably of similar
origin, impacted the earth at high speed in the El Indio -
Guerrero area of the Texas - Mexican boder after following
a long trajectory through the atmosphere. By the time a
search team arrived, what remained of the object had been almost
totally incinerated. Such material as could be recovered was
transported to the A.E.C. facility at Sandia, New Mexico, for
study.

Implications for the National Security are of continuing importance in that the motives and ultimate intentions of these
visitors remain completely unknown. In addition, a significant
upsurge in the surveillance activity of these craft beginning
in May and continuing through the autumn of this year has caused
considerable concern that new developments may be imminent.
It is for these reasons, as well as the obvious international
and technological considerations and the ultimate need to
avoid a public panic at all costs, that the Majestic-12 Group
remains of the unanimous opinion that imposition of the
strictest security precautions should continue without inter-
ruption into the new administration. At the same time, contingency plan MJ-1949-04P/78 (Top Secret - Eyes Only) should
be held in continued readiness should the need to make a
public announcement present itself. (See Attachment "G".)

TOP SECRET / MAJIC
EYES ONLY

· · · · · · · · · · · · · ·
· TOP SECRET ·
· · · · · · · · · · · · · ·

EYES ONLY   COPY <u>ONE</u> OF <u>ONE</u>.

ENUMERATION OF ATTACHMENTS:

• ATTACHMENT "A"........Special Classified Executive
                       Order #092447. (TS/EO)

• ATTACHMENT "B"........Operation Majestic-12 Status
                       Report #1, Part A. 30 NOV '47.
                       (TS-MAJIC/EO)

• ATTACHMENT "C"........Operation Majestic-12 Status
                       Report #1, Part B. 30 NOV '47.
                       (TS-MAJIC/EO)

• ATTACHMENT "D"........Operation Majestic-12 Preliminary
                       Analytical Report. 19 SEP '47.
                       (TS-MAJIC/EO)

• ATTACHMENT "E"........Operation Majestic-12 Blue Team
                       Report #5. 30 JUN '52.
                       (TS-MAJIC/EO)

• ATTACHMENT "F"........Operation Majestic-12 Status
                       Report #2. 31 JAN '48.
                       (TS-MAJIC/EO)

• ATTACHMENT "G"........Operation Majestic-12 Contingency
                       Plan MJ-1949-04P/78: 31 JAN '49.
                       (TS-MAJIC/EO)

• ATTACHMENT "H"........Operation Majestic-12, Maps and
                       Photographs Folio (Extractions).
                       (TS-MAJIC/EO)

· · · · · · · · · · · · · ·
· TOP SECRET ·
TOP SECRET / MAJIC
EYES ONLY

EYES ONLY   T52-EXEMPT (E)

TOP SECRET / MAJIC
EYES ONLY   0 0 7

⁕ TOP SECRET ⁕

EYES ONLY   COPY ONE OF ONE.

ATTACHMENT "A"

⁕ TOP SECRET ⁕

EYES ONLY TOP SECRET / MAJIC   T52-EXEMPT (E)
EYES ONLY   0 0 7

A-3
TOP SECRET
EYES ONLY
THE WHITE HOUSE
WASHINGTON

008

September 24, 1947.

MEMORANDUM FOR THE SECRETARY OF DEFENSE

Dear Secretary Forrestal:

  As per our recent conversation on this matter,
you are hereby authorized to proceed with all due
speed and caution upon your undertaking. Hereafter
this matter shall be referred to only as Operation
Majestic Twelve.

  It continues to be my feeling that any future
considerations relative to the ultimate disposition
of this matter should rest solely with the Office
of the President following appropriate discussions
with yourself, Dr. Bush and the Director of Central
Intelligence.

Harry Truman

TOP SECRET
EYES ONLY

008

APPENDIX B

LETTER FROM GENERAL TWINING
TO GENERAL SCHULGEN

This letter, which was published in the January 1969 Condon Report, was only classified Secret, and so could not discuss information that was classified Top Secret or above.

23 September 1947

SUBJECT: AMC Opinion Concerning "Flying Discs"
     TO: Commanding General
          Army Air Forces
          Washington 25, D.C.

ATTENTION: Brig. General George Schulgen
            AC/AS-2

1. As requested by AC/AS-2 there is presented below the considered opinion of this Command concerning the so-called "Flying Discs." This opinion is based on interrogation report data furnished by AC/AS-2 and preliminary studies by personnel of T-2 and Aircraft Laboratory, Engineering Division T-3. This opinion was arrived at in a conference between personnel from the Air Institute of

Technology, Intelligence T-2, Office, Chief of Engineering Division, and the Aircraft, Power Plant and Propeller Laboratories of Engineering Division T-3.

2. It is the opinion that:

a. The phenomenon reported is something real and not visionary or fictitious.

b. There are objects probably approximating the shape of a disc, of such appreciable size as to appear to be as large as man-made aircraft.

c. There is a possibility that some of the incidents may be caused by natural phenomena, such as meteors.

d. The reported operating characteristics such as extreme rates of climb, maneuverability (particularly in roll), and action which must be considered evasive when sighted or contacted by friendly aircraft and radar, lend belief to the possibility that some of the objects are controlled either manually, automatically or remotely.

e. The apparent common description of the objects is as follows:

(1) Metallic or light reflecting surface.

(2) Absence of trail, except in a few instances when the object apparently was operating under high performance conditions.

(3) Circular or elliptical in shape, flat on bottom and domed on top.

(4) Several reports of well kept formation flights varying from three to nine objects.

(5) Normally no associated sound, except in three instances a substantial rumbling roar was noted.

(6) Level flight speeds normally above 300 knots are estimated.

f. It is possible within the present U.S. knowledge—provided extensive detailed development is undertaken—to construct a piloted aircraft which has the general description of the object in subparagraph (e) above which would be capable of an approximate range of 7000 miles at subsonic speeds.

g. Any developments in this country along the lines indicated would be extremely expensive, time consuming and at the considerable expense of current projects and therefore, if directed, should be set up independently of existing projects.

h. Due consideration must be given the following:

(1) The possibility that these objects are of domestic origin—the product of some high security project not known to AC/AS-2 or this Command.

(2) The lack of physical evidence in the shape of crash recovered exhibits which would undeniably prove the existence of these objects.

(3) The possibility that some foreign nation has a form of propulsion possibly nuclear, which is outside of our domestic knowledge.

3. It is recommended that:

a. Headquarters, Army Air Forces issue a directive assigning a priority, security classification and Code Name for a detailed study of this matter to include the preparation of complete sets of all available and pertinent data which will then be made available to the Army, Navy, Atomic Energy Commission, JRDB, the Air Force Scientific Advisory Group, NACA, and the RAND and NEPA projects for comments and recommendations, with a preliminary report to be forwarded within 15 days of receipt of the data and a detailed report thereafter every 30 days as the investigation develops. A complete interchange of data should be effected.

4. Awaiting a specific directive AMC will continue the investigation within its current resources in order to more closely define the nature of the phenomenon. Detailed Essential Elements of Information will be formulated immediately for transmittal thru channels.

N. F. TWINING
Lieutenant General, U.S.A.
Commanding

APPENDIX C

INSIDER INFORMATION UNCOVERED DURING AUTHENTICATION OF MAJESTIC-12 DOCUMENTS

This appendix lists information that was not known to UFO researchers before we began authenticating the Eisenhower briefing, the Truman-Forrestal memo, and the Cutler-Twining memo.

DONALD MENZEL'S CONNECTIONS AND TALENTS

1. Longer continuous association with NSA and predecessor Navy agency than anyone else (30 years as of 1960).
2. Top Secret Ultra clearance and work with CIA.
3. Classified work for many major contractors.
4. Close connections with Vannevar Bush from 1934 on.
5. Extraordinary discretion concerning classified matters (brought out in 1,300 pages of testimony at his loyalty hearings).
6. Expert cryptanalyst; taught cryptanalysis before World War II.
7. Expert knowledge of another symbolic language (Japanese).
8. Frequent trips to New Mexico on government expense account during 1947 and 1948.
9. Suddenly left consulting position at ERA in summer of 1947 to work on highly classified matter.

10. Strong engineering orientation, which is very unusual for an astronomer.
11. Close connections with Detlev Bronk, Lloyd Berkner, and various space scientists.
12. Head of Naval Reserve Communications Unit 1-1, Cambridge, Massachusetts.
13. His papers at Harvard require three different permissions for access, rather than being easily accessible.

SPECIAL DATES

1. November 18, 1952. Date of MJ-12 briefing. Eisenhower was briefed in Pentagon vault, although no record has yet been found of the briefing. References to other still-classified briefings for Eisenhower on this date found in OSD files. General Twining was definitely at one of the Pentagon briefings with Eisenhower.
2. September 24, 1947. Date of Truman-Forrestal memo. Only date in last eight months of 1947 when Bush met with Truman. Forrestal was also present. Bush and Forrestal met prior to Truman meeting, and left together.
3. August 1, 1950. Date when Walter Bedell Smith was named permanent member of MJ-12. Only date in first 10 months of 1950 when Smith met with Truman. The meeting was off the record and not publicized.
4. September 19, 1947. Briefing notes preliminary analytical report—directed by General Twining—given on this day. Twining flew from Ohio to Washington, D.C. on September 18, and returned to Ohio on September 19.

OTHER ESSENTIAL INFORMATION

1. The Cutler-Twining memo has neither a signature nor an /s/. Years after the memo was found, it was discovered that Cutler was out of the country on that date, and so could not have signed the memo.

2. James Lay had an off-the-record meeting with Eisenhower at 2:30 P.M. on July 14, 1954—the date of the Cutler-Twining memo—and a phone conversation with Eisenhower at 4:30 P.M. that day.

3. The typeface of the Cutler-Twining memo is exactly the same size and style as used in other NSC memos between 1953 and 1955.

4. The phrase "your concurrence in the above change of arrangements is assumed" apparently used by Cutler and Lay in highly classified memos to avoid necessity of response.

5. Placing a slant red pencil mark through the security marking—as appears on the Cutler-Twining memo—is standard procedure for declassifiers at repositories.

6. The use of a period after the date on the Truman-Forrestal memo was found to be standard style for the office of Vannevar Bush.

7. The supposedly odd date format of *day month comma year* occurs in numerous examples in published works as well as in items sent by both Walter Bedell Smith and Roscoe Hillenkoetter.

8. The discovery of a memo from Lay to Cutler dated July 16, 1954, in which Lay speaks of keeping the pressure off Cutler when he returns by taking care of things.

9. It was standard practice for highly classified memos to obscure the subject rather than to spell it out clearly.

10. There can be identical signatures by the same person, although they are very likely not to be consecutive signatures.

11. During and after the 1952 election campaign, Eisenhower was briefed by Walter Bedell Smith, then head of the CIA, on national security and defense matters.

12. General Robert Montague, although little known by the public, was an appropriate person for membership in MJ-12 because of his position at Fort Bliss, which included command of White Sands Missile Range; his appointment as head of the Armed Forces Special Weapons Centre at Kirtland; and because he was well-known to General Twining, his West Point classmate.

13. Government documents of that time period were occasionally

typed using one typewriter for the text and a different one for the date.

14. The numerical portion of the date on the Truman-Forrestal memo ("24, 1947.") was done on a different typewriter than that used for the text of the letter.

15. Many government offices of that time period used varying formats, styles, and typewriter faces for their classified memos, letters, and so on, rather than always being consistent.

16. Huge numbers of documents from the Truman and Eisenhower administrations are still classified even after recent classification review. The Eisenhower Library has at least 100,000 pages of classified NSC material still unreviewed and unavailable.

17. James Forrestal's papers at Princeton require permission for access rather than being open.

18. Dictation Onionskin—the type of paper used for the copy of the Cutler-Twining memo found in the National Archives—was made only in bid lots from 1953 through the mid-1970s.

SOME EXCLUSIONS TO THE FREEDOM OF INFORMATION ACT

The following is a list of exclusions to material that can be requested under FOIA. These are regulations that apply just to FBI material, and they illustrate the almost insurmountable stumbling blocks that face any researcher looking for UFO material.

SUBSECTIONS OF TITLE 5, UNITED STATES CODE, SECTION 552

(b) (1) (A) specifically authorized under criteria established by an Executive order to be kept secret in the interest of national defense or foreign policy and (B) are in fact properly classified pursuant to such Executive order;

(b) (2) related solely to the internal personnel rules and practices of an agency;

(b) (3) specifically exempted from disclosure by statute (other than section 52b of this title), provided that such statute (A) requires that the matters be withheld from the public in such a manner as to leave no discretion on the issue, or (B) establishes particular criteria for withholding or refers to particular types of matters to be withheld;

(b) (4) trade secrets and commercial or financial information obtained from a person and privileged or confidential;

(b) (5) inter-agency or intra-agency memorandums or letters which would not be available by law to a party other than an agency in litigation with the agency;

(b) (6) personnel and medical files and similar files the disclosure of which would constitute a clearly unwarranted invasion of personal privacy;

(b) (7) records or information compiled for law enforcement purposes, but only to the extent that the production of such law enforcement records or information (A) could reasonably be expected to interfere with enforcement proceedings, (B) would deprive a person of a right to a fair trial or an impartial adjudication, (C) could reasonably be expected to constitute an unwarranted invasion of personal privacy, (D) could reasonably be expected to disclose the identity of a confidential source, including a State, local, or foreign agency or authority or any private institution which furnished information on a confidential basis, and, in the case of a record or information compiled by a criminal law enforcement authority in the course of a criminal investigation, or by an agency conducting a lawful national security intelligence investigation, information furnished by a confidential source, (E) would disclose techniques and procedures for law enforcement investigations or prosecutions, or would disclose guidelines for law enforcement investigations or prosecutions if such disclosure could reasonably be expected to risk circumvention of the law, or (F) could reasonably be expected to endanger the life or physical safety of any individual;

(b) (8) contained in or related to examination, operating, or condition reports prepared by, on behalf of, or for the use of an agency responsible for the regulation or supervision of financial institutions, or

(b) (9) geological and geophysical information and data, including maps, concerning wells.

SUBSECTIONS OF TITLE 5, UNITED STATES CODE, SECTION 552A

(d) (5) information compiled in reasonable anticipation of a civil action proceeding;

(j) (2) material reporting investigative efforts pertaining to the enforcement of criminal law including efforts to prevent, control, or reduce crime or apprehend criminals, except records of arrest;

(k) (1) information which is currently and properly classified pursuant to Executive Order 12356 in the interest of the national defense or foreign policy, for example, information involving intelligence sources or methods;

(k) (2) investigatory material compiled for law enforcement purposes, other than criminal, which did not result in loss of a right, benefit or privilege under Federal programs, or which would identify a source who furnished information pursuant to a promise that his/her identity would be held in confidence;

(k) (3) material maintained in connection with providing protective services to the President of the United States or any other individual pursuant to the authority of Title 18, United States Code, Section 3056;

(k) (4) required by statute to be maintained and used solely as statistical records;

(k) (5) investigatory material compiled solely for the purpose of determining suitability, eligibility, or qualifications for Federal civilian employment or for access to classified information, the disclosure of which would reveal the identity of the person who furnished information pursuant to a promise that his identity would be held in confidence;

(k) (6) testing or examination material used to determine individual qualifications for appointment or promotion in Federal Government service the release of which would compromise the testing or examination process;

(k) (7) material used to determine potential for promotion in the armed services, the disclosure of which would reveal the identity of the person who furnished the material pursuant to a promise that his identity would be held in confidence.

APPENDIX E

AIR FORCE RESPONSE TO SENATOR PATTY MURRAY

When Senator Patty Murray of Washington requested information about the events in Roswell in July 1947, Lieutenant Colonel Shubert of the Air Force sent her this one-page letter, dated August 25, 1993. (Following this letter is my own response to Shubert.)

The Honorable Patty Murray
United States Senator
2988 Jackson Federal Building
915 2nd Avenue
Seattle, Washington 98174

Dear Ms. Murray:

This is in reply to your inquiry to the Secretary of Defense in behalf of Mr. Michael C. Atkins regarding events occurring near Roswell, New Mexico, in July 1947.

The Air Force possesses no records regarding this incident. We are not aware that any other governmental department or agency, other than the National Archives, possesses any records pertaining to UFOs.

As information, the Air Force began investigating UFOs in 1948 under a program called Project Sign. Later, the program's name was changed to Project Grudge and, in 1953, it became known as Project Blue Book. On December 17, 1969, the Secretary of the Air Force announced the termination of Project Blue Book. The decision to discontinue UFO investigations was based on a number of factors, including reports and studies by the University of Colorado and the National Academy of Sciences, as well as past UFO studies and the Air Force's two decades of experience investigating UFO reports.

As a result of these investigations, studies, and experience, the conclusions of Project Blue Book were: 1) no UFO reported, investigated and evaluated by the Air Force has ever given any indication of threat to our national security, 2) there has been no evidence submitted to, or discovered by, the Air Force that sightings categorized as "unidentified" represent technological developments or principles beyond the range of present-day scientific knowledge and, 3) there has been no evidence indicating that sightings categorized as "unidentified" are extraterrestrial vehicles.

Similar information is being sent to several Members of Congress in response to their inquiries.

We appreciate your interest in this matter and trust this information is helpful.

Sincerely,
THOMAS W. SHUBERT, Lt Col, USAF
Congressional Inquiry Division
Office of Legislative Liaison

Feb. 11, 1994

Thomas W. Shubert, Lt. Col. USAF
Congressional Inquiry Division
Office of Legislative Liaison
Office of the Secretary
Department of the Air Force
Washington, DC 20330-1000

Dear Colonel Shubert:

Mr. Michael C. Atkins has sent me a copy of your letter of August 25, 1993, to Senator Patty Murray of Washington State, concerning UFOs. I am writing to inform you that whoever provided the information in the letter has provided both inaccurate information and misleading information, as will be established below.

Perhaps I should add that I have had a serious professional interest in UFOs since 1958, have lectured on the subject "Flying Saucers <u>ARE</u> Real" to more than 600 colleges and 100 professional groups in all 50 states, provided testimony to the congressional hearings of July 29, 1968, and written 62 papers about UFOs in addition to coauthoring <u>Crash at Corona</u>, a book about the U.S. government's recovery and coverup of crashed saucers in New Mexico in 1947.

To simplify the exposition, I will use the term USAF to include both the Air Force and the Army Air Force, which was the proper name until September 1947. I will also use the term "you" rather than "the letter to Senator Murray."

1. USAF began its investigation into flying saucers (the term UFO was invented by USAF Captain Edward Ruppelt after 1950) at least as early as June 1947, NOT in 1948 as you state. There were many newspaper articles throughout the U.S. indicating great government concern with the well over 1,000 flying disc reports made in more than 40 states shortly after the publicity given to pilot Kenneth Arnold's sighting of nine objects in Washington State on June 24, 1947. Ruppelt's comments will be enclosed.

A. Serious USAF investigation focused on the crashed saucer recovered outside Roswell, New Mexico in early July 1947. USAF
Colonel William Blanchard, Commander of the 509th
Composite Bomb Group and Roswell Army Air Field, ordered
his Intelligence Officer, Major Jesse Marcel, to accompany a
rancher, who had brought very strange wreckage into the office
of Roswell Sheriff Wilcox, back to the site of the discovery of
the wreckage with a Counter Intelligence Corps (later OSI)
Officer on July 6, 1947. Not incidentally, the 509th dropped the
atomic bombs on Hiroshima, Nagasaki, and in Operations
Crossroads in the Pacific in 1946. Colonel Blanchard eventually
became a four-star USAF general and USAF vice chief of staff.
All officers of the 509th were hand-picked. The 509th was part
of the 8th Air Force.

B. When Major Marcel returned to the base on July 8 with a vehicle loaded with pieces of the very strange wreckage, Colonel
Blanchard ordered USAF Lt. Walter Haut to issue a press release indicating that wreckage of a flying disc had indeed been
recovered. He also ordered Major Marcel to get a B-29 crew to
take the major and some of the wreckage to Wright Field in
Ohio with a stop at 8th Air Force HQ in Fort Worth, Texas.

USAF General Roger Ramey, Commander of the 8th Air
Force, received instructions prior to Major Marcel's arrival to
cover up the story and never to talk about the wreckage again
through his chief of staff, Colonel T. J. DuBose (later a USAF
general), who got them directly from USAF General Clements
McMullen, who was basically acting as Commander of the
USAF SAC under USAF General Kenney. Testimony from
both Marcel and DuBose (both deceased) is on file and readily
available. General Ramey ordered Marcel to say nothing and
told the press (which was waiting because Haut's press release
went out on the newswire about noon New Mexico time) that
the wreckage they were observing was that of a radar reflector
from a weather balloon.

Ramey had replaced the real wreckage with the radar reflec-

tor foil-like material and got away with this intentional deception for 31 years until I got involved. An FBI memo (enclosed)
indicates the wreckage was NOT that of a weather balloon and
was shipped on a special flight to Wright Field. The notion that
Blanchard and Marcel couldn't recognize the wreckage of a
radar reflector from a weather balloon is absurd, as is the notion that pieces of one could cover an area 3/4 mile long and
hundreds of feet wide and that the wooden sticks couldn't be
broken, burnt, or cut and would have strange pastel symbols.
General Ramey's cover story went out about four hours after
Haut's. Both releases were too late for morning papers. Haut's
made it into evening papers from Chicago west. I will enclose
copies of several of these. Some include the text of the release.

   The Roswell story is told in detail in the three books and
about eight long papers that have been published. Walter Haut
is alive and well (in Roswell), as is Jesse Marcel, Jr., M.D., pilot,
flight surgeon, and member of military aircraft accident investigating teams who also handled the very unusual material. Both
have given notarized testimony.

C. General Nathan Twining's Sept. 23, 1947 formerly Secret letter (enclosed) concerning UFOs clearly indicates that significant effort had been put into the flying saucer problem by then,
   long before Sign, Grudge, and Blue Book. The National
   Archives copy of the original lists five top technical men from
   AMC as contributing to the letter. Twining was head of the Air
   Materiel Command and later went on to become vice chief and
   then chief of staff of the USAF, and eventually served as chairman of the Joint Chiefs.

2. The notion that Project Blue Book and its predecessors, Sign and
Grudge, were the sum total of Air Force UFO investigations as implied in your letter is easily demolished.

A. A Jan. 31, 1949 FBI memo states that Army and Air Force
   Intelligence (NOT Sign and Grudge or later Blue Book) consider the subject of flying saucers Top Secret. I certainly could-

n't find any Top Secret or TS Plus files in the Blue Book material.

B. The problem of unidentified aerial objects is directly related to the mission of the Air Defense Command with its continent-wide radar net, computers, closed communications system, and instrument aircraft ready to be scrambled to identify and monitor the characteristics of uncorrelated targets. Whether one is seeking Soviet aircraft and missiles or flying saucers matters not; the technical effort is the same. Project Blue Book had a major, a sergeant, a few secretaries, a bunch of filing cabinets, and a once-a-month visit from a quiet astronomer. There were no computers, radars, instruments, or closed communications system. Perhaps of most importance, it had no need-to-know for Air Defense Command data. It accepted and occasionally investigated civilian reports. Of far greater interest are reports from military personnel.

C. According to the very memo that resulted in the December 1969 closure of Project Blue Book (the October 20, 1969 memo from General Carroll Bolender—copy enclosed), "Moreover reports of UFOs which could affect National Security are made in accordance with JANAP 146 or Air Force Manual 55-11 and are not part of the Blue Book system. . . . However, as already stated, reports of UFOs which could affect national security would continue to be handled through the standard AIR FORCE procedures designed for this purpose. . . ." It should be noted that Blue Book had not even been on the distribution list for these reports. Any reasonable person would certainly expect that objects which could affect national security would be of far greater significance than mere civilian uninstrumented observations. It is obvious that any USAF claim that all Air Force investigations were subsumed under the heading of Blue Book, Sign, and Grudge is false.

D. I do have on hand copies of two formerly Top Secret Air Force Intelligence UFO-related documents. Neither had anything to do with Blue Book, Sign, and Grudge. Both relate, as might be expected from item 2A above, to Air Force Intelligence. Copies are enclosed. There are surely more where these came from, just waiting to be released.

3. The conclusions of Project Blue Book as noted in your letter make no more sense today than they did in 1969. They are very well written propaganda:

A. Penguins in Antarctica have also given "no indication of being a threat to our national security." They are certainly real. The best question about UFOs is are <u>any</u> of them intelligently controlled extraterrestrial spacecraft. The evidence, including some very interesting data from Project Blue Book Special Report 14, clearly indicates that some are.

B. If any of the functions noted—reporting, investigation, evaluation—were performed by some other agency, such as the CIA, DIA, ONI, NRO, this first statement could be technically true, but totally meaningless. This same limitation applies to the statement about the evidence "submitted to or discovered by the <u>Air Force</u>." In addition, such information would almost by definition be extremely highly classified and could not be disclosed. After all, a country which has an annual black budget of $34 billion, according to a Pulitzer Prize-winning journalist, must have cover stories to protect "black" programs. Obviously, I should also note as a scientist who worked on a host of far-out, exciting, eventually cancelled, highly classified R & D programs, that trips to the stars do NOT represent technological developments or principles beyond the range of present-day scientific knowledge any more than a trip to the moon was beyond the range of scientific knowledge in 1947. It just took a huge effort and tons of money to go from principles to practice.

Conclusion 3 is frankly absurd. Anybody who studies the large-scale scientific studies noted in my enclosed paper "The Case for the Extraterrestrial Origin of Flying Saucers" will find that the conclusion that <u>some</u> UFOs are ET spacecraft is inescapable. For example, USAF Project Blue Book Special

Report 14 (essentially never mentioned in official USAF statements for obvious reasons) demonstrates that 21.5 percent of
the 3,201 sightings investigated could NOT be identified, completely separate from the 9.5 percent which were labeled
Insufficient Information. The probability that the Unknowns
were just missed Knowns was shown to be less than 1 percent. It
was found that the better the quality of the sighting, the more
likely to be an Unknown. It is clear that the combination of appearance and incredible flight behavior rule out an earth origin
for those pre-1955 Unknown sightings. If any terrestrial source
could duplicate that flying behavior back then, we earthlings
would no longer be building F-16, F-17, F-18, MIG 29,
Mirage 5, etc., aircraft.

The press release which was very widely distributed when
BBSR 14 was completed, like your letter, was totally misleading, including this statement by the then secretary of the USAF:
"On the basis of this report, we believe that no objects such as
those popularly described as flying saucers have overflown the
United States. Even the Unknown 3% could have been identified as conventional phenomena or illusions if more complete
observational data had been available." The fact is that the
Unknowns were, as noted above, 21.5 percent of the total, not
3 percent, and were completely separate from the Insufficient
Information cases.

Parenthetically, I should note that it is hilarious for the
USAF over and over again to suggest that ONLY 500 or 600
sightings couldn't be explained. Fewer than 1 percent of naturally occurring isotopes are fissionable, or of chemicals cure dis-
eases, or of people are 7 feet tall, or of the matter in a ton of
good grade gold ore is gold. Would any rational person say no
isotopes are fissionable, or no chemicals cure disease, or no one
is 7 feet tall, or the ore is worthless?

4. Your paragraph 2 makes this incredible statement: "We are not
aware that any other governmental department or agency, other than
the National Archives, possesses any records pertaining to UFOs." If

the USAF is not so aware, it certainly should be. Let me educate you. The CIA admitted finding over 900 pages of material concerning UFOs and released a list of 57 documents originating with other agencies, including the State Department and the DIA and 18 from the NSA. The NSA, when taken to court and forced to do a search, admitted finding 239 UFO documents with 79 originating with other agencies, including 23 from the CIA, which somehow hadn't found them when doing its initial search.

Of course the NSA refused to release any of its 160 UFO documents even to Judge Gerhard Gesell on the grounds of national security. Everybody and his brother has been collecting UFO data. I should add that, as described in the enclosed piece, "The Cosmic Watergate," the CIA also hadn't found the 200 UFO documents referenced internally in the 900 released pages, none of which were classified above Secret. I have been to 15 archives. There should have been loads of TS material. Also Maxwell AFB had quite a number of documents relating to UFOs, but NOT part of the Blue Book system. The US Army had numerous CIRVIS reports relating to UFOs. Somebody needs to do some homework.

5. If the Air Force has no unreleased UFO-related data, then why did the USAF Office of Special Investigations instruct its many units to violate its own procedures should they receive a Freedom of Information request about UFOs from me? Their memo is enclosed. The only "reasonable," if unethical, reason is the intent to hide data from the public. It probably violates all kinds of rules and regulations.

In summary, Colonel Shubert, an apology is in order to Senator Murray and the other members of Congress to whom your office provided such false and misleading information. It is time to at least get educated about the facts and to stop misrepresentation to the American people and their elected representatives. I have my finger on the pulse of the country after all my lectures. Perhaps you need information from somebody like me who has been on the hot seat? The GAO should certainly be given the data about Roswell. It may well be that you don't know where it is. Perhaps Majestic-12 or some such organization does. As former President Nixon found out, mis-representation to the American people can eventually have serious consequences.

Most cordially, and looking forward to your response,

Stanton T. Friedman
cc: Senator Patty Murray, Congressman Steven Schiff, others

APPENDIX F

DIRECTORS OF CENTRAL INTELLIGENCE

Name	Tenure
Souers, Sidney	January 23, 1946-June 10, 1946
Vandenberg, Hoyt	June 10, 1946-May 1, 1947
Hillenkoetter, Roscoe	May 1, 1947-October 7, 1950
Smith, Walter	October 7, 1950-February 9, 1953
Dulles, Allen	February 26, 1953-November 29, 1961
McCone, John	November 29, 1961-April 28, 1965
Raborn, William, Jr.	April 28, 1965-June 30, 1966
Helms, Richard	June 30, 1966-February 2, 1973
Schlesinger, James	February 2, 1973-July 2, 1973
Colby, William	September 4, 1973-January 30, 1976
Bush, George	January 30, 1976-January 20, 1977
Turner, Stansfield	March 9, 1977-January 20, 1981
Casey, William	January 28, 1981-January 29, 1987
Webster, William	May 26, 1987-August 31, 1991
Gates, Robert	November 6, 1991-January 19, 1993
Woolsey, R. James	February 5, 1993-January 10, 1995
Deutch, John	May 10, 1995-

SOURCES

LARGE STUDIES

Bloecher, Ted. *Report on the UFO Wave of 1947*. NICAP, 1967. Information on 853 UFO sightings for June-July 1947. Introduction by Dr. James E. McDonald.

Fuller, Curtis, ed. *Proceedings of the First International UFO Congress*. New York: Warner Books, 1980, 440 pages.

Gilmour, Daniel J., ed. *The Condon Report: Scientific Study of Unidentified Flying Objects*. New York: Bantam Books, 1969, 965 pages. Information on 117 sightings, of which 30 percent could not be identified, and much more miscellaneous data. Directed by physicist Dr. Edward U. Condon of the University of Colorado, Boulder. Sponsored by the Air Force. Cost of study $539,000.

Hall, Richard, ed. *The UFO Evidence*. NICAP, 1964, 184 pages. Edited by Richard Hall for the now-defunct National Investigations Committee on Aerial Phenomena. Information on more than 740 "unknowns" culled from more than 4,500 cases. Separate chapters on sightings by commercial and military pilots, law enforcement officers, and scientists, as well as a chapter on evidence for intelligent control of some UFOs. An update about twice as large should be available from the Fund for UFO Research by the end of 1996.

Hendry, Allan. *The UFO Handbook*. Garden City: Doubleday, 1979, 297 pages. Mostly about IFOs.

Hynek, J. Allen. *The UFO Experience: A Scientific Inquiry*. New York: Ballantine, 1974, 309 pages.

Jacobs, Dr. David Michael. *The UFO Controversy in America*. Bloomington: Indiana University Press, 1975, 362 pages. Adapted from Ph.D. thesis, History, University of Wisconsin at Madison.

McCampbell, James M. *Ufology*. Millbrae, CA: Celestial Arts, 1976, 185 pages.

McDonald, Dr. James E. "Statement on UFOs." McDonald's detailed, 70-page paper from the 1968 Congressional UFO Symposium, with detailed information on more than 40 cases. Available from UFORI, PO Box 958, Houlton, ME 04730-0958 ($10 including postage).

Mutual UFO Network. *Annual Symposiums.* Every year since 1969 there has been a UFO Symposium sponsored by MUFON, with proceedings published including all presented papers. Many papers by Ph.D.s, M.D.s, etc. Some volumes have been well over 200 pages. For information, write MUFON, 103 Oldtowne Road, Seguin, TX 78155.

Olsen, Thomas M. "The Reference for Outstanding UFO Reports," 1966.

Our Extraterrestrial Heritage—From UFOs to Space Colonies. January 1978. 117 pages. Proceedings of a symposium (including 14 papers) sponsored by the American Institute of Aeronautics and Astronautics, Los Angeles.

Phillips, Ted. *Physical Traces Associated with UFO Sightings.* CUFOS, 1975, 160 pages. More than 800 cases.

Proceedings of the April 30–May 2, 1976 CUFOS Conference. CUFOS, 1976, 320 pages. Thirty-five papers, three appendixes.

Project Blue Book Special Report Number 14. Air Force, 1955. Work done by Battelle Memorial Institute, Columbus, OH, for the Air Force. Privately published version with introduction by Dr. Bruce Maccabee may be available from Center for UFO Studies, 2457 West Peterson Avenue, Chicago, IL 60659. It has information on more than 3,000 UFO sightings (more than 600 of which are "unknowns") with categorizations, quality evaluations, statistical cross-comparisons, more than 240 charts, tables, graphs, and maps.

Rodeghier, Mark. *UFO Reports Involving Vehicle Interference.* CUFOS, 1981, 144 pages.

Ruppelt, Captain Edward J. *The Report on UFOs.* Garden City: Doubleday, 1956, 277 pages. Ruppelt was the first head of Project Blue Book.

Sachs, Margaret. *The UFO Encyclopedia.* New York: G. P. Putnam's Sons, 1980, 408 pages.

Sagan, Carl and Thornton Page, eds. *UFOs: A Scientific Debate.* Cornell University Press, 1972, 310 pages. Proceedings of the December 1969 Boston symposium on UFOs sponsored by the American Association for the Advancement of Science. It includes 15 papers and discussion by professionals including McDonald, Menzel, Sagan, and others.

Saunders, Dr. David R. and R. Roger Harkins. *UFOs? YES! Where the Condon Committee Went Wrong.* New York: Signet, 1968, 256 pages.

Spencer, John and Hilary Evans, eds. *Phenomenon: Forty Years of Flying Saucers.* New York: Avon, 1988, 413 pages.

Story, Ronald D., ed. *The Encyclopedia of UFOs.* Garden City: Doubleday, 1980, 440 pages.

Thesis–Antithesis. September 1975. 150 pages. Proceedings of a Symposium on UFOs and the Future sponsored by the American Institute of Aeronautics and Astronautics and the World Future Society, Los Angeles.

U.S. Air Force. *Projects Grudge and Blue Book Reports 1-12.* Originally Secret. NICAP, 1968, 235 pages. Covers 1951-1953.

U.S. Congress. *Symposium on UFOs, July 29, 1968.* 247 pages. Congressional hearings, with testimony from twelve scientists, including McDonald, Hynek, Harder,

Sprinkle, Friedman, Menzel, and Sagan. Available from NTIS, 5285 Port Royal Road, Springfield, VA 22161 (Item PB179541).

GOOD GENERAL BOOKS

Bondarchuk, Yurko *UFO Sightings, Landings, Abductions: The Documented Evidence.* Toronto: Methuen, 1979, 208 pages. Introduction by Stanton T. Friedman. (Republished as Signet paperback *UFO Canada,* 1981.)

Downing, Dr. Barry H. *The Bible and Flying Saucers.* Philadelphia: J. B. Lippincott, 1968, 221 pages (Avon paperback, 1970, 191 pages).

Edwards, Frank. *Flying Saucers Serious Business.* New York: Lyle Stuart, 1966, 319 pages.

Fuller, John. *Incident at Exeter.* New York: G. P. Putnam's Sons, 1966.

———. *Aliens in the Skies: The New Battle of the Scientists.* New York: G. P. Putnam's Sons, 1969, 217 pages. Includes much of the information presented at the July 1968 Congressional hearings, but without the references.

Haines, Dr. Richard F. *UFO Phenomena and the Behavioral Scientist.* Scarecrow Press, 1979, 450 pages (13 articles).

———. *Melbourne Episode—Case Study of a Missing Pilot.* Los Altos, CA: LDA Press, 1987, 275 pages (LDA Press, PO Box 880, Los Altos, CA 94023-0880). The full story of missing pilot Frederick Valentich.

———. *Project Delta: A Study of Multiple UFOs.* Los Altos, CA: LDA Press, 1994, 250 pages. Information on 473 cases.

Hall, Richard. *Uninvited Guests—A Documented History of UFO Sightings, Alien Encounters & Coverups.* Santa Fe: Aurora Press, 381 pages (including 156 pages of appendixes).

Hynek, Dr. J. Allen, Philip Imbrogno, and Bob Pratt. *Night Siege: The Hudson Valley UFO Sightings.* New York: Ballantine Books, 1987, 208 pages.

Jung, Dr. Carl G. *Flying Saucers: A Modern Myth of Things Seen in the Sky.* New York: Signet, 1969.

Keyhoe, Donald E. *The Flying Saucers Are Real.* New York: Fawcett, 1950 (Tandem paperback, 1970).

———. *Flying Saucers from Outer Space.* New York: Holt, Rinehart and Winston, 1953, 256 pages.

———. *The Flying Saucer Conspiracy.* New York: Holt, Rinehart and Winston, 1955.

———. *Flying Saucers TOP SECRET.* New York: G. P. Putnam's Sons, 1960.

———. *Aliens from Space.* Garden City: Doubleday, 1973, 276 pages (Signet paperback, 1974).

Lindemann, Michael. *UFOs and the Alien Presence: Six Viewpoints.* Santa Barbara, CA: The 2020 Group, 1991, 233 pages. Includes interviews with Linda Howe, Stanton Friedman, Budd Hopkins, Robert Lazar, and others. (The 2020 Group, 3463 State Street, Suite 264, Santa Barbara, CA 93105.)

Michel, Aime. *Flying Saucers and the Straight Line Mystery.* Paris: S. G. Phillips, 1958.

Vallee, Dr. Jacques. *Anatomy of a Phenomenon: Unidentified Flying Objects in Space—A Scientific Appraisal.* 1965, 210 pages. (Ace paperback, 1966).

———. *Dimensions: A Casebook of Alien Contact.* New York: Contemporary Books, 1988, 304 pages.

———. *Confrontations: A Scientist's Search for Alien Contact.* New York: Ballantine Books, 1991, 273 pages.

———. *Revelations: Alien Contact and Human Deception.* New York: Ballantine Books, 1991, 273 pages.

Vallee, Dr. Jacques and Janine. *Challenge to Science: The UFO Enigma.* New York: Henry Regnery, 1966, 268 pages (Ballantine paperback).

Walters, Edward and Frances. *The Gulf Breeze Sightings.* New York: William Morrow, 1990, 348 pages. Introduction by Budd Hopkins, photographic analysis by Dr. Bruce Maccabee.

PH.D. THESES

Bullard, Dr. Thomas Eddie. "Mysteries in the Eye of the Beholder: UFOs and Their Correlates as a Folkloric Theme Past and Present." Indiana University, 1982, 608 pages.

Flaherty, Dr. Robert Pearson. "Flying Saucers and the New Angelology: Mythic Projection of the Cold War and the Convergence of Opposites." UCLA, 1990, 726 pages.

Jacobs, Dr. David M. "The Controversy over Unidentified Flying Objects in America: 1896-1973." University of Wisconsin, Madison, 1973.

McCarthy, Dr. Paul. "Politicking and Paradigm Shifting: James E. McDonald and the UFO Case Study." University of Hawaii, 1975, 303 pages.

Milligan, Dr. Linda Jean. "The UFO Debate: A Study of a Contemporary Legend." Ohio State University, 1988, 624 pages.

Parnell, Dr. June Ottilie. "Personality Characteristics on the MMPI, 16PF, and ACL of Persons Who Claim UFO Experiences." University of Wyoming, 1986, 110 pages.

Rojcewicz, Dr. Peter Michael. "The Boundaries of Orthodoxy: A Folkloric Look at the 'UFO Phenomenon.'" University of Pennsylvania, 1984, 738 pages.

Schutz, Dr. Michael Kelly. "Organizational Goals and Support—Seeking Behavior: A Comparative Study of Social Movement Organizations in the UFO (Flying Saucer) Field." Northwestern University, 1973, 448 pages.

Stone Carmen, Dr. Jo. "Personality Characteristics and Self-Identified Experiences of Individuals Reporting Possible Abduction by Unidentified Flying Objects (UFOS)." United States International University, 1992, 131 pages.

Strentz, Dr. Herbert Joseph. "A Survey of Press Coverage of Unidentified Flying Objects, 1947-1966." Northwestern University, 1970, 355 pages.

UFO ABDUCTIONS

Bowen, Charles. *The Humanoids: A Survey of Worldwide Reports of Landings of Unconventional Aerial Objects and their Occupants.* 1969, 256 pages.

Fiore, Dr. Edith. *Encounters: A Psychologist Reveals Case Studies of Abductions by Extraterrestrials.* New York: Ballantine, 1989, 277 pages.

Fowler, Raymond E. *The Andreasson Affair.* Englewood Cliffs, NJ: Prentice-Hall, 1979, 239 pages (Bantam paperback, 1980, 1988).

————. *The Watchers: The Secret Design Behind UFO Abduction.* New York: Bantam
     Books, 1990, 386 pages.
Fuller, John G. *The Interrupted Journey: Story of the Abduction of Betty and Barney Hill.*
     New York: Dial Press, 1966, 350 pages (many paperback editions).
Fund for UFO Research. "Final Report on Psychological Testing of UFO Abductees."
     Fund For UFO Research, 1985, 49 pages. Report demonstrates that UFO ab-
     ductees are not mentally disturbed people.
Hopkins, Budd. *Missing Time.* New York: Marek, 1981.
————. *The Intruders: The Incredible Visitations at Copley Woods.* New York: Random
     House, 1987, 223 pages.
Jacobs, Dr. David M. *A Secret Life: Firsthand Accounts of UFO Abductions.* New York:
     Simon and Schuster, 1992, 336 pages. Introduction by Dr. John Mack.
Lorenzen, Coral and Jim. *Flying Saucer Occupants.* New York: Signet, 1967, 215 pages.
Mack, Dr. John E. *Abduction: Human Encounters with Aliens.* New York: Charles
     Scribner's Sons, 1994, 432 pages.
Strieber, Whitley. *Communion: A True Story.* New York: William Morrow, 1987, 300
     pages.
Turner, Dr. Karla. *Into the Fringe: A True Story of Alien Abduction.* New York: Berkley
     Books, 1992, 242 pages.
Walters, Ed and Frances. *UFO Abductions in Gulf Breeze.* New York: Avon, 1994, 294
     pages.
Walton, Travis. *Fire in the Sky.* New York: Marlowe, 1996, 370 pages.

CRASHED SAUCERS

Berlitz, Charles and William Moore. *The Roswell Incident.* 1980. New York: Grosset
     & Dunlop, 1980, 184 pages (Berkley paperback, 1988). Some excellent material,
     though marred by irrelevant and unjustified sensationalism about astronaut sight-
     ings and other claims.
Eberhart, George, ed. *The Roswell Report: An Historical Perspective.* CUFOS, July 1991
     ($15). Has both original and reprinted articles.
————. "The Plains of San Agustin Controversy, July 1947." FUFOR/CUFOS, June
     1992, 88 pages. Several papers and rebuttals and exhibits relating to a Chicago
     conference of Roswell researchers.
Friedman, Stanton T. "Update on Crashed Saucers in New Mexico." 1991 MUFON
     Conference paper, 18 pages. Delineates the history of the Roswell investigation.
     Available from UFORI, PO Box 958, Houlton, ME 04730-0958 ($4).
Friedman, Stanton T. and Don Berliner. *Crash at Corona.* New York: Paragon House,
     1992, 217 pages (Marlowe paperback, 1994). Copies autographed by Friedman
     ($21.45 hardcover, $15 softcover, postpaid) available from UFORI, PO Box 958,
     Houlton, ME 04730-0958.
Moore, W. L. "Crashed Saucers: Evidence in Search of Proof." 1985 MUFON
     Conference Paper, 49 pages. Demolishes the Scully story and covers findings of
     Friedman and Moore after 1980. Available from UFORI ($8).
Randle, Kevin. *A History of UFO Crashes.* New York: Avon Books, 1995, 276 pages.
Randle, Kevin. *Roswell UFO Crash Update.* Global Communications, 1995, 190 pages.

Randle, Kevin and Donald Schmitt. *UFO Crash at Roswell.* New York: Avon, 1991, 327 pages. Lots of research and some unjustified claims.

———. *The Truth About the UFO Crash at Roswell.* New York: M. Evans, 1994, 251 pages (Avon paperback, 1994, 314 pages). Both hardcover and softcover have a number of new scenarios for which there seems to be little support.

Scully, Frank. *Behind the Flying Saucers.* New York: Henry Holt, 1950, 230 pages. Scully, a Hollywood reporter was apparently taken in by some conmen about a crash near Aztec, New Mexico.

Stringfield, Leonard H. *UFO Crash Retrievals: The Inner Sanctum, Status Report VI.* July 1991, 142 pages. Published by LHS, 4412 Grove Avenue, Cincinnati, OH 45227 ($18.50).

———. *UFO Crash Retrievals: Search for Proof in a Hall of Mirrors, Status Report VII.* February 1994, 67 pages. Published by LHS, 4412 Grove Avenue, Cincinnati, OH 45227 ($16.50).

MAJESTIC 12

Cameron, Grant and T. Scott Crain. "UFOs, MJ-12 and the Government." ca. 1992, 113 pages. Available from MUFON, 103 Oldtowne Road, Seguin, TX 78155-4099 ($20.50).

Friedman, Stanton T. "Update on Operation Majestic-12." MUFON paper, 1988, 20 pages. Available from UFORI, PO Box 958, Houlton, ME 04730-0958 ($4).

———. *Final Report on Operation Majestic 12.* 1991, 108 pages. Available from UFORI ($14).

———. "Crashed Saucers, Majestic 12, and the Debunkers." MUFON 1992 Conference, 20 pages. Available from UFORI ($4).

———. "Operation Majestic 12? YES!" August 1994, 37 pages. Refutes anti-MJ-12 arguments in Randle's June 1994 paper. Available from UFORI ($4).

Moore, W. L. and Jaime H. Shandera. "The MJ-12 Documents: An Analytical Report." 1991. Available from Fair Witness Project, 4219 W. Olive Avenue, Suite 247, Burbank, CA 91505 ($25).

Randle, Kevin D. "Conclusions on Operation Majestic Twelve." June 1994, 30 pages. Available from UFORI ($4).

Strieber, Whitley. *Majestic.* New York: G. P. Putnam's Sons, 1989. A *novel* stimulated by the reality of the Roswell incident.

VIDEOS

There is a huge variety of UFO videos. Some are just like home movies of lectures and/or interviews given at conferences. At many Whole Life expos and other random conferences, a videographer films each presentation. Others have been made for theater or major TV exposure. Standing well above the rest is UFOs Are Real. This 93-minute movie produced in 1979 was intended for theaters and has been shown frequently on TV in New York, Los Angeles, and many other cities. It has many excellent production values.

There are interviews with abductee Betty Hill, Star Model builder Marjorie Fish, and abductees Travis Walton and Mike Rogers (featured in the fictionalized movie *Fire in the Sky*). It includes a wide variety of still and motion pictures including the 1979 New Zealand UFO footage shot from an aircraft by a professional photographer, the Catalina Island footage, and testimony from Dr. Bruce Maccabee, Dr. James Harder, Dr. George Mitchell, Dr. Richard Haines, Lieutenant Colonel Larry Coyne, Lieutenant Colonel Jesse Marcel Sr. (his first filmed interview), and Lieutenant Colonel Wendelle Stevens. A number of very intriguing documents are featured as well, including the September 23, 1947 memo from General Twining to Brigadier General Schulgen, and a letter to the United Nations from astronaut Gordon Cooper.

Among the cases featured are the Betty and Barney Hill abduction, the Travis Walton case, the Iranian jet case, the Coyne helicopter case, and the Roswell incident. Nuclear physicist Stanton Friedman was co-scriptwriter, technical advisor, on location, and in the film. Copies are available ($19.95, plus $3 shipping and handling) from Odyssey Group, 270 N. Canon Drive, Suite 1402-R-1, Beverly Hills, CA 90210 or by calling 1-800-544-4365.

Flying Saucers Are Real. Illustrated lecture by Stanton T. Friedman, filmed outdoors at the Kennedy Space Center, 1993, with many visuals. 84 minutes. Available from UFORI, PO Box 958, Houlton, ME 04730-0958 ($25).

Recollections of Roswell. Testimony from 27 witnesses compiled by Fund for UFO Research. 105 minutes. Available from UFORI ($25).

The UFO Controversy. Four 30-minute interviews with Stanton Friedman, 1992: A. Crashed Saucers. B. Operation Majestic-12. C. UFO Technology. D. Why the Coverup? Why Come Here? Why Not Talk to Us? Available from UFORI ($25 postpaid).

UFOs: The Best Evidence. George Knapp, compiler and editor, 1994. Vol. 1: "The Visitors." Vol. 2: "Strange Encounters." Vol. 3: "The Government Coverup." Available from Altamira Communications, 9457 Las Vegas Boulevard S., Suite G, Las Vegas, NV 89123, or call 1-800-575-5525.

UFOs: The Real Story. CD-ROM. Unity Publishing with Stanton T. Friedman. Interactive multimedia: videos, audios, stills, interview with Stanton Friedman. Available from Unity Publishing, 106 Main Street, Suite 194, Houlton, ME 04730-0958 ($39.95, plus $3 shipping and handling).

SOVIET UFO MATERIALS

Gindilis, L. M., D. A. Men'kov, and I. G. Petrovskaya. "Observations of Anomalous Atmospheric Phenomena in the USSR: Statistical Analysis." Soviet Academy of Sciences (NASA translation), 1979, 53 pages. Investigation of 256 UFO sightings compiled by Professor Felix Zigel.

Hobana, Ian and Julien Weverbergh. *UFOs from Behind the Iron Curtain.* Translation published by Souvenir Press, 1974, 309 pages.

Vallee, Dr. Jacques. *UFO Chronicles of the Soviet Union: A Cosmic Samizdat.* New York: Ballantine Books, 1992, 212 pages.

UFO COVERUP

Blum, Howard. *Out There: The Government's Secret Quest for Extraterrestrials.* New York: Simon and Schuster, 1990, 300 pages. No index, riddled with errors and undocumented claims.

Fawcett, Lawrence and Barry Greenwell. *Clear Intent: The Government Coverup of the UFO Experience.* Englewood Cliffs: Prentice Hall, 1984, 264 pages.

Friedman, Stanton T. "UFOs: Earth's Cosmic Watergate." 1980, 22 pages. Available from UFORI, PO Box 958, Houlton, ME 04730-0958 ($4 postpaid).

Good, Timothy. *Above Top Secret: The Worldwide UFO Coverup.* London: Sidgwick and Jackson, 1987, 590 pages, many documents.

———, ed. *The UFO Report 1991.* London: Sidgwick and Jackson, 1990, 254 pages.

———. *Alien Update.* New York: Arrow, 1993, 296 pages.

Weiner, Tim. *Blank Check: The Pentagon's Black Budget.* Warner Books, 1990, 273 pages. Weiner has won two Pulitzer Prizes and it shows. Nothing about UFOs, but well documented material about government secrecy.

UFO ORGANIZATIONS

The Center for the Study of Extraterrestrial Intelligence (CSETI). Dr. Steven Greer, Director, PO Box 15401, Asheville, NC 28813.

Center for UFO Studies (CUFOS). 2457 W. Peterson Avenue, Chicago, IL 60659. Publishes quarterly *International UFO Reporter,* $25/year. About 1,000 members.

Fund for UFO Research. PO Box 277, Mt. Rainier, MD 20822. Raises funds for UFO research. No memberships. Send SASE for free information about available publications, especially government documents and research done for it.

Mutual UFO Network (MUFON). 103 Oldtowne Road, Seguin, TX 78155. Publishes Monthly *MUFON Journal,* $30/year. Over 5,400 members. Has annual MUFON Symposium (twenty-sixth was held in 1995) with papers by professional people and proceedings available at the conference.

UFO Research Institute (UFORI). PO Box 958, Houlton, ME 04730-0958. Publishes videos and UFO publications. No memberships. Send SASE for free catalog.

UFO Newsclipping Service. Monthly. Route 1, Box 220, Plumerville, AR 72127.

Arcturus Book Service, 1443 SE Port St. Lucie, Port St. Lucie, FL 34952. Carries huge stock. Write for catalog.

PERIODICALS

The Flying Saucer Review. PO Box 162, High Wycombe, Bucks. England HP13 5DZ. Annual subscription, US $35.

UFO Magazine (England). 66 Boroughgate, 1st floor, Otley Near Leeds, England LS21 1AE. Annual subscription, US $30.

ANTI-UFO ORGANIZATION

Committee for Scientific Investigation of Claims of the Paranormal (CSICOP). 3965 Rensch Road, Amherst, NY 14228-2713. Debunking group. Publishes *Skeptical Inquirer.*

SEARCH FOR EXTRATERRESTRIAL INTELLIGENCE (SETI)

Billingham, Dr. John, ed. *Life in the Universe.* Cambridge: MIT Press, 1981, 461 pages, 35 articles. No references to UFOs.

Billingham, Dr. John and Dr. Bernard Oliver, co-directors. *Project Cyclops: A Design Study of a System for Detecting Extraterrestrial Intelligent Life.* NASA Report CR 114445, 1971, 243 pages.

Dickinson, Terence. "The Zeta Reticuli Incident." 32-page, full-color booklet published in 1974 by Astronomy Magazine. All aspects of the Betty Hill star map and Marjorie Fish's 3D models. Lists all sunlike stars in our neighborhood. Available from UFORI, PO Box 958, Houlton, ME 04730-0958 ($5 postpaid).

———. "Update on the Zeta Reticuli Incident." 1980, 4 pages. Refutes anti-star map arguments. Available from UFORI ($1).

Drake, Dr. Frank and Dava Sobel. *Is Anyone Out There?* New York: Delacorte Press, 1992, 272 pages. The authors are absolutely certain there are no visitors to earth and no interstellar travel, although they give no good basis for their belief.

Friedman, Stanton T. "Ufology and the Search for ET Intelligent Life." 1973. Debunks SETI specialists such as Carl Sagan. Available from UFORI ($4).

———. "SETI, Sagan, Science." May 1993, 27 pages. Debunks Sagan's article on abductions in Parade and challenges SETI specialists on their reasoning and failure to do their homework on UFOs and interstellar travel. Available from UFORI ($4).

Morrison, Dr. Philip, Dr. John Billingham, and Dr. John Wolfe, eds. *The Search for Extraterrestrial Intelligence.* NASA SP-419, 1977, 276 pages. The discussion about interstellar travel is absurd.

Sagan, Dr. Carl. *The Cosmic Connection: An Extraterrestrial Connection.* Garden City: Doubleday, 1973, 274 pages.

———, ed. *Communication with Extraterrestrial Intelligence.* Cambridge: MIT Press, 1973, 428 pages.

Shklovski, Dr. I. S. and Dr. Carl Sagan. *Intelligent Life in the Universe.* New York: Delta, 1968, 508 pages. Only pages 13-21 are devoted to UFOs, mostly a court case about Saturnian quartz mine stock fraud.

UFOS AND TECHNOLOGY

Friedman, Stanton T. "Flying Saucers & Physics." 1974 MUFON paper, 17 pages. Available from UFORI, PO Box 958, Houlton, ME 04730-0958 ($4).

————. "Flying Saucer Technology," "Flying Saucer Energetics," and "UFO Propulsion Systems" in 1980 International UFO Conference Proceedings.

MacVey, John W. *Interstellar Travel: Past Present and Future.* New York: Stein and Day, 1977, 253 pages. Neglects much research.

Mallove, Dr. Eugene F. and Gregory L. Matloff. *The Starflight Handbook: A Pioneer's Guide to Interstellar Travel.* New York: John Wiley and Sons, 1989, 274 pages.

BOOKS AND ARTICLES BY AND ABOUT DEBUNKERS

Friedman, Stanton T. "Flying Saucers, Noisy Negativists and Truth," 1985. MUFON paper debunks debunkers Klass, Sagan, the Amazing Randi, etc. Available from UFORI, PO Box 958, Houlton, ME 04730-0958 ($4).

Jacobs, Dr. David. "The Debunkers." In the Proceedings of the First International UFO Congress, 1980, pages 123-138.

Klass, Philip J. *UFOs Identified.* New York: Random House, 1968.

————. *UFOs Explained.* New York: Random House, 1974, 369 pages (Vintage paperback, 1976, 438 pages).

————. *UFOs: The Public Deceived.* New York: Prometheus.

————. *UFO Abductions: A Dangerous Game.* New York: Prometheus Books, 1988, 200 pages.

Menzel, Dr. Donald H. *Flying Saucers.* Cambridge: Harvard University Press, 1953.

Menzel, Dr. Donald H. and Mrs. Lyle Boyd. *The World of Flying Saucers: A Scientific Examination of a Major Myth of the Space Age.* Garden City: Doubleday, 1963, 302 pages.

Menzel, Dr. Donald and Dr. Ernest Taves. *The UFO Enigma.* Garden City: Doubleday, 1977, 297 pages.

Oberg, James E. *UFOs & Outer Space Mysteries: A Sympathetic Skeptic's Report.* Norfolk, VA: Donning, 1982, 192 pages.

Sagan, Carl. *The Demon-Haunted World: Science as a Candle in the Dark.* New York: Random House, 1995, 460 pages.

Shaeffer, Robert. *The UFO Verdict: Examining the Evidence.* Prometheus Books, 1980, 242 pages.

Tacker, Lieutenant Colonel Lawrence J. *Flying Saucers and the US Air Force.* Philadelphia: Van Nostrand, 1960. 89 pages of text, 75 pages of appendixes, including USAF Regulation 202-2 and JANAP 146(D).

INDEX

WALTER HUBER
1793 - 245 ROAD
NEW CASTLE, CO. 81647

WALTER HUBER
1793 - 245 ROAD
NEW CASTLE, CO. 81647

WALTER HUBER
1793 - 245 ROAD
NEW CASTLE, CO. 81647